# New Deal Labor Policy and the American Industrial Economy

# New Deal Labor Policy and the American Industrial Economy

## by Stanley Vittoz

The University of North Carolina Press   Chapel Hill and London

Library of Congress Cataloging-in-Publication Data

Vittoz, Stanley.
  New Deal labor policy and the American industrial economy.

  Bibliography: p.
  Includes index.
    1. New Deal, 1933–1939.   2. Labor policy—United
States—History—20th century.   3. Trade-unions—
United States—Political activity—History—20th century.
4. United States—Politics and government—1933–1945.
5. United States—Economic conditions—1918–1945.
I. Title.
HD8072.V715        1987        331'.0973        86-24911
ISBN 0-8078-1729-5

Designed by Jessica Letteney

For Julie

# Contents

# Acknowledgments

Authors customarily acquire many debts in the course of writing their books, and my own case is no exception. I wish to express my appreciation to the numerous archivists and librarians who skillfully and patiently assisted my research efforts; to John Schlosser, who took time out from his own studies at Stanford University to examine local sources on my behalf; to Wilhelm Fink Verlag München, publishers of *Amerikastudien*, and Geron-X, Inc., publishers of *Politics and Society*, for permission to adapt material that originally appeared in those journals; to Pat Gorman and Joan Plonski for typing the penultimate draft of the manuscript; and to Lewis Bateman and the rest of the editorial staff at the University of North Carolina Press for their expert professional guidance throughout the publishing process. I also was fortunate in having financial support for one or another phase of the study from the Hoover Presidential Library Association, the Dalhousie University Research Development Fund, and the Adolph G. Rosengarten Fund, Department of History, University of Pennsylvania.

Although any errors in either fact or interpretation that remain are mine alone, this book would be a far less creditable contribution to historical scholarship than it is without the insight that I gained from discussions with many friends and colleagues who took an interest in my work. I am especially grateful to Lee Benson, Fred Block, Steve Fraser, Ellis Hawley, and Michael Katz for their helpful criticism and unflagging encouragement as this project neared completion. To both Gabriel Kolko and Norman Pollack, who taught me the importance of striving to attain an independent critical vision, I owe a debt of intellectual inspiration that extends far beyond the scope of the ideas presented here. Most of all I wish to thank Julia Lynn Vittoz, whose discerning advice and tremendous personal generosity are embodied in every dimension of the effort that was invested in producing this volume.

Beijing
February 1986

# New Deal Labor Policy and the American Industrial Economy

# Introduction

No other single contribution to the theory of industrial society has had an impact comparable to that of Karl Marx's brilliantly inspired critique of capitalism. Although Marx's stature as a modern thinker automatically places him in a rank shared by the likes of Charles Darwin and Sigmund Freud and is recognized commensurately by intellectual historians the world over, the ability of his work to command an advantage over other lines of thought that also have found their way into the contemporary view of the human condition is most pronounced in Europe. There, the industrial working class, honored in all the classic texts as the living manifestation of capitalist irrationality, has been idealized by the master's epigones with remarkably little deviation from the original prophecy as the ultimate bearer of social revolution and historical reason. Those who defend capitalism in the United States and contend that their assessment of it is unaffected by any particular ideological influence, however, strongly dispute the universal significance of what Marxists believe to be the fundamental contradictions of the system. They ordinarily do so by pointing to the presence of "countervailing" centers of power in society and by attempting to show that all major interest groups that constitute the American polity, including the industrial working class, historically have had a materially viable, therefore legitimate, stake in the preservation of the established social order.

Each of these competing conceptions of the modern social process harbors its own particular weakness. In the case of the former the working class may be charged with nothing less damning than the betrayal of historical reason in the event that it fails to live up to its revolutionary responsibilities. In the case of the latter there is a tendency to accord far too much significance to the normative and benign aspects of the American social order, in which unusually durable middle-class values and popular expectations are commonly believed to prevail. Those who propound a Marxist view often exaggerate the disintegrative potential of social stratification, whereas their conservative adversaries appear to be all but blind to the likelihood that in the modern age a growing number of Americans merely endure rather than actively endorse the formal behavioral prescriptions of capitalism. All such differences in point of view and the frequent intrusion of certain characteristic frailties of analysis notwithstanding, however, most contemporary observers—radical and conservative alike—generally agree that the more or less unique political and interpersonal arrangement existing in the United States thus far has provided the basis for a remarkably stable, deeply continuous social formation.

An irrepressible interest in, as well as a certain puzzlement about, the phenomenon of social continuity as alluded to above led me to the study of government labor policy and the economic foundations of industrial politics in the United States between the world wars. No other period or aspect of twentieth-century American history is as heavily laden with questions that bear directly on the nature and resilience of American capitalism, its material dynamism and institutional staying power, its remarkably persistent social and intellectual "prestige,"[1] long after the day when the cultural principle of absolute self-reliance ceased to have much popular currency.

Nor is it a coincidence that my interest in the topic was stimulated originally by a group of radical scholars who contributed vitally during the 1960s to the birth of a new, sharply critical, revisionist orientation in American historical writing. Their main vehicle in this enterprise was a highly influential series of studies on the rise and impact of "corporate" liberalism during the Progressive era and what is now widely recognized as the essentially conservative function of much of the social and economic reform for which the modern period of United States political history is primarily noted.[2]

Individual emphasis, sometimes reaching the point of serious disagreement, is as natural and commonplace among these historians as it is among others who may be identified with a particular school of thought. Nevertheless, certain core theses are associated with this unusually distinctive body of literature, ordinarily dubbed "New Left" historiography. One angle of vision in particular that stands out in the radical approach involves a provocative claim concerning the ultimate locus of power in America, with profound implications for the age-old riddle of American exceptionalism.[3] The revisionists sensed, above all else, that the terms of debate on one of the chief paradoxes of American history—the failure of capitalist exploitation to produce a significant political turn toward socialism—would be permanently altered if it could be shown that an ideologically advanced governing perspective in the highest reaches of society had enabled the nation's ruling interests to devise an effective strategy for the *containment* of freewheeling popular democracy. Verification that such a shift in power had actually occurred was offered in a small outpouring of critical books and essays, the common tendency of which was to invest rather heavily in the idea that key elements of the American corporate elite had been favored with both the self-interested foresight and the practical ingenuity to channel every routine expression of working-class discontent since the turn of the century into institutionalized, politically sterile oppositional activity that might readily accommodate a sufficiently rationalized version of the capitalist system.

If we combine the containment and rationalization theses as the revisionists intend, it is difficult to imagine a more direct repudiation of the traditional pluralist conception of American politics. As logic would have it in the radical interpretation, much that passes for reform within the existing system should actually be seen as a potential step on the path to a more subtle form of social control. Undeterred in their belief that a popularly inspired—hence "democratic"—commitment to the public welfare is synonymous with the meaning of modern liberalism, Americans have been treated to the perpetration of a phenomenal bourgeois sham.

By the early 1970s, this bleak outlook had been fashioned into the most sweeping critique of American institutions and political culture ever produced by Americans themselves. Succumbing to a profound sense of what Gabriel Kolko has described as "radical pessimism,"[4] an intellectually uninhibited band of young revisionist scholars proceeded to render an interpretation of the recent past in which the self-consciously conservative machinations of an avant-garde element of the American upper class had largely been successful in absorbing, diverting, or otherwise pacifying the substance and occasional cry of lower-class resentment. The ruling elite, we may deduce from this scenario in the accumulation of power, achieved its hegemonic status primarily on the strength of its capacity to manipulate and adjust the operational parameters of the socioeconomic system, always in such a way as to avoid upsetting the basic institutional structures of capitalism. Ultimately this viewpoint was supposed to explain why moderate reform, including trade unionism and the characteristically ambiguous "collectivist" aims of progressive liberalism,[5] repeatedly appear in the American experience to have helped preserve the integrity of capitalist social relations, even though it was capitalism's gravely limited capacity to meet the requirements of genuine human sociability that had originally come under attack by reformers and radical social critics.

The argument in many respects was deeply persuasive. Corporate liberal and allied revisionist currents,[6] as they began to surface some two decades ago, ultimately produced a landmark interpretive reorientation among historians with respect to the origins and impact of "progressive" reform during the early years of the twentieth century. This was particularly true insofar as that extensively examined episode seemed to bear certain negative implications for the basic accuracy of what had long been presumed to be a generally antagonistic relationship between business and the state in American politics. Before long the corporate liberal model had been extended to the next period of heightened reform activity in twentieth-century American history—the 1930s and the New Deal. Among the earliest contributors to a critically intoned revisionist perspective on the politics and policies of that era, Barton Bernstein, Paul Conkin, and Howard Zinn addressed what they took to be the essentially conservative, system-saving achievements of New Deal reform.[7]

Their assessment was not an altogether novel one. William Leuchtenburg, in a highly acclaimed, moderately critical survey of the period published in 1963, had already observed that "the New Deal could advance impressive claims to being regarded as a 'savior of capitalism.'" As if to neutralize any suggestion of personal disapproval on that score, however, Leuchtenburg also credited the New Deal with having "achieved a more just society by recognizing [certain interest] groups which had been largely unrepresented" previously in the record of American politics.[8]

The revisionists, by contrast, were not so generous. For them, the pursuit of justice and the general well-being of those among the populace in greatest need of material sustenance and genuinely principled political support all too frequently were subordinated to the primary policy objectives of Franklin Roosevelt and the New Dealers, which by all accounts centered on the attainment of economic recovery through the restoration of business prosperity. The customary requirements of the capitalist system and the overriding importance of the profit motive, in other words, are seen by the revisionists as explaining the regrettably limited responsiveness of public authority to legitimately urgent expressions of public need, even in the comparatively dramatic and otherwise highly contingent political climate of the 1930s. The improved interest-group representation that for Leuchtenburg was one of the New Deal's most praiseworthy accomplishments struck the more critical-minded analysts as being distinctive only by virtue of its symbolic and formal importance and substantively leaving almost everything to be desired from the point of view of vast numbers of Americans—the powerless, the unorganized—who were largely left behind the march of contemporary liberal reform.[9]

As the revisionists of the early to mid-1960s managed to turn scholarly sensitivities gradually in the direction of greater skepticism toward the alleged "progressivism" of the Progressive era, so the similarly engaged revisionists of the late 1960s and early 1970s managed with comparable effect to discredit the most unabashedly partisan, post–World War II liberal celebrations of New Deal history. That the New Deal and the New Dealers ultimately were held hostage to a fundamentally biased configuration of social power under capitalism is no longer an intellectually suspect proposition in the view of most historians. On the contrary, historians and other analysts now generally agree that the New Deal, though evidently the bane of laissez-faire, was never in an especially favored position to exceed the comparatively narrow boundaries of American political culture. A different assessment might be in order had the New Deal been driven by an unambiguous desire to achieve basic institutional change in the United States. The plain fact of the matter, of course, is that it was not. This clearly had been one of the limiting characteristics of Progressivism; and during the 1930s the inspiration for reform in America once again was easily subdued by certain stubbornly persistent institutional habits of the past.[10]

It is essential nevertheless that we not lose sight of the primary question lying before us. The main point, in my opinion, is not to argue that the New Deal failed to produce any genuine or meaningful reform but rather critically to assess the actual proportions of change and social adjustment that did occur in a specific instance in which the potential for democratic reform within the framework of capitalism was substantially realized. This formulation of the central evaluative issue in our effort to understand the politics of the 1930s is the one that I find most congenial to an assessment of New Deal labor policy. Federal labor policy during the 1930s was the product of a conspicuously accelerated incidence of intense interaction between the agencies of the state, on one hand, and society's principal antagonists during the Depression era— labor and capital—on the other. It is also the one vitally important component of New Deal reform which has been least effectively accounted for thus far in the general development of the revisionist project. Indeed, the corporate liberal model as applied to the Progressive era, when by most accounts labor policy and labor reform were more often directed toward undermining or deflecting rather than accommodating union power, appears in certain major respects not to fit the New Deal context very well at all. During the 1930s, organized labor was the beneficiary of several tangible concessions in the sphere of federal policy, particularly the adoption of the National Labor Relations Act of 1935. There were some unusually "fair" contests of power in the legislative arena beginning in 1933, which unlike any previous wave of dramatic political events in twentieth-century American history significantly affected the more elemental struggle that was being waged simultaneously in the far reaches of the nation's industrial hinterland between labor and capital, not infrequently to the objective advantage of the former.

The obvious question that is raised, in reference to the primary evaluative problem that those of us engaged in the revisionist project repeatedly confront, is whether New Deal labor policy can be characterized simply as another proverbial "triumph of conservatism." Here I find myself essentially in agreement with those critics who argue that it is not enough to dwell on the indisputable fact that New Deal labor policy failed to achieve a truly radical, institution-shaking reapportionment of wealth and power in American society generally and between labor and capital specifically. Any historically valid estimate of the alleged conservatism of New Deal labor policy on the basis of that criterion alone, as Jerold Auerbach among others has correctly observed,[11] merely begs the question of how and why the New Deal labor reform that did occur actually came to pass.

A few scholars in the revisionist camp have attempted to grapple with this problem by pointing to certain documentable instances of business support for labor reform during the New Deal era, up to and including what some have interpreted as a significant amount of "corporatist" backing for the Wagner Act.[12] Were there in fact certain capitalists whose unusually high level of social awareness and whose search for increasingly rationalized modes of factory management ultimately allowed them either to support or quietly to acquiesce in the adoption of such measures? And if so, what practical, goal-specific relationship may there have been between the apparently "liberal" inclinations of business on one hand and the content of the law on the other?

To a considerable extent, these are the questions from which the present study takes its investigative cue. Specifically, I have attempted to delineate more systematically and in greater detail here than one may find in any previously published volume the precise nature and proportions of business support for New Deal labor policy in instances when the alignment of senti-ment both for and against such policy among industrial employers in particular seems to bear directly on the problem of determining the actual guiding forces of New Deal reform. In this regard I have already suggested that I share the general revisionist estimate of New Deal labor policy as having been conserva-tive in effect. But the present work clearly departs from what I have pointed to (not too unfairly, I hope) as a dominant thread of analysis in the currently reigning revisionist perspective at the level of historical causation.

Typically, New Deal labor policy was not the creation of a group of wily capitalists and their highly placed political allies. The facts bear out this statement. There is, I believe, compelling evidence upon which to argue that the origins and eventual institutionalization of New Deal labor policy had very little to do with the manipulative ingenuity of an ideologically sophisticated corporatist element of the American business elite. On the contrary, I think it is almost impossible not to consider the labor reform of the Roosevelt years, in the most general sense, as the largely spontaneous product of a plurality of contending interests whose ideal aims and practical expectations were freely represented in all the great political contests of the Depression era.

This does not mean, insofar as the case of New Deal labor policy may be considered to bear a certain representative significance, that we must therefore restore what once was a mantle of exclusive respectability in the field of American political analysis directly to the "pluralists." There is, most as-suredly, no need for that, if an integrated theory of the state, politics, and class can be articulated and validated empirically in relation to the manifold pecu-liarities of American history and society. Minimally, this theory would have to yield to the evident reality of countervailing power as a political fact of life in a formal democracy like the United States, to the partially facilitative role of the state in that regard, and to the periodic but no less meaningful frustration of specific business interests—even the interests, upon occasion, of the so-called corporate liberals. Finally, though not as to gainsay the foregoing, any such theory would also have to take into account the impact and overall importance, amid all the other pertinent factors, of a fundamentally biased configuration of social power within which the institutional structures of capitalism have remained virtually sacrosanct.[13]

This book does not provide an elaborate theoretical framework of the sort called for above. But it does attempt to provide a systematic description and analysis of New Deal labor policy in the context of my deeper concern about the need for a broadly applicable integrated theory of the state, politics, and class to enhance our collective capacity to understand the operative lineaments of power generally in modern American society. As such, my approach to the more abstract theoretical implications of industrial politics in the United States, like my approach to the subject matter of this book specifically, is informed by two general hypotheses.

First, I proceed on the basis of the not very startling assumption that ever since the rise of the factory system in this country, if not before, labor has constituted the preeminent material liability of capital because of labor's status as a prime element in the cost of production, calculated within the specific competitive structure of individual industrial product markets. Second, although I do not argue the point at length, I assume that labor in the United States as elsewhere in the modern bourgeois world has operated as the foremost ethical liability of capital. The periodic mobilization of public resentment in response to exploitive practices that denote a significant disregard for the contemporary symbols of economic justice attests to the existence of just such a "liability." The exact potency of this element in American history is virtually impossible to gauge. But if labor during the past century or more has suffered an obvious decline in its ability to maintain a position of strategic independence in the world of work and enterprise, we can at least speculate about the extent to which that process at various stages along the way must have aggravated the irreducibly contingent nature of mass loyalty in capitalist society generally.

Ultimately I am positing here the existence of two overlapping but potentially contradictory dimensions of modern economic life, exemplified by the dual imperative of "doing business" both profitably and in a manner that consistently meets with the moral approval of society as a whole. What has to be determined as precisely as possible is how the critical elements of this dilemma have been resolved, time and time again, frequently via the intervention of the state and the mediation of law,[14] in such a way as to leave the deeply implanted institutional roots of capitalism in the United States completely intact, if not more firmly anchored than ever before. The answer to this question, moreover, must be obtained, as I have already implied, without resort to the instrumentalist fallacy of assuming that in every instance of determinative historical significance capitalists, because their position of primacy as a class in American society has always been sustained, are therefore necessarily the most likely candidates for recognition as the prime-moving group behind the processes of rationalization, social adjustment, systems maintenance—call it what you will.

The forces and events that combined to shape the origins of New Deal labor policy stand as a marvelous case in point. Industrial relations in the United States during the 1930s were upset, rearranged, and at least in some respects "rationalized" with unprecedented ferocity. This change took place, however, in a historical context that at times was deeply affected by a palpable crisis of public confidence in the social responsibility of business per se and that soon would provide the occasion for America's original flirtation with Keynesian solutions to the worrisome persistence of capitalist stagnation. This is not to say that in the course of the Depression upheaval businessmen ever fully lost their capacity for political initiative and cultural influence in the United States, but certainly insofar as the politics of federal labor policy were concerned, the managers of American industry seem to have been forced as never before into an essentially defensive posture. Capitalism easily survived its greatest ordeal ever in American history. But those capitalists who were engaged in business directly as the employers of industrial labor suffered that ordeal through bitter contests of power with labor and the state much more frequently than they did in peaceful collaboration with either of the latter two parties. Against the backdrop of certain directly related patterns of development in American industrial politics predating the onset of the Depression, and in the immediate context of what strikes me as having been an exceptionally fluid relationship between labor, capital, and the state generally during the 1930s, the main purpose of this book is to provide a substantive evaluation of the effect of that highly changeable tripartite relationship on the characteristic departures in federal policy during the Roosevelt era which at the time were heralded by all as the very embodiment of labor's New Deal.

I cannot claim in the pages that follow to have fulfilled the long-standing need for a comprehensive political history of New Deal labor policy. Our lack of a modern study of that scope is evidence of the continuation of a significant void in the historiography of the Great Depression. I do believe that I have provided a reasonably full picture of the economic calamity that, among other things, was responsible for a vastly heightened public awareness about the competing claims of labor and capital in the United States during the 1930s. But the specific aims of numerous lobbyists and opinion makers who collectively played an important role in facilitating the popular acceptance of a new direction in federal policy affecting the interests of everyone directly involved with the operation of an industrial sector engulfed in crisis still await the detailed historical synthesis they so obviously deserve.

Although I am aware of how much else must be weighed in the balance if we are ultimately to have the fullest possible explanation of who got what and why out of the arena of reform during the 1930s, the present study focuses primarily on one key aspect of the larger historical question. In a sense, my interest rests more with the economic implementation of New Deal labor policy than with its political or legislative origins, even though the latter necessarily stands prominently in the overall narrative design of the volume. I have carefully scrutinized the actions of both managers and workers in se- lected sectors of the industrial economy with an eye to demonstrating the highly contingent and sometimes helpless nature of their response to the dynamics of federal labor policy reform during the height of the New Deal. I argue, in particular, that the response of industrial employers to the intense coupling of politics and economics during the Roosevelt era, although far from random in nature, nevertheless was not what one would expect to find on the basis of (exclusively) either the old progressive/pluralist or the newer revision- ist interpretations of New Deal reform.

The former interpretation, generally speaking, characterizes New Deal la- bor policy as having been distinctly prolabor, and therefore antibusiness, in nature. The latter interpretation, in its least radical but most frequently appli- cable formulation, argues that by extending a helping hand to the industrial worker New Deal labor policy actually gave many industrialists essentially what they wanted, too: federal regulation of the terms of employment, which it was hoped would alleviate the relentless and pervasive pressure to trim pro- duction costs that entrepreneurs experienced during the depths of the Depres- sion. This, in turn, would have the effect of dampening the forces of price deflation and also provide at least one of the necessary conditions for a restoration of business profitability.

We shall see in the present study that the accuracy of either of these interpretations—the progressive/pluralist and the revisionist—depends to a large extent upon the specific legislation in question. A less obvious but equally important question that also must be answered, because we presum- ably want to know how various employer interests viewed the legislative building blocks of New Deal labor policy, is what the specific conditions of entrepreneurial survival happened to be at a particular time on an industry-by- industry basis. As a rule, industrial employers reacted with stark dissimilarity when faced with the inroads of government authority bent on labor reform during the 1930s. Often, different employers in the same industry had perfectly sound business reasons for manifesting either support for or opposition to specific policy initiatives, depending upon the strength or weakness of their position in the competitive structure of a given product market.

There was, in fact, only one instance during the entire Depression decade when industrial employers rose up and expressed themselves in unison on a question of federal labor policy and that was to indicate their solid opposition to the Wagner National Labor Relations Act of 1935. That there was only one such instance does not diminish the importance of the measure because the adoption of the Wagner Act surely signaled one of the most remarkable victories for the principle of affirmative action in the annals of American public policy. Although I would not go so far as to say that this particular occurrence represents an entirely unruffled factual feather in the cap of the old progressive/pluralist interpretation of New Deal reform, and that consequently we should dismiss the primary contention of the revisionist perspective out of hand, there is no question that the advent of the Wagner Act indicates a need to integrate an account of routine interest-group struggle within a political and social universe bounded by the exigencies of advanced capitalism. New Deal labor policy, created willy-nilly out of the politics of the Depression, was not a totally one-sided affair. But the final position taken in this study is that it is entirely possible to concede such a legitimate point to pluralism without concluding that the revisionist critique of liberal reform must therefore be historically baseless as well. If the case of the Wagner Act gives a curious twist to the main interpretive issues at stake here, all it actually proves is that the evolution of New Deal labor policy should be viewed, not as part of an abstract formulation for the continued domination of one social class by another, but rather as a contingent element of the state's effort simultaneously to resolve the economic system's greatest crisis ever while destabilizing the institutional structures of capital as little as possible.

# Part One

# Economic Foundations of Industrial Politics before the New Deal

# 1 Lean Years

Many of the chief causes as well as the unusual length and severity of the Great Depression in the United States can be linked to gross sectoral imbalances that plagued the domestic economy practically from the beginning of the decade that ended with the historic financial crash of 1929. At the root of it all, several analysts have argued, lay a highy disproportionate increase in the accrual of profits to business engaged in the oligopolistic production of capital equipment and a steadily growing assortment of other goods typically classified as luxury consumer durables. That imbalance, combined with an increasingly unequal distribution of income in favor of the wealthier classes of society generally after World War I, had the effect of promoting an unusually rapid increase in both individual and corporate savings relative to consumption expenditures. The expanded flow of capital funds into the securities market, a natural result of increased private saving, was not matched by a corresponding growth in the level of productive investment, except perhaps in that particularly dynamic—but not yet dominant—sector of the manufacturing economy occupied by relatively new lines of enterprise such as the automotive, electrical equipment, aircraft, and petrochemical industries. Rather, the tremendous proliferation of purely speculative or otherwise fundamentally unsound outlets during the second half of the 1920s, both at home and abroad, tended to restrict the rate of capital formation relative to what might have occurred had a significantly larger proportion of accumulated wealth been disbursed domestically for consumptive purposes.[1]

Since at least the mid-nineteenth century, the overall growth of the American labor force had been a necessary, if not entirely sufficient, condition for a high rate of internal capital formation and sustained industrial expansion. The failure of the labor supply to grow in complete conformity with increased demand during every phase of the developmental process had the complementary effect of encouraging a progressively greater capital-output ratio and the relative displacement of labor by machinery. The massive immigration of European workers, which accelerated enormously during the thirty or so years divided by the turn of the century, stimulated both capital formation and technological innovation, bolstering the growth process while the scarcity of labor relative to capital in periods of peak demand continually encouraged a more efficient combination of productive agents.[2] Then, during World War I, a watershed in the secular trend was reached with the shift from debtor to creditor status by the United States in world capital markets. This change automatically opened the way for a corresponding adjustment in the stream of internationally produced values, which, along with the imposition of unusually severe constraints on the growth of the domestic labor supply during the war, substantially altered the comparative costs of investment in the factors of production.[3]

The net results were absolutely unprecedented. During the first ten years after the war the price of capital declined by 50 percent relative to the price of labor and the ratio of total manufacturing capital invested to units of labor-time worked increased by one-third.[4] Supplemented by the stimulus of previous outlays, these expenditures soon paid off in a burst of new technological enhancements, including a particularly significant advance in the electrification of industrial machine processes. Whereas only about 30 percent of the nation's manufacturing capacity was electrically powered in 1914, by 1929 the proportion had risen to 70 percent. Between 1919 and 1929, horsepower per worker in manufacturing increased by nearly 50 percent compared to a gain of only 15 percent during the previous decade. Similar advances were attained in steam railroads, for which horsepower per employee during the 1920s increased by a rate almost three times greater than that from 1909 to 1919. In agriculture and mining the increase exceeded 50 percent in both decades.[5]

The most astounding development of all was that between 1919 and 1928, coincident with an almost 50 percent increase in aggregate production, overall factory employment declined by about 6 percent. Additional data compiled by Solomon Fabricant reveal that out of a listing of 307 separate manufacturing industries more than half registered a net decline from 1919 to 1929 in the total number of wage earners employed, a statistically unique phenomenon in this century.[6] Yet at the same time, manufacturing productivity increased by an average of 72 percent, nearly three times the rate for the entire private domestic economy, and after at least six decades of a steadily declining ratio, output per unit of capital input also increased by better than one-half. By contrast, output per unit of labor time in manufacturing increased during each of the two preceding decades by less than 13 percent.[7]

One major consequence of the production trends described above was that the traditional dependence of American industry on a continual influx of low-cost immigrant labor never returned after the war.[8] The nonagricultural work force increased between 1920 and 1930 by more than one-fourth, a rate considerably greater than during the previous decade. After the war, however, additions to the work force were absorbed almost entirely by increased employment in the construction, trade, service, and finance sectors of the economy, as the proportion of the total labor force engaged in manufacturing declined by approximately 7 percent.[9]

The demand for factory labor did increase in some industries, of course. Employment generally increased during the 1920s in industries characterized by a financial capacity for the ready adoption of innovative production techniques and more efficient methods of factory organization, a much above average reduction in unit labor costs, and a particularly large increase in marketable output. But employment tended to increase only slightly or even to decline in industries in which capital innovation was slow and improvements in productivity and output only moderate.[10] Between 1922 and 1929, the aggregate production of durable consumer goods and capital equipment, including nonresidential construction, increased by approximately 70 percent compared to only a 30 percent increase in output for perishable and semi-durable goods.[11] Now, however, the relatively greater demand for labor among the former group of industries was met more or less adequately by interindustrial shifts in employment from those sectors, including mining and steam railroads, that had been competitively overdeveloped by the inflated demands of production for war.

There had been a general acceleration in the rate of internal migration to regions of the country where the demand for labor was greatest soon after the beginning of hostilities in Europe.[12] This accentuated version of a standard migratory pattern was first induced by higher factory wages between 1914 and 1918[13] and then sustained during the postwar decade by economically depressed conditions in the agricultural sector. Specifically, there was an unusually pronounced population movement from farming, rural, and industrially underdeveloped areas in the eastern half of the nation to the principal industrial subregions of the Northeast and upper Midwest.[14]

For our purposes here, it is of greatest importance that the emergent pressures which prompted these migrations were not confined within the framework of what at first glance might easily be mistaken for a neatly self-adjusting economic system. On the contrary, what must be appreciated about the combined force of each of the prevailing factors just described (increased productivity and labor force growth and mobility) is that it contributed materially to a situation after the war in which the slowly accumulating contradictions of an otherwise burgeoning economy eventually would come home to roost. Most notable among these in the short run was the collapse of entrepreneurial fortunes in several major branches of American industry. Rail transportation and mining were among the hardest hit, along with garment manufacturing and textiles. Having expanded and evolved through several generations of economic development to what many New Era business analysts deemed the peak of "maturity," these industries were troubled not so much by localized shortages of labor during infrequent periods of heightened overall demand as they were repeatedly beset by severe competitive dislocations—attended by a superabundance of labor, high unemployment, and steadily deteriorating wage standards—during prolonged periods of stagnation or, as was often the case, sudden marketwide contractions.[15]

The details of the phenomenon were extraordinarily complex, but the essence of the matter is perfectly clear. The emergence of several distinctly uncomplementary structural tendencies during the 1920s indicated a profound overall weakness in the American economy, and this was particularly true of certain irregularities in the distribution of industrial income. It has been well established that the average earnings of all employed factory labor, for example, rose during the decade at a rate far below the corresponding increase in manufacturing productivity. Between 1923 and 1929, the real hourly wages of production workers in manufacturing advanced at an annual compound rate of less than 1.4 percent, despite a marked stability in consumer prices, and the ratio of real hourly earnings to output per unit of labor time in the same broad occupational category declined by an average annual rate of 3.6 percent.[16] This trend, moreover, reflected the making of a unique economic situation. Although precise estimates of the magnitudes involved may vary, the 1920s appear to have been the only decade thus far in the twentieth century in which capital's share of the national income increased precipitously at the same time that labor's share was subject to a considerable reduction.[17]

On balance, there probably was no more important source of material disparity during the 1920s than the one produced by this highly unusual reversal of past trends in the distribution of factor income shares. Its basic causal significance in relation to the coming of the 1929–32 economic collapse is almost universally accepted among historians of the interwar period, and rightly so. There is, however, yet another, subsidiary, dimension of the more general distributional question that I would like to raise briefly as a means of introducing one of the central interpretive themes of the present work. For in addition to the effect of a critical maladjustment in the income shares of capital and labor during the 1920s, there were other, far less unusual incongruities in the realm of material existence that also had a major impact on the political-economic dynamics of the era, not the least important of which was the typically uneven distribution of labor's reward.

Wage standards and employee income varied widely throughout the decade, from industry to industry, as well as between different groups of workers in the same industry, depending principally upon the competitive structure of the product market and the relative strength of organized labor. Although the downward spiral in prices and production that began in the late fall of 1920 was accompanied by a general decline in the wages of nonunion labor, for example, it is clear that organized workers were relatively successful at preventing sharp reductions in hourly rates. Concomitantly, during the course of the economic upturn in 1922–23, nonunion workers typically were able to recoup only about half of their total depression losses. By the end of 1923, even though production and employment had substantially recovered from the depths of the postwar slump, nonunion wage rates were still between 10 and 25 percent below their 1920 levels; workers in the organized trades, after successfully resisting major wage cuts in 1921–22, ordinarily were receiving compensation equal to or above the predepression rate. The wage differential between these two groups widened as the decade progressed. By 1929, union rates, although representing the income potential of only about 11 percent of the nonagricultural labor force, ranged from 16 to 27 percent above the corresponding average for nonunion workers, whose earnings in absolute terms were still approximately the same as they had been in 1914.[18]

These data would appear to indicate a fairly consistent correlation between union power and wage security throughout the first postwar decade. It is not fanciful, in any event, to suppose that such a correlation actually did exist. And a closer examination of certain distinctively labor-intensive industries, in which trade unions periodically exercised greater than average autonomous influence in the marketplace even during the typically "lean years" of the 1920s, should allow us to establish reasonably sound evidence upon which to judge what I shall contend was the single most important (although highly variable) aspect of labor's role in the American economy for the duration of the interwar period.

In the bituminous mining industry, for example, perhaps the ideal case for the illustrative purposes that I have in mind here, a significant difference can be found between the proportion of income claimed by groups of workers whose union support remained more or less intact after 1921 as opposed to those employed in coal fields where the miners' union was either destroyed or greatly weakened during the course of the postwar depression. The difference, however, was essentially negative, or defensive in character, in that even those workers whose interests were represented with uninterrupted consistency by the miners' union merely were able to maintain their income share, and other groups subject to the same general economic conditions typically lost ground. Roughly the same situation prevailed in the garment manufacturing industry, whose workers, with the assistance of relatively strong industrial unions, were able to maintain their level of income reasonably well in the face of a much more substantial decline for manufacturing labor as a whole. In the cotton textile industry, in which independent employee unions had never gained much of a foothold and which were virtually absent in the southern branch of the trade, there was very little opportunity for workers—North or South—to resist downward pressure on wages and working conditions.[19]

Within the rather hastily drawn and otherwise entirely provisional tally of situational comparisons rendered above, there inheres, I would like to argue, a simple but vitally important economic common denominator: the variable factor of labor, and especially union labor, in the calculus of entrepreneurial risk-taking. It is not my intention at this point to comment upon the wisdom of anything that has ever been said about the proletariat's notoriously acquiescent political behavior in the United States relative to the experience of the rest of the advanced capitalist world. Nor do I have any reason in the context of the present study to dwell on the widely acknowledged inability of trade unions in this country to affect appreciably the distribution of national income.[20] The only particular characteristic of American labor that I am interested in having recognized here is that it constitutes one of the foremost organizational liabilities of certain vital sectors of the modern American economy, chiefly in its capacity as an element of the cost of production, calculated in terms of the specific competitive structure of individual industrial product markets.

The economic foundations of industrial politics in cotton textiles, garment manufacturing, and bituminous coal mining during the 1920s and early 1930s, the details of which will be explored in the remainder of this and the following two chapters, embody almost perfectly the critical structural relationships noted above. In the earlier history of all three of these old American industries, in which the livelihood of countless thousands of the country's citizens was still being determined at the beginning of the Depression era, one may discern the emergence of something resembling a structured pattern of competitive interests that in each case displays a striking correspondence to the patterning of indigenous managerial opinion on the most appropriate response to various public policy issues of vital concern to labor. Because of a certain consistency of record on that score more generally in American industry as well, this element, or condition of "correspondence," as I call it, has been adopted as the basic contextual underpinning for six of the eight chapters of this work. I thus avail myself of an expository paradigm that can be employed both descriptively and analytically, first for purposes of establishing certain distinctly continuous aspects of business' confrontation with the economics of labor during both interwar decades, and second, for purposes of constructing what I take to be a generally viable comparative framework within which to evaluate business' reaction to that which was actually "new" in New Deal labor policy. And with that, let us turn finally to the test of application. A reasonable place to begin, for reasons that will become clear soon enough, is with the pre–New Deal history of the cotton textile industry.

# The Decline of "King Cotton"

The cotton textile industry in the United States has always been highly competitive. Although significant concentration is now common in certain specialized product lines, the four leading producers have seldom accounted for more than 10 percent of the industry's total product. Until the late 1930s, the level of concentration was much lower, with the largest concerns in the industry subject to the constant threat of displacement by newer and stronger competitors.[21]

The greatest period of expansion in the industry occurred between 1880 and 1914, with the South—principally the Carolinas, Georgia, and Alabama—claiming the lion's share of new productive capacity. In 1880 there were about twenty times as many spindles in the North as in the South, whereas by 1910 the North's predominance in total spindleage had been reduced to only 60 percent. The thirty-year increase in New England and points west amounted to about seven million spindles, compared to a gain of more than ten million units in the South. Moreover, at least half the increase in southern spindleage took place after the turn of the century, indicating a generally accelerated tendency to the displacement of northern dominance.[22] By 1910 the southern branch of the industry enjoyed a monopoly on the production and sale of coarser goods. The rapid diversification of product lines in both regions would soon precipitate a struggle over the developing market for medium-grade cloth, which the northern sector of the industry would ultimately lose.[23]

Entry barriers were far less formidable in the southern branch of the industry at the turn of the century than they were in the older production centers of the Northeast, primarily because the market for coarser goods had grown much more rapidly in recent years than had the market for delicate product lines. As a consequence of high market demand and lower regional investment requirements, cotton mills in the South tended to be smaller than in the North. But what the average southern producer lacked in relative overall capacity, he effectively regained in the form of higher profits and the distinct prospect of continued expansion. This favorable situation induced the southern producer to invest readily in newer and more efficient production facilities, whereas northern mill owners generally were reluctant to undertake further capitalization of their interests in light of an apparently irreversible decline at the hands of their more competitive southern counterparts.[24]

Although the discriminatory effect of regional freight differentials and the relative proximity of many southern textile producers to the supply of raw cotton were partly responsible for the southern competitive advantage, the comparative cost of labor was consistently the most important entrepreneurial consideration.[25] The production of finer grades of cloth in New England customarily required the employment of large numbers of experienced European and French Canadian operatives, whereas the type and scale of production that developed in the South after 1880 was amenable to employment of an indigenous and highly vulnerable unskilled work force. Upward pressure on wages in the heavily industrialized Northeast, a natural consequence of the diversified demand for labor there, was only partially counteracted by the effect of immigration, whereas southern textile producers enjoyed an advantage in this regard by virtue of the relative absence of intraregional competition for the nonagricultural labor supply.[26]

The North-South wage differential narrowed dramatically after the turn of the century (by as much as 50 percent between 1900 and 1909 alone), coincident with a tremendous expansion in the market for cotton goods ordinarily produced only by southern mills. Indeed, until after World War I, demand and mill capacity in the South frequently outstripped the resources of the adult labor force, accounting for the appearance of significant regional wage gains even during periods when textile wages in New England were either stationary or falling. These adjustments, however, never provided any real competitive relief to the northern branch of the industry, particularly because southern mill interests consistently were able to retard the march toward interregional wage parity by employing substantial numbers of children in their operations.[27]

In 1905, women over the age of fifteen occupied a significantly lower proportion of the textile labor force in the South than in any other region of the country. In the case of child labor, however, the situation was exactly the opposite. The number of children under the age of sixteen employed in New England textile factories declined from about 17,700, or 14 percent of the industry's regional labor force in 1880, to 9,400, or approximately 6 percent of the regional labor force in 1905. In the South, the relative incidence of child labor declined only slightly, from 25 to 23 percent, during the same twenty-five-year interval, as the total number of children employed in the rapidly expanding southern mills increased from about 4,100 in 1880 to over 27,500 in 1905.[28]

Beginning as early as 1867 in Massachusetts, cotton textile manufacturers in New England and the upper mid-Atlantic states were subject to legal restrictions on the employment of minors. These restrictions were not uniformly well enforced. But by 1905, presumably knowledgeable contemporaries were of the opinion that such laws had proven sufficiently prohibitive to account for the better part of the net regional decline in the incidence of child labor.[29]

Between 1900 and 1915, all of the major southern textile states also adopted some form of child labor legislation, formulated at the behest of a politically influential coalition of local anti-child-labor committees.[30] The southern legislation, however, was not well enforced, nor did it prescribe standards on a par with those administered in the northeastern states.[31] As a consequence, the preexisting geographic lopsidedness in the competitive structure of the cotton textile industry remained largely undisturbed. The resultant situation nearly predetermined the alignment of interests within the industry for or against every relevant initiative in the arena of national reform thereafter, beginning with the proposed Federal Child Labor Act of 1916, which sought to prohibit the interstate shipment of goods produced by workers under the age of sixteen. Here, in an unmistakable preview of things to come, a measure that was opposed nearly unanimously by the southern branch of the industry nevertheless frequently won the support of textile interests in the Northeast.[32]

The cotton textile industry, in common with many others, generally prospered during World War I. Soon after the armistice, however, a worldwide decline in consumer demand forced the price of some U.S. product lines down by as much as 50 percent. Textile manufacturers shared in the general business recovery of 1922, but by the end of the following year the industry once again was plagued by excess capacity and falling profits, a condition from which there was to be little relief until the 1940s.

Before 1923, the expansion of the southern sector of the industry was accommodated more or less satisfactorily by a broadening in both the domestic and export markets for cotton goods. From that year forward, however, continued southern expansion came increasingly at the expense of the New England market share.

The most lucrative line of production during the 1920s was in industrial fabrics, a virtual monopoly of the southern sector of the industry. Moreover, in addition to the South's accelerated diversification into medium-grade lines, by 1923 finer goods, produced almost exclusively in New England, increasingly were subject to market competition from silk and rayon products.[33] Almost from the beginning of the postwar decade, therefore, the interregional wage differential had a new and greater impact on the overall competitive structure of the industry. The disparity between northern and southern rates had been narrowing steadily since the turn of the century, but in 1928, cotton textile workers in the South were still earning an average of 31 percent less per hour than their counterparts in the North. Four years later, just before the National Recovery Administration (NRA) cotton textile code went into effect, the differential held at about 26 percent. More revealing yet, U.S. Bureau of Labor Statistics data indicate that in 1927, for example, cotton textile wages averaged approximately 59 percent of value added in production among the top four producing states in the Northeast, compared to only about 51 percent among the top four producing states in the South. There was, by the same calculus, an averge 20 percent difference in the wage bill between the leading northern producer, Massachusetts, and the leading southern producer, North Carolina.[34] As a result, even before the onset of the Great Depression, scores of northern producers were forced either to go out of business, let some of their properties stand idle, or move their operations to the South to take advantage of markedly lower production costs, especially wages.[35]

Between 1923 and 1933, the southern sector of the industry managed to acquire about two and a half million additional spindles. At the same time the northeastern states lost more than eight million production units, indicating a substantial industrywide decline in physical capacity. That decline, however, was more than offset by a tremendous proliferation of double-shift operations, especially in the South. In 1923, industrywide spindle running time averaged slightly fewer than 3,000 hours per active production unit, whereas ten years later the average had increased to more than 3,500 hours per unit. The increase in operating hours per active spindle during this period in the textile-producing states of the Northeast was relatively slight—from 2,439 in 1923, to 2,666 in 1933. Most of the increase occurred in the southern states, where operating hours per active unit rose from 3,505 in 1923, a figure well above the national average for that year, to 3,913 in 1933. The clear disparity in regional production schedules and their relative rates of change reflected a pattern of development in direct correspondence to the rapid removal of the industry's center of operations from New England to the South. Over a period of ten years, the South's lead over the North in the number of operating hours per active production unit increased from approximately a 44 to a 47 percent margin. In addition, in the South, an average of 97 out of every 100 spindles in place during the 1920s were being run, compared to an active rate of fully 10 percent lower in the northeastern states.[36]

An important accompaniment to (as well as partial cause of) the shifting center of production in cotton textiles after World War I was a predominantly southern-based effort to reduce operating costs on an increased marketable volume of product by the adoption of a second shift, or "night work." This practice peaked between 1928 and 1933, long after the problem of overproduction had become apparent to the entire industry. Indeed, the contradictions of such a policy were as obvious to textile producers as they were economically inescapable.[37] The wholesale price of cotton goods declined between 1928 and 1932 by 46 percent, completely sapping the ability of countless producers to remain competitive, especially those who could least easily bear the burden of unit labor costs that had fallen during the same five-year interval by about one-third less than the drop in prices. In 1929, a peak year for corporate profits in the economy as a whole, profits in the cotton textile industry failed to reach a level even comparable to that attained during the 1920–21 depression. The trouble, of course, had begun much earlier. In 1926, for instance, a good year for manufacturing profits generally, the number of cotton textile firms reporting deficits greatly exceeded those reporting even marginal net income. Unit for unit, the industry's losses that year outweighed total receipts by approximately 70 percent. Profits were up between 1927 and 1929, but large losses occurred again between 1930 and 1932. During the latter year, about 75 percent of the industry recorded a net deficit.[38]

There can be no question that the cotton textile industry in the United States was in serious difficulty during the 1920s, both in the South and in New England. In 1923, the ratio of profits to receipts was about the same in both regions: 10.84 and 10.82 percent, respectively. During 1924, however, the ratio dropped to 1.6 percent in the North and to 2.13 percent in the southern states. Both sectors experienced nearly parallel recoveries during 1925, but in 1926 profits took another dive from which most southern producers would never completely recuperate. Over the next two years, northern interests managed better than a fivefold recovery, but the average rate of return among southern interests improved by no more than a factor of two. In 1929, the ratio of profits to receipts was still somewhat greater in the North than in the South. And although losses suffered during the depths of the Depression in the southern sector of the industry were generally less severe than those experienced in the North, there were no regional exemptions from the consecutive deficits of 1930, 1931, and 1932.[39]

The story of cotton textiles from this point on in many ways is a strikingly familiar one in the annals of twentieth-century American business history. The cumulative effect of persistent deflationary pressure since 1923, a succession of profitless trading seasons during the early 1930s, a proliferation of double-shift operations throughout the industry, and the inevitable failure of voluntarist efforts to eliminate the problem of overproduction ultimately disposed major producer interests—northern and southern alike—to seek a political response to an apparently steadily widening and otherwise uncontrollable breach in the competitive rationality of the product market.

Historically, the earliest indication of a clear tendency in this direction occurred in connection with the founding and subsequent activity of cotton textile trade associations. Organized along local, state, and eventually regional lines, such groups were formed to improve communication between affiliated manufacturers on technological and marketing developments within the industry. The first truly regional association appeared in New England in 1865, and the rise of similar organizations in the Southeast followed shortly thereafter. They gradually became more involved in the industry so that by soon after the turn of the century several different trade groups were operating well-funded voluntary service agencies, which increasingly performed as political lobbies for their members as well as the main force behind the development and extension of specialty markets.[40]

By 1900, cotton textile management's growing infatuation with associationist strategies of business organization had inspired the first wave of serious experimentation with voluntary agreements to curtail production, aimed at stabilizing the industry's price structure during periods of market contraction. Among a variety of such schemes, "open-pricing" (a practice sanctioned by law under the provisions of the 1914 Federal Trade Commission Act) was probably the most commonly employed method of combating short-term deflationary pressures, not only in cotton textiles but in numerous other industries as well.[41] The philosophy behind such agreements was to persuade the manufacturers of a given commodity willingly to share production information, whereupon they would presumably find it both desirable and possible to regulate output and thus be in a position to avoid any widespread or chronic overaccumulation of inventories. If this process was carried out successfully, prices and market shares throughout the industry would stabilize.

On numerous occasions after the turn of the century, fairly sizable groupings of temporarily aligned textile interests moved optimistically toward the goal of controlling some of the worst manifestations of a constantly fluctuating product market, generally through the use of open-pricing and an assortment of parallel collaborative restraints. Disappointment over the outcome, however, ran high. Sooner or later, most nonbinding arrangements for the elimination of competitive disorder in the production of cotton textiles, including the practice of open-pricing, failed. They failed because the extent and duration of compliance by producers with cooperative regulatory guidelines rarely had more than a marginal impact on entrepreneurial fortunes. The competitive structure of the cotton textile industry was far too vulnerable even to the most minor or short-term economic dislocations to be greatly affected by the willingness of a few key management groups to submit to the organizational principles of voluntarism.[42] The experimental method can and frequently does take a good deal of time to produce widely accepted results, however, and so it would be in the case at hand. Ever hopeful that the simple strategies of old might yet somehow avail them of the means with which to remedy the increasingly complex problems of the present, with a view to stabilizing competition, despite a succession of disappointments, industry leaders in both the North and the South confidently recommended voluntary action throughout the economically troubled postwar years.

This latest reassertion of the voluntarist strategy was occasioned by a repetition of the classic scenario in cotton textiles: a long-term shift in the balance of production and trade from the northern to the southern branch of the industry, which was undergoing a process of acceleration during the 1920s, was accompanied in mid-decade by a series of additional competitive dislocations stemming from a general decline in the growth of the industry's traditional markets. As in the past, when the problems arising from such pressures became serious enough, major producer interests responded by seeking the establishment of a suitable organizational apparatus through which to monitor, and hence control, industrywide trade practices. Preliminary steps toward that end were ventured in June 1926, when committees of both northern and southern mill interests representing about one-third of the industry met in New York to discuss the possibility of effecting an interregional agreement on production and pricing.

This and subsequent deliberations that led to the creation of the Cotton Textile Institute (CTI) in the fall of 1926 had been initiated by a group of aggressive southern manufacturers, although the end result was not their achievement alone.[43] Heretofore, the northeastern interests had been reluctant to participate in anything resembling a national trade association because the locus of power therein might make an accommodation of certain regional economic imperatives impossible. But now many of these manufacturers seemed to be humbled by the sense that an increasingly precarious business situation virtually compelled their support of any plan that might bring stability to the industry, especially if it could prevent the further removal of cotton mills from the Northeast to the South. The supreme desperation of the New Englanders at this point is perhaps best reflected in the decision that the CTI was to be barred, except upon formal amendment of its by-laws, from encouraging any extraneous political activity that could radically upset basic economic relationships within the industry, such as, for example, long-standing regional differentials in the hours and wages of labor. This provision was obviously a concession to the overwhelming dominance of the southern sector of the industry and to the nearly blind hope that the northeastern interests might ultimately derive some benefit should manufacturers in the South successfully bring the deflationary spiral in their region under control.

Although far from unanimous, in the end agreement was reached on the creation of a national trade association dedicated to two relatively unambitious tasks: building industrywide support for open-pricing in selected product lines and an attempt to alleviate the problem of stagnant demand through the administration of a general research and development program. Before long, however, the inadequacy of these conventional measures was evident to every member of the new association. As in the past, cooperative pricing among fewer than practically all competing units within the industry could not command enough force to have a truly redeeming economic impact. After a trial of several months, new mills were still being constructed in the South and competitive price reductions continued unabated as a growing volume of goods in newer and cheaper product lines cut further into established market shares.[44]

Labor's position in the cotton textile industry during the 1920s was extremely weak. The International Workers of the World and communist-led National Textile Workers Union pushed into southern textile centers in the wake of a series of spontaneous strikes initiated by unorganized mill hands late in the decade. But the "revolt in the Piedmont" was brutally and effectively crushed by the manufacturers at every turn.[45]

Textile unions in the North were not much better off. The entire membership of the United Textile Workers, a loyal American Federation of Labor (AFL) affiliate, was employed in the northeastern branch of the industry. In 1929, however, that membership amounted to only about thirty thousand individuals, or less than 3 percent of the industry's total work force; in basic cotton textiles only about 2 percent of the labor force was organized.[46] At the close of the decade, therefore, given the absence of uniform state or federal controls on wage levels and hours of work, labor's tremendous strategic vulnerability could only contribute to the perpetuation of an overall structure of competitive uncertainty that threatened the economic survival of the textile producers.[47]

By the end of 1927, not coincidentally, many textile manufacturers had already decided that the only effective way to control competition within the industry would be sharply to curtail the volume of night work. Several large southern producers suggested that they in particular could find little reason to support the Cotton Textile Institute unless the association was willing to sponsor an industrywide attack on the night shift. Most producers in the Northeast were already operating under state laws that severely restricted the employment of women and children on the second shift (in Massachusetts the nighttime employment of women and minors was prohibited altogether), thereby eliminating one of the primary business incentives associated with the appearance of the problem in the first place. In the South, such laws generally were much less restrictive. For southern mills, the universal elimination of night work would have meant the end of a long-standing competitive advantage. But with the shift of manufacturing dominance within the industry to the South[48] and the general decline in both world and domestic markets for cotton goods relative to the industry's overall productive capacity, the important issue for many southern producers during the later 1920s was less the maintenance of their regional competitive advantage than a need to control the proliferation of competitive dislocations within their own sector of the industry.[49]

In the South, local wage differentials were not a critical factor in the intraregional structure of competition. In 1927, for example, the total wage bill accruing to North Carolinian mill operations was only about 2 percent greater, calculated as a proportion of value added in production, than in either South Carolina or Alabama, and only 3 percent greater than in Georgia. Of more significance was the uneven imposition of laws affecting the employment of women and minors, which largely determined the relative ability of manufacturers in the various textile-producing states to supplement the locally available force of male workers in night-work operations. In the South, of course, the specific terms of such labor legislation as did exist varied from state to state just as in any other region. And because textile producers in the Northeast already recognized the importance of implementing marketwide restrictions on employment as a means of resolving the competitive hiatus between the two major geographic divisions of the industry, it is not surprising that the same policy issue was eventually designated as the key to a more evenly balanced competitive relationship between the ascendant southern interests as well.[50]

In late 1928, a poll indicated that at least half the manufacturers in the southern sector of the industry were opposed to night work and hence favored the adoption of uniform controls on the employment of women and children as a means of reducing the current level of production. Although to many this issue had become a matter of economic survival, as in the past the industry's ability to secure compliance with a given plan of action was seriously limited. For the CTI to pursue any substantive policy without alienating a large segment of the membership would require the consent of much more than a simple majority of the association's subscribers. In the absence of a proper consensus, therefore, in 1928 and again the following year, the institute's executive committee was compelled to ignore the issue of night work, even though it directly affected the problem of overproduction—thereby once again casting doubt on the prospect that an effective response to the problem of runaway competition could ever be mounted strictly from within the industry. The association, however, continued to support voluntary open-pricing and even went so far as to sanction a number of semiautonomous production curtailment agreements. At least two of these measures received the tacit approval of the Hoover administration and approached the rigor of general industrial codes. But neither was sufficiently inclusive in its market coverage to withstand the severe deflationary shocks to which the cotton textile product market was pitilessly exposed in the months ahead. A powerful minority of the nation's cotton textile interests, representing about 37 percent of the industry's total spindleage, was still operating beyond the bounds of the institute's oversight in mid-1929.[51]

The onset of the Great Depression aggravated the problems already confronting a deeply troubled textile industry. As a result, between October 1929 and October 1930, the Cotton Textile Institute gained enough new operators in its membership rolls to account for an additional 10 percent of current capacity. This increase enhanced the internal appeal of long-standing proposals for the adoption of cooperative, industrywide production controls. Unable to muster a sufficiently broad consensus on the desirability of eliminating night work altogether, however, out of sheer desperation certain key producers now also began to seek the federal government's endorsement of independent recommendations for the adoption of a uniform workweek throughout the industry. Finally, in February 1930, after numerous high-level conferences and much prodding by several of the country's most powerful textile executives, CTI officials agreed to encourage subscriptions to a new plan whereby individual producers would pledge voluntarily to limit their day-shift operations to a maximum of fifty-five hours per week and their night-shift operations to a maximum of fifty hours per week. The scheme was initially received with enthusiasm by an industry urgently in need of relief from what was rapidly developing into the worst economic crisis that American textile operators had ever faced. By the following October, manufacturers operating a total of nearly 23 million spindles, or approximately 75 percent of the active equipment in the industry, had subscribed to the "55-50" plan, and the overall numbers were steadily on the rise. A few months later, in January 1931, more than four-fifths of the total mill capacity involved in the manufacture of such standard product groups as fine goods, print cloths, sheeting, and carded yarn were operating under the terms stipulated in the institute's curtailment program. Of the equipment not covered by the agreement, 3.75 million spindles were located in New England, where many mills were already operating fewer hours per week than the officially prescribed maximum.[52]

Still, as Louis Galambos has aptly pointed out, "55-50 was at best a stopgap measure." In the North, 57 mills (4,443,097 spindles) and in the South, 224 mills (4,522,914 spindles) rejected the plan. Many New England cotton textile interests suggested that even if the entire industry were to subscribe, the overall reduction in output still would not be sufficient to stabilize the product market's extremely volatile price structure. Ultimately, almost everyone, including some of the plan's foremost proponents in the South, realized that the only genuine solution to the industry's overcapacity problem lay in the total elimination of night work.[53]

In October 1930, in the wake of yet another price reduction and amid assurances that it would receive the steadfast support of at least two-thirds of the industry, CTI's executive committee was authorized by the association's board of directors to announce the initiation of a new industrywide program that would endeavor to "eliminate, as soon as possible . . . the employment of women and minors under eighteen years of age between the hours of 9 p.m. and 6 a.m."[54] The agreement was scheduled to go into effect on 1 March 1931, provided that at least 75 percent of the industry's total spindleage and an equal proportion of the "night runners" were by that time committed to the plan. Moreover, for the agreement to remain in effect, it was determined that the total number of subscriptions should be increased to represent, first 80 and then 85 percent of the industry by the beginning of March in each of the two succeeding years.

As the March 1931 deadline approached, 83 percent of the entire industry and 79 percent of the night runners had subscribed to the institute's latest curtailment scheme. These figures represented a somewhat greater proportion of the industry than technically required to initiate the agreement. Yet the tally varied tremendously, depending upon the geographical region and the market serviced. Fully one-third of all southern producers, for instance, refused to have anything to do with the effort, and in at least one product line, as many as 75 percent of the firms running a night shift elected to withhold compliance. Indeed, despite an unusually strong initial show of support for the plan, resistance to the idea of voluntary production curtailment was still recognized by most knowledgeable observers as a serious enough problem "to keep the industry in [at least] a temporary state of demoralization."[55] The situation had not greatly improved by the following March, when the continuing subscription goal of 80 percent was only narrowly met, an accomplishment that probably can be attributed at least in part to the persuasive efforts of Secretary of Commerce Robert P. Lamont and a group of influential bankers who controlled the flow of credit to the nation's financially troubled textile manufacturers.[56]

By the spring of 1932 it had become clear to CTI officials, as well as to scores of independent producers, that the limits of the association's cooperative appeal were rapidly being reached. The success of the institute's curtailment plan was still seriously threatened by a group of ardent noncooperators, who represented an uncomfortably substantial proportion of the industry's total productive capacity. Such operations tended to be smaller than average in size and to have been in business for a relatively short period of time. And although there is no conclusive evidence to indicate that these aggressive competitors necessarily enjoyed higher short-term profits than the "cooperators," they nonetheless managed to occupy a consistently threatening position in the overall competitive structure of the product market. Ultimately their attitude would force the abandonment of all hope that the industry's economic problems could ever be solved through the application of strictly voluntary internal controls.[57]

The crisis in cotton textiles now deepened rapidly. In most product lines the disparity between orders and inventories widened beyond any reasonable expectation of natural adjustment. In February 1932 the southern office of *Textile World* called its readers' attention to the profoundly discouraging fact that even in the midst of an unprecedented collapse in consumer demand the industry was still operating at approximately 94 percent of capacity, with mills in the South averaging over 100 percent of their normal daytime schedules.[58] Although by this time almost nine-tenths of the industry was technically observing the current prohibition on the employment of women and children at night, CTI officials soon discovered that a substantial proportion of "sub-scribed" capacity nevertheless was hedging on the spirit, if not the letter, of the agreement by normally running an all-male second shift. A survey of some 712 southern mills, for example, revealed that although two and a half million spindles had abandoned night work altogether, approximately 43 percent of the industry's spindleage was still operating on double shifts out of the unrelieved necessity to cut unit labor costs on an increased marketable volume of product.

In an effort to deal with the situation, both the institute and the largely southern-based American Cotton Manufacturers Association attempted to se-cure subscriptions to an agreement that would seek to eliminate the night shift for a period of one year beginning 15 October 1932. This plan, however, never had a chance because a sudden late summer surge in demand sent cotton manufacturers into a frenzy of increased production and an unusually vicious scramble for new orders. Word soon followed that in the all-important narrow sheeting and print cloth groups, compliance with the agreement to eliminate night work for women and children had fallen below the critical 80 percent level, whereupon the institute was forced to announce that mills in these product groups were no longer obligated to honor their subscriptions. The issuance of that news prompted an additional string of defections from the cooperative fold, which in turn precipitated a temporarily critical decline in the association's role as an effective organizational force within the industry.[59] Early in the fall of 1932 it was estimated that perhaps 30 percent of all the manufacturers in the trade, producing up to half of the industry's total out-put, had resumed day-night operations in excess of the recommended 55-50 schedule.

These reports came in such rapid succession and were so dispiriting in nature that they prompted a reappraisal of the institute's long-preferred ap-proach to the elimination of excessive competition within the industry. In mid-November, at what CTI president George A. Sloan reportedly described as "the most representative meeting of the leaders of the cotton textile industry in the United States in the past six years," it was formally agreed that any cooperative program that might attract the interest of certain manufacturers more than others henceforth should be pursued under the independent auspices of the several product divisions. The chief idea was to preserve something of the old organizational forms while leaving the definition of specific collective goals to the determination of smaller producer groups.[60] By this time, how-ever, no one really believed that any application of the standard voluntary framework could ever satisfactorily meet the industry's most fundamental organizational needs. It was equally apparent that there remained but one viable alternative. And, indeed, the issue had already been settled. Only a month or so before the November meeting, the institute's membership in convention had approved—calmly and with uncharacteristic dispatch—a resolution that at long last authorized the association and its representatives to mount a determined legislative and political attack on the manifold dysfunctional aspects of the entire labor-production-price nexus.[61] To the leaders of the American cotton textile industry, the coming of the New Deal would provide both an inspiration and an opportunity.

# 2 Protocol of Peace

      Before the New Deal, key management figures in the American cotton textile industry constantly labored to devise a workable strategy for the control of production schedules and price competition. Although leading operators in the South as well as the North were convinced that greater economic stability could be achieved by regularizing the terms of employment, their efforts almost wholly neglected to anticipate the reaction of organized labor because trade unions in the textile industry were not an economic power that management was compelled to respect. This situation contrasted sharply with that in the garment manufacturing industry, in which the independent status of trade unions was integral to the dynamics of business competition.

    To a greater extent perhaps than any other industry in the country, garment manufacturing in the United States is, and always has been, characterized by an exceedingly competitive market structure. Extremely low capital requirements and the destabilizing influence of frequent style changes, as well as highly diversified product specialization, have had the combined effect of continually undermining the security of established market shares within the industry.

    New York City traditionally has been the center of the trade, particularly in the manufacture of women's apparel. Throughout the period under consideration here, the wholesale value of women's wear turned out by New York shops formed a steadily increasing proportion of the national aggregate: 64 percent in 1899, 69 percent in 1909, and 74 percent in 1921. By contrast, the national market share of producers in Boston, Philadelphia, Chicago, Cleveland, and several other less significant locations underwent a gradual decline. In Philadelphia, for instance, where the local product constituted 7.8 percent of the value of the industry's total output in 1909, ten years later the figure had fallen to 5.8 percent, and it fell another full point by 1921. In Cleveland, the proportion declined from 3.3 percent in 1909 to 2.5 percent in 1921. At the same time, however, New York did not pick up all, or even most, of the slack. After 1909, and especially after 1912, Los Angeles, Cincinnati, Toledo, St.

Louis, and Rochester also moved ahead considerably in the trade. Despite the growing predominance of the New York market, then, by the turn of the century the women's clothing industry in the United States was moving just as clearly toward greater geographic dispersion, a tendency that became even more pronounced after the beginning of World War I.

Decentralization in the clothing industry was also taking place at the same time on another, more decisive, level. To an ever-increasing extent after the turn of the century, entrepreneurial success in the garment trades came to depend upon the preservation of an exceedingly specialized division of labor caused by a tremendous proliferation of the so-called jobber-contractor system, especially in the New York-Philadelphia-Baltimore eastern hub of the women's clothing industry. Because of frequent style changes and the seasonal character of the trade, there were few advantages to large-scale, totally integrated production operations. One government study conducted during the 1930s found that even in the less segmented men's wear industry, medium-sized factories realized an average annual return on net worth of 9.2 percent, small factories 7.2 percent, and relatively much larger operations only 3.6 percent. In the manufacture of women's clothing, the small shop enjoyed an even greater competitive edge, and job-contracting typically provided the only means for otherwise unprofitable operations to compete in a sufficiently broad sphere of an incredibly diversified product market. Thus, although the number of fully self-contained establishments producing women's clothing in the United States increased between 1909 and 1919 by 48.7 percent, the number of contract shops mushroomed during the same period by a phenomenal 158.8 percent. In addition, the number of workers employed in the former type of operation declined slightly and employment in the latter increased by almost 90 percent. Moreover, although the total number of workers employed in contract shops in 1919 still represented less than one-fifth the number then employed in all regular, or "inside," establishments engaged in the production of ladies' garments, the ratio would rise monumentally during the years immediately ahead.[1]

Profit margins in the garment industry have always been extremely narrow, with approximately one-third of all sales revenue traditionally consumed by labor costs. Indeed, market shares and profits have most frequently turned on the variability of that expenditure alone. Certainly in the manufacture of women's apparel, the wage factor is unsurpassed by any number of other vital business considerations ranked in order of economic importance. This situation was manifest clearly for the first time in 1910, when a group of established inside producers in New York City decided to seek a working accommodation with union officials in an effort to bring at least a modicum of stability to the competitive structure of an excessively turbulent product market. Once

established, this arrangement became the basic framework for the most durable system of union-management cooperation in the history of modern American capitalism.[2]

Labor organizations made their first appearance in the New York garment
trades during the late 1870s, although most of the early ones led a very short
and unstable existence. A good initial example occurred in 1883, when the
members of the newly formed Dress and Cloak Makers' Association called the
first "immigrant strike" for a ten-hour day and a piecerate amounting to an
average $15 weekly wage. The strike was a success, but the union disinte-
grated almost immediately after a settlement had been reached, a sequence of
events that became the standard scenario for the rise and decline of unions in
the garment industry for the next twenty-five years.[3] Typically, working conditions would be allowed to become unbearable before workers resorted to
collective action. "Then would come a strike in the nature of a crusade fought
with great heroism by an improvised organization." The confrontation generally would end in "a formal and much acclaimed victory," only to be "followed
by a loss of interest in the union and an undermining by bosses and workers of
the hard won standards."[4]

The instability of the early garment unions was endemic to the trade.
Initially, even the ethnic and cultural homogeneity of the work force in the
New York clothing industry failed to result in the organizational cohesion one
might expect. Any potential commitment on the part of the individual garment
worker to the long-term interests of the collective was subject to constant
erosion as a result of the completely open entrepreneurial structure of the
industry. As a consequence, for example, the Jewish clothing worker was
commonly perceived as someone who regarded his job as little more than a
"stop gap." Individual tradesmen constantly shifted to other occupations, until
sometimes they became the employers of newer arrivals. It was not unheard-of
for "the labor crusader of yesterday" to become "the unconscionable sweat
shop boss of today." With the merchant capitalist in a key position to dictate
wages through low rates paid to the contractor and removed from the direct
hiring of labor, it is not difficult to see how the unions generally "lacked a
fulcrum for a permanent raising of the conditions in the trade."[5]

Time and experience, nonetheless, eventually worked to the benefit of
labor. In the spring of 1891, at a convention of delegates from various garment
unions in Brooklyn, Boston, and Philadelphia, the United Garment Workers of
America was formed, soon gathering under its influence most of the independent locals in the industry. Ideological controversy between radicals and mod-
erates quickly divided the organization, however, and in 1900 the workers in
the women's wear branch parted company and formed a separate national
union.[6]

The International Ladies' Garment Workers' Union (ILGWU) functioned from the beginning as a semi-industrial union. It offered membership to all workers, regardless of skill or nationality, and organized them in locals corresponding to the various sectors and job classifications of the trade. In large production centers such as New York or Philadelphia, union officials encouraged the formation of so-called joint boards, which united separate locals in each metropolitan region under centralized, coordinated leadership. This strategy initially met with less than complete success. Throughout its early years the ILGWU was ravaged by internal dissension, and more than once it appeared that the union might soon collapse of its own factional weight. Then, in 1909–10, circumstances turned in its favor as two successive strike victories greatly enhanced workers' confidence in the organization's long-term prospects.[7]

The first significant opportunity for the ILGWU came in the fall of 1909 in the shirtwaist trade, then one of the newer branches of the women's garment industry. Drawing its labor supply largely from among unmarried Jewish and Italian women between the ages of sixteen and twenty-five, the waist trade's relatively late entrance into the industry enabled it to bypass the sweatshop stage and made it more susceptible to advanced methods of production ordinarily associated with only the largest and most modern clothing workshops. The trade was highly seasonal, however, and the workers were still subject to some of the worst abuses of the industry.

The sequence of events that eventually culminated in a general strike of historic proportions began in July 1909 with a dispute in a shop owned by Rosen Brothers of New York. The company refused to pay the rate demanded by the shop's inside subcontractors (usually male tradesmen, who in turn employed from three to eight women helpers), whereupon the latter successfully induced all the employees in the shop—some two hundred workers—to go on strike. The Ladies' Waist Makers' Union, Local 25, readily came to the assistance of the subcontractors, and after a struggle of five weeks, the firm conceded and came to an acceptable agreement with the union.

The settlement at Rosen Brothers was followed almost immediately by two other work stoppages that soon became the center of attention throughout the trade. One of these was a strike in the shop of Leiserson on Tenth Street; the other was against the infamous Triangle Waist Company, one of the largest firms in the trade, employing several hundred workers. Both establishments offered unflagging resistance to the union and its supporters, which by late November 1909 had inflamed the situation sufficiently to produce a general strike involving between twenty and thirty thousand waist- and dressmakers employed by more than five hundred shops throughout the city. Some New York employers began sending their orders to factories in Philadelphia, but in mid-December the strike spread to that city as well. By the following February, when the strike was finally terminated, hundreds of shirtwaist manufacturers in both Philadelphia and New York were compelled to reach individual settlements with the union, which generally compromised formal recognition in return for the employer's pledge to reduce hours and raise wages. Recognition or not, however, the union's limited achievements were laudable enough in the eyes of workers in the shirtwaist trade to bring approximately ten thousand additional members into the ranks of the local, whose official rolls before the strike had numbered only a minute fraction of the new influx.[8]

Less than six months after the conclusion of the waistmakers' strike, the ILGWU organized the New York cloak and suit trade with even greater success. Again, a general strike was involved, known in the annals of the garment industry as the "Great Upheaval." But whereas the shirtwaist strike had been the product of an essentially spontaneous outburst of worker discontent, the struggle in the cloak trade developed as a consequence of more careful planning and preparation within the union. .

There were two broad phases in the growth and development of the cloak and suit trade that affected the interests of the ordinary garment worker after 1890. The first phase, as explained in one of the classic studies of labor in the women's clothing industry, "consisted in the crowding out of the older wealthy large-scale manufacturers or 'warehousemen' by newly hatched small manufacturers." According to data compiled by the U.S. Commission on Industrial Relations, in 1890 fully 90 percent of all cloaks and suits in the women's trade "had been made by contractors in the employ of a few large manufacturers," whereas ten years later "only 25 percent were so made." In 1900 all signs pointed to eventual displacement of the contractor by the smaller inside shop.

> The small manufacturer made his own samples. He generally obtained his cloth and other raw materials on credit by arrangement with some bank. He sold his product to jobbers who became the middlemen between the small manufacturer and the larger or smaller buyers of the country. Most of the small manufacturers were recent immigrants from Russia, Austria, and Poland. Their shops were generally located in the districts of the East Side, on Division Street, East Broadway, Wooster Street, and so on. They were called the "moths of Division Street" in contrast with the large "warehousemen" who were the "giants of Broadway." In ten years these "moths" devoured the "giants." The competitive power of the small manufacturer lay in his methods of operation. He did not send designers to Paris, but was his own designer. He kept no show rooms and employed no models. He saved on rent by staying in small and overcrowded shops. . . . The labor employed in such shops was the cheapest available. A small margin of profit was considered a sufficient reward. In this way the older firms of Jonasson, Friedlander, Blumenthal and others were either forced into bankruptcy or reduced to

subordinate places in the trade, while the firms of Sadowski, Beller, and similar newcomers pushed forward.[9]

The second phase was a repeat of the first:

> The former "moths" grew fat, underwent a metamorphosis, and became "giants" in their turn. In the early years of the new century, they began to move away from their old haunts to Broadway and into the streets adjoining Fifth Avenue and into the Avenue itself. The new "giants" also began to rent large shops with show rooms and to imitate the methods of their former competitors. Confronted by the same problems of high rent and of other fixed expenses, as the large manufacturers of the decade before, they also had recourse to "outside" contractors. On the other hand, a new crop of "moths" was hatched. The new "moths" moved up to Broadway and the adjoining streets, but operated on the old "Division Street" system. By 1910 this second movement had gone far enough to arouse the anxieties of the new "giants."[10]

The cloak and suit trade harbored a built-in tendency toward competitive disintegration. This pattern was typical of the clothing industry as a whole. The material well-being of the ordinary garment worker seemed condemned to a condition of perpetual uncertainty. The unsafe and unsanitary physical environment in the clothing shops, which duplicated the conditions of life in the tenement house and urban slum, changed little through the years before and after the turn of the century. Even technical improvements that came into use from time to time in the average production facility were hardly ever unaccompanied by further impositions on the worker. Every time a more efficient sewing machine came on the market, for instance, it was not uncommon for workers to be required to buy their own, and often they would elect to do so because of the attractions of greater productivity associated with the piece-rate system. Even in shops that furnished machines, responsibility for their maintenance and the cost of various accessories generally fell to the operator, as did an additional charge for electricity in shops with equipment adapted for its use.[11]

These practices were strongly resented by labor throughout the industry. From the ordinary garment worker's point of view, however, there is no question that the system of inside subcontracting represented the greatest evil of all, for it tended to perpetuate an elaborate hierarchy of exploitive interests within the shop and a structure of built-in incentives to keep wages down:

> The subcontractors and their few favorites would earn fair and even high wages, while the majority of the workers would be condemned to "starvation" wages. There were sub-contracting pressers, for instance, who made $100 and $150 a week, while the "helpers" who worked for them

would "go home" at the end of a week's work with $6 or $8. . . . [Moreover, with the general proliferation of subcontracting after the turn of the century], wages seem to have remained stationary and in some cases even to have fallen. In 1900 the [U.S.] Industrial Relations Commission reported that during the busy season the average operator could earn from $15 to $20 a week, a baster could make $9 to $15 a week, while a presser could earn $12 to $15. An expert operator would earn during the busy season as much as $40 a week. In 1910 the average wage in the busy season was estimated between $15 and $18 a week for operators and at $14 a week for pressers. The wages of cutters had been $24 a week as far back as 1890, while in 1910 the number of cutters who were earning that wage was but a small portion of the total number engaged in the trade.[12]

Such disparities, which were automatically compounded by "home work, sweating, contracting and sub-contracting . . . 'exaggerated overstrain due to piece payment,' and the fact that the trade was the 'refuge of the immigrant,' stamped upon the industry a character of 'deplorable industrial chaos.' " It was clear, moreover, "as a result of two decades of observation and experience, that no inherent force was in operation to remedy matters." Technical and market conditions "allowed free play to every newcomer in the industry." Nor as yet was there any political barrier to "the overrunning of the trade by ever fresh and 'green' immigrant workers." Consequently, even those "few employers with progressive ideas who might have attempted to place the trade on a higher plane, were continually hampered by 'cut-throat' competition."[13]

Yet, miraculously, it was in this highly unstable economic atmosphere that the ILGWU finally succeeded in its bid for recognition as the principal bargaining agent for more than 150,000 workers engaged throughout the country in the manufacture of women's apparel. The first phase of the process was initiated early in July 1910, when nine garment locals in New York called a metropolitanwide general strike in an effort to extend union control throughout the city's cloak, suit, and skirt trades. Support for the strike was overwhelming among union and nonunion employees alike, who thereupon marched forth to confront the shopowners as a firmly united front.

In the needle trades, as in many other fields of American enterprise, employers' associations were originally conceived as a means of collectively resisting unionization of the industry's labor force. Such, at least, was the avowed purpose of the Cloak, Suit and Skirt Manufacturers' Protective Association, an organization formed and representing its position in the summer of 1910 with a public announcement that its members as individual employers were "quite prepared to go down in ruin" rather than accept the extension of union power in their shops.[14] This militantly combative posture, however, was characteristic of only the earliest phase of the struggle. The association quickly fell victim to reality as many of the smaller shopowners, for whom a prolonged work stoppage could prove particularly disastrous, began almost immediately to pursue their own independently negotiated settlements. Ultimately, therefore, with the competitive welfare of its members at stake, the manufacturers' association had little choice but to come to terms with the union and eventually did so in a series of bargaining conferences held under the "impartial" chairmanship of renowned jurist Louis D. Brandeis.

Even as the first Brandeis conference convened in late July, the membership of the Cloak, Suit and Skirt Manufacturers' Protective Association consisted of fewer than one hundred of the largest producers in the trade. The association's strategy took shape accordingly and was revealed by A. E. Lefcourt, president of the group, when he confided his hope to John A. Dyche, general secretary-treasurer of the ILGWU, that the union's influence soon could be extended throughout the industry "to protect the legitimate manufacturers from the small fry who are cutting into their trade." Later in the summer, during another in the same sequence of meetings with union officials, Julius H. Cohen, general counsel for the manufacturers, reiterated the association's "realistic" attitude toward the situation when he commented to the other side that "we accept absolutely now the proposition that you should have a strong union."[15] With this remarkable utterance, Cohen was indicating the associated manufacturers' hope that the "Protocol of Peace"—as the agreement that finally emerged from the Brandeis conferences came to be called—would ultimately contribute to the union's total penetration of the industry, thereby stabilizing competition and offering established producers a certain degree of protection against the traditional hazards of the trade. Ideally, the manufacturers sought the elimination of inside subcontracting and other built-in "cost reducers" that allowed virtually unrestricted access to the market. Toward this end, the negotiators for the manufacturers' association agreed to a modified, or "preferential," union shop, as well as to the general principle of assisting the union to expand its organizational reach throughout the industry. Indeed, from the employer's standpoint, the acceptability of the entire protocol arrangement depended on the ability of the ILGWU effectively to control nonunion competition. Concomitantly, whenever the union suffered even a moderate setback in the effectiveness of its market coverage—as occurred during the business slump of 1913–14, for example—the manufacturers' organization would automatically undergo a test of allegiance in direct proportion to any resulting increase to the individual shopowner in the business cost of observing one's obligation under the terms of the original modus vivendi with the international.[16]

From its inception in 1910 through the unusually prosperous years of World War I, the organizational principles embodied in the protocol movement enjoyed considerable, if somewhat stormy and uneven, success. Arrangements similar to that between the ILGWU and the cloak, suit, and dress manufacturers eventually were concluded in most of the other specialty trades of the New York garment industry. The longevity of any of these agreements depended not only on how well the initial compact could be policed but also on whether and how readily an ever greater proportion of the producers in a given product market could be brought into control. The primary organizing strategy at this level of struggle in all branches of the trade involved the repeated use of "authorized strikes," wherein the union, with the mutual consent and cooperation of the associated employers, would conduct marketwide work stoppages designed to bring as many independent nonunion shops and their contractors as possible under the general purview of the protocol.[17]

Initially, the agreement with the ILGWU in the cloak, suit, and dress trades had been signed by only 75 to 100 employers. Yet by August 1913, out of an estimated 1,885 inside and contract shops throughout New York City, some 533 were reportedly operating under the protocol. Numerically, the associated manufacturers still represented a minority interest. But this was less significant than the fact that the same group of establishments—for the most part leaders in the trade—accounted for about one-half of the entire regional product, a situation that prevailed with only minor variations in most of the other divisions of the women's wear industry.[18]

The men's clothing industry, by contrast, was much more decentralized geographically than the women's trade, making any arrangement between employers and the union similar to the protocol a more intractable interregional problem and the representational interests of labor in general that much more difficult to look after. In this respect, certainly, the old United Garment Workers of America was unable to match the largely creditable performance of the ILGWU. The record of the insurgent Amalgamated Clothing Workers of America after its formation as an industrial union in 1914, however, was impressive. Behind its banner, the total number of organized workers in the men's wear industry increased dramatically during the war. Chicago, Cleveland, Rochester, Baltimore, Toronto, and Montreal, cities where larger "inside" operations tended to prosper, were fairly well covered by the union throughout the 1920s. During the same period, however, the union's position was extremely tenuous in Boston, Buffalo, Cincinnati, and virtually all major production centers west of Chicago—almost any place where local economic forces and the pattern of entry into the market allowed particularly small-scale manufacturers to flourish. The men's wear industry in New York City was partially secured in 1924, but Philadelphia remained beyond the union's effective control until the end of the decade.[19]

Although garment manufacturers shared in the general prosperity of World War I, ultimately they, too, no less than the embattled entrepreneur in any other highly competitive consumer goods industry, were forced to adjust to the harsh realities of a depressed postwar economy. In the case of garments, a general expansion of capacity between 1914 and 1918 in response to increased wartime demand[20] was followed during the contraction of the early 1920s by a sharp rise in the incidence of outside job-contracting, particularly in the manufacture of women's clothing, and both the men's and women's industries experienced the widespread flight of establishments from unionized markets in search of almost any business environment that offered the prospect of a reduced wage bill. With typical ease and unprecedented frequency, production facilities were removed from established garment districts in metropolitan New York and transplanted to various outlying communities where, after the war, labor was both plentiful and cheap: "Trucks loaded with sewing machines and accompanied by skilled machinists reached their destination at night. They toiled and hammered, building tables and shelves, and soon another factory was completed, ready for someone to turn on the electric switch, fully equipped to produce, with youthful strength and energy, with newly evolved methods, without interference from unions or the usual disorder in the garment trade, in a new setting."[21]

Still, many producers were unable to cut their losses quickly enough to survive. Even in the notoriously malleable women's wear industry, hundreds of manufacturers were driven from the market by heavy postwar competition. The greatest absolute decline in the number of both inside and contract shops between 1919 and 1933 took place after 1929, when each type of establishment was affected more or less equally.[22] Previously, however, inside operations had borne the greater part of the industry's internal economic burden. Statistics show a decline of 6 percent in the total number of regular shops in the women's trade across the country between 1919 and 1929, compared to an increase in the number of contract shops of more than 32 percent during the same economically fragile ten-year period.[23] The available data indicate that in the men's wear industry, the number of regular shops declined only marginally from 1923 to 1929 and that contract shops were attrited at a rate of almost 17 percent. The decline in the number of establishments was more pronounced than in the women's trade, although the characteristic predominance of inside production in the manufacture of men's wear would appear to have survived the contraction of the 1920s almost intact.[24] Ultimately, however, there was no refuge anywhere within either branch of the industry that would have enabled the producer long to escape the general devastation being wrought by the intense competitive pressures of the period. The entire collectivity was affected, as were all manifestations of working and business life therein, especially the former cohesiveness of the manufacturers' associations and the unique relationship that the organized shopowners had developed in recent years with the garment unions.[25]

In 1921, about 85 percent of both the shops and the workers engaged nationally in the manufacture of women's coats and suits were functioning on an "inside" basis. By 1925, only 25 percent of the establishments so engaged in the New York market, as well as only about 30 percent of the workers, were involved exclusively in inside operations. As a consequence, membership in the main employers' association servicing those trades declined from 440 establishments employing more than 21,000 workers in 1916, to 188 establishments employing fewer than 7,500 workers in 1924. In addition, some 30 percent of the remaining member establishments were engaged to varying degrees in outside job-contracting. Formed in 1923 as the successor to the employer's organization that signed the original Protocol of Peace, the Industry Council of Cloak, Suit and Skirt Manufacturers managed to increase association membership by an additional 100 to 150 shops during the relative prosperity of 1925–26. But this accomplishment could be sustained only as long as the threshold of entrepreneurial jeopardy did not fall below certain tolerable limits, which of course occurred on an unprecedented scale during the early 1930s. By January 1933 the industrial council was able to list only 165 establishments as official subscribers. Membership in the leading association of dress and waist manufacturers underwent a similar decline, corresponding to a marked increase in the proportion of the trade's total output produced by nonunion contract shops from about 25 percent in 1919 to approximately 40 percent in 1930.[26]

The rapid deterioration of business conditions in the clothing industry and the attendant decline of the employer associations had a profoundly unsettling effect both on the unions and on the material position of labor during the 1920s. In the men's trade, total employment and the proportion of workers employed under union contract declined sharply between 1923 and 1929, but both employment and production in nonunion markets showed a distinct increase. The wage differential between organized and unorganized markets seems to have remained reasonably stable, but there was a gradual downward trend in average rates throughout the postwar decade. With the beginning of the Depression, the pace of the downward spiral accelerated, so that by 1932 wages had fallen from a point only slightly below the 1929 average for comparable union rates in other industries to 36 percent below that level and from 23 percent above to 2 percent below average nonunion rates.[27]

Labor suffered a similar fate in the women's industry. Not only did ILGWU membership decline between 1930 and 1932 by more than 38 percent, but the union was forced to accept a series of humiliating wage reductions to protect the solvency of organized employers in danger of being driven from the market by nonunion competition.[28] Given the objective conditions of the trade, garment manufacturers naturally turned to competitive wage reductions as their first line of defense.[29] And yet, for the organized employer, this situation presented a supreme irony. He was aware that round after round of wage trimming, even if attained with the cooperation of the union, could only accelerate the deflationary spiral and further jeopardize established market shares. Indeed, he never imagined that the situation as it was then developing could be remedied by anything less than a reinvigorated union strong enough to drive "free-lance competition" from the industry forever. In 1930, however, the realities of the marketplace temporarily assured that the garment manufacturers' deeper apprehensions about this course of developments would be subordinated to the imperatives of short-term economic survival.[30]

The idea of the protocol, then, if not the original commitment, lingered on into the Depression era. The manufacturers had come to look upon the garment unions as an organizational tool and a competitive weapon indispensable to the purposes of economic control. When a three-year agreement between the ILGWU and the cloak, suit, and skirt manufacturers came up for renegotiation in 1929, representatives of the industrial council readily confirmed their intention to uphold the basic principle behind the associated employers' earlier advocacy of a system of industrywide collective bargaining as the best means of restoring the trade to some reasonable measure of economic good health. "We were, indeed, fully aware of the weakened condition of the union," one spokesman for the manufacturers later explained. But "rather than take advantage of that helplessness and create further disorganization, we sat down with its leaders and conferred with them in behalf of a new agreement and vouchsafed our support to the strengthening of the demoralized union. We did that because we believed that a powerful union and a correspondingly powerful association would be the most effectual means of re-establishing high standards in our industry."[31]

The first desperate months of the Great Depression emphasized the crucial significance of the link between union security and the economic fate of the garment industry.[32] Wage-cutting was rampant. There were reports that the sweatshop had undergone a revival of major proportions in the small towns of the East, and union spokesmen in the men's trade charged that work ordinarily paying $40 a week in New York City was now being channeled to "hide-away shops" in New Jersey and Pennsylvania where the job could be done at rates as low as $6.[33]

The already widely acknowledged desirability of bringing the entire industry under the collaborative organizational wing of national unions and employer associations was now more apparent than ever. Clearly, this would have been an exceedingly difficult task even under the best of circumstances; in 1932, with the competitive situation completely out of control, it was an impossibility. Both the unions and the manufacturers' associations were immobilized by the collapse of every operating standard in the industry, and no end to the further deterioration of economic conditions was in sight. It was precisely at this juncture, however, when the prospects for a purely internal effort to rationalize market forces in the industry seemed so bleak, that new options and opportunities began to emerge in the realm of national politics. American industry, upon the ascendancy of Franklin Roosevelt and the Democrats in the spring of 1933, was about to become the beneficiary of a "new deal," and it was from the garment trades that the disciplining hand of the interventionist state would receive one of the most appreciative welcomes.[34] After nearly four years of raging economic depression, nothing could have been more self-evident to the great majority of clothing manufacturers than the need for a publicly sanctioned institutional framework for the negotiation and administration of industrywide employment standards capable of withstanding those elements of commercial life that had made such a mockery of the regulatory precepts embodied originally in the Protocol of Peace.

# 3 | The Miners' Bargain

Union bargaining power had an important impact on the imperatives of entrepreneurial survival in the bituminous mining industry during the 1920s. The details of the issue strongly complement the main interpretive themes advanced in the preceding treatment of the garment manufacturing and cotton textile industries. In fact, a close examination of the economic foundations of industrial politics in the mining of soft coal should make it possible to perceive with utmost clarity the general pattern or direction of what I would characterize as a historically unique structure of forces and interests that emerged by the end of the first postwar decade to play a premier role in the course of events culminating in June 1933 with the New Deal's endorsement of many of the American labor movement's most fundamental organizational goals.

In the business of coal mining, the success or failure of the labor force to present a well-organized bargaining front nearly always has been a principal economic concern in relation to the simple dynamics of competition within the industry. In bituminous mining, specifically, there has been a tradition of union strength since the 1890s in the so-called Central Competitive Field, which consists of districts where the mineral is extracted in Indiana, Illinois, Ohio, and western Pennsylvania. The long-standing commercial primacy of this region deteriorated quickly after World War I, however, because of the accelerated growth of output in southern Appalachia and other outlying districts where mining operations, and ultimately the sale price of coal, were much less likely to be influenced by the economic constraints of a unionized work force. The situation in this respect had become so pivotal to the economics of the industry by the end of the 1920s that unless union operators could rid themselves of any further obligation to abide by the relatively costly terms of the standard wage agreement, they found themselves having much to gain by the advent of circumstances that forced their more cost-efficient competitors to bear up under the same obligation—that is, to recognize, and to bargain with, the union. When the time came, therefore, even though the perception of individual interests was still governed purely by the logic of the market, mine

operators engaged in that branch or segment of the bituminous industry historically most vulnerable to the exercise of union power were in the right frame of
mind to view the coming of the New Deal with notable equanimity.

The soft coal industry in the United States traditionally has suffered the
disintegrative effects of an extremely volatile price structure; the opposite has
generally been true of anthracite mining. That two branches of the same basic
industry could diverge so radically is primarily an issue of geography. Thus,
whereas the mining of anthracite is confined almost exclusively to only three
counties in northeastern Pennsylvania, bituminous coal has been extracted for
decades on a much wider scale in thirty or more different states of the Union.
As a result, in anthracite mining a relative balance has prevailed since the turn
of the century between demand, production, and developed capacity. In bituminous mining, however, there has been a persistent tendency for developed
capacity to exceed secular demand because of the far greater availability of
soft coal across a much wider geographic range of production and market
environments.[1]

First and foremost, the territorial extent of deposit has affected the relative
level of concentration peculiar to each branch of the industry. Statistics show,
for example, that in 1920, 80 percent of the nation's anthracite coal was mined
and marketed by only twenty competing firms. By 1937, according to data
compiled by the Anthracite Coal Industry Commission, 94.7 percent of the
mineral's recoverable tonnage was controlled by ten companies, which in
addition to being the largest in the trade, were also associated with the same
financial interests as the major anthracite-carrying railroads.

The bituminous industry has always been characterized by a tremendous
diffusion of market power. Accordingly, and in sharp contrast to the situation
in anthracite mining, in 1920 the top three hundred companies engaged in the
extraction of bituminous coal controlled only about 57 percent of the industry's
total product. The proportion had increased to 67 percent by 1930, but this was
hardly an unprecedented figure. The ratio had been about the same in 1905 and
was even higher before the turn of the century, when at one point the market
share of the industry's three hundred largest companies peaked at 71 percent.[2]

This extremely fluid structure of power, woven from a vast and always
changing number of competing units, in conjunction with occasional periods
of radically fluctuating demand, accounts for the long history of economic
chaos in bituminous mining. Every time there was a significant increase in
demand, developed capacity and the level of production tended to expand
rapidly because of the natural abundance of soft coal, on one hand, and the
exceedingly modest capital outlays normally required to initiate new operations, on the other. As long as demand and prices continued to rise, both old
and new capacity, as well as any increase in overall output, usually enjoyed at
least a tolerable minimum of market security. In bituminous mining, however,

sharp upswings in demand during this century have been notoriously short-lived. And with every downward adjustment has come a new wave of ruthlessly competitive pricing, against which the individual producer's only defense was a compensatory reduction of operating costs. Indeed, on several occasions the pressures in this direction have been so severe as to force major blocs of marginal capacity out of the market. Yet any derivative respite from the deflationary spiral generally has been only temporary and of steadily diminishing consequence. This is because of the entrepreneurial propensity in the mining of bituminous coal to resume operations out of momentarily idled capacity at the earliest indication of an upturn in market prospects or the attainment of even the most trifling competitive advantage. The result has been a fairly clear long-range pattern of development, wherein the vulnerability of the industry to repeated economic dislocation was both continually reproduced and deepened over time by the normal operation of the market's own contradictory structure of incentives and rewards.[3]

Because the cost of labor in bituminous mining during the period under consideration averaged between 60 and 80 percent of value added in production and more than half of all mine labor was paid on a piece-rate basis, competition in the industry centered on the economic and strategic determinants of the wage bill. Well before the turn of the century, the rigid interdependence between labor costs and profitability in bituminous mining led some operators to begin experimenting with union-management compacts designed to combat ruinous price competition during periods of declining demand. In bituminous mining, however, any organizational basis for the continuation of such activity was necessarily diminished by the gross instability of the industry's market structure. In this respect, the situation was a little more stable in anthracite mining. Something of a watershed seems to have occurred with the arbitrated settlement of a lengthy and bitterly fought strike in 1902, after which management in the coke industry consistently engaged in an industrywide contractual relationship with the United Mine Workers of America (UMW) that by the time of World War I had become reasonably secure.[4]

By the end of the nineteenth century a vast railway network had created a situation that made the gradual integration of previously isolated soft coal markets irresistible. This system included an increasingly large bloc of new capacity in southern Appalachia, the growth of which had been subsidized indirectly by the railroads. Lower freight rates were offered to shippers in outlying districts, thereby broadening substantially the economic terrain upon which established producers in other regions of the country were forced to negotiate their survival.[5] The result was a growing interest among these producers in the extension of geographically uniform market relations so as to deny any serious competitive advantage to the marginal interloper.

The first concerted effort in this regard was undertaken in 1886 by a group of major producers in Illinois, Indiana, Iowa, Ohio, Pennsylvania, and West Virginia. Specifically, their aim was to standardize interdistrict labor costs through the implementation of a joint wage agreement with the National Federation of Miners and Mine Laborers. Union rivalry and a sharp decline in coal prices in 1887, however, precipitated an immediate round of intense competition, which undermined any possibility of stabilizing market relations within the industry through cooperative means.

In 1898 another, more successful, joint agreement was reached between the United Mine Workers of America and union operators in Illinois, Indiana, Ohio, and western Pennsylvania. These mining districts were all indigenous to what since has become known as the Central Competitive Field. Much like New York garment manufacturers at a somewhat later date, the Central Competitive Field operators hoped that extending joint recognition to the miners' union not only would bring under control and stabilize wage competition between the initial signatories to the agreement but also that the compact might eventually be broadened to include producers in West Virginia and other important outlying nonunion fields, which increasingly threatened the Central Competitive Field's domination of the regional market for soft coal. It was taken for granted from the beginning, therefore, that the long-term utility of the interstate compact would depend on the ability of a strong national miners' union to bring an ever-increasing proportion of the national coal market within the organizational framework of the Central Competitive Field's scheme of monitored competition.[6]

This time a few more positive, if necessarily limited, accomplishments were achieved both for the union and for the collaborating operators. For varying periods during the first decade and a half after the turn of the century, the UMW managed to organize certain districts in Alabama, Iowa, central Pennsylvania, western Kentucky, Tennessee, Michigan, Montana, Wyoming, and Washington, as well as to maintain a separate interstate agreement with union operators in Kansas, Missouri, Oklahoma, and southwestern Arkansas. For the most part, however, producers in West Virgina, who clearly posed the greatest competitive threat to the market security of interests in the Central Competitive Field, successfully evaded the union until at least 1918, and operators in the increasingly productive districts of northeastern Kentucky almost without exception also resisted the efforts of the UMW throughout the prewar period.[7]

From the turn of the century through the mid-1930s, the combined output of the six leading bituminous mining states—Illinois, Indiana, Ohio, Pennsylvania, Kentucky, and West Virginia—accounted for an average of more than 80 percent of the industry's total product. Indeed, even though production grew apace in several other regions (especially the West), the primary cause of the economic turmoil that plagued the industry continually during these years was directly attributable to the deteriorating market position of producers in the Central Competitive Field as compared to that of producers in the newer and rapidly expanding fields of Kentucky and West Virginia, where coal is lodged in shallower seams and is generally of better quality than that which is mined farther to the north. During the period 1910 to 1914, for instance, the latter group of interests saw a 5 percent increase in the proportion of their combined output. This increase was almost wholly at the expense of production in Ohio, which finally was all but completely halted by a long and bitter strike that lasted in many parts of the state from early 1914 well into the following year. In the end, however, the effect of competition from southern mining operations came to constitute a significant burden to the entire Central Competitive Field as well, as the growth of demand in both the regional and lake trade continually lagged behind the overall increase in interregional production. Thus, in Illinois, where mining output had grown more rapidly after 1910 than anywhere else in the Central Competitive Field, as 1914 drew to a close it was reported that no less than 25 percent of that state's capacity had fallen into bankruptcy.[8]

A tremendous increase in the demand for soft coal during World War I —both domestically and internationally—enabled the Central Competitive Field, upon the reactivation of much previously idled capacity, to claim approximately a 70 percent share of the industry's marketable product in the upper Appalachian region. The number of active bituminous mines in all regions of the United States combined increased from approximately 5,600 at the beginning of the European war to just under 9,000 by the time hostilities ended in 1919. And yet, wartime demand was sufficiently great to account for more than a twofold increase in the average market value of the industry's gross domestic product.

Soft coal production in the United States declined during 1919 by more than one-fifth in the wake of a year-end strike by workers employed in union mines, which at the time accounted for just over 70 percent of the industry's overall capacity. This loss of production resulted immediately in serious market shortages, which drove prices sharply upward, setting the economic stage for the eventual entry of new "speculative," usually nonunion, operations.

The price spiral did not end, however. During 1920 prices climbed even higher as a result of yet another shortage, brought on by a railway switchmen's strike and a simultaneous increase in the European demand for U.S. coal. The export market remained reasonably attractive the following year also because of a prolonged work stoppage by British coal miners, which helped to cushion the negative effect of the 1921 depression on the level of domestic purchases. Indeed, upward pressure on American coal prices was sustained fairly consistently throughout the first four years after the war, as numerous bottlenecks continued to hamper production at full capacity.

The most serious interruption came in April 1922, when 140,000 anthracite and 460,000 bituminous miners struck for an average of 122 days—a situation in the latter case that brought to a halt fully 60 percent of the industry's current production. In addition, a railway shopmen's strike drastically limited coal deliveries, which increased substantially the overall magnitude of domestic shortages. Then, in 1923, the French occupied the Rurh and ended the flow of German coal to many of its traditional European markets, once again diverting additional demand to American supplies. Output increased and prices began to level off as striking U.S. coal miners returned to work during the late summer and early fall of 1922. Because of sustained foreign demand, however, prices remained reasonably buoyant through at least the first six to eight months of 1923, which in turn worked as a natural—even if now partially moderated—inducement to the continued development of new capacity. All told, between 1921 and 1923 nearly 1,300 new bituminous mines were opened in the United States, which in comparative terms amounted to a phenomenal rate of expansion. Whereas the overall productive potential of the industry had risen by an increment of roughly 31 million tons a year during the very active period of growth from 1899 to 1910 and then declined to an average rate of only 14.5 million additional tons per annum from 1910 to the end of the war, between 1919 and 1923 the yearly increase in bituminous mine capacity climbed to an unprecedented average of something in excess of 50 million tons.[9] But events were soon to show that the rational limits of the industry's expansion had finally been reached.

During the last quarter of 1923, in a sudden break with the general pattern of the recent past, bituminous coal prices began a precipitous decline, reaching a level in the month of December about 27 percent below the market average at the beginning of the previous year. This decline was only the first phase of a deflationary cycle from which the industry was to realize little better than sporadic relief until well into the following decade.

Between 1923 and 1929, operations in more than three thousand active mines, representing approximately 23 percent of the industry's total capacity, were halted. Yet coal prices continued to fall, a phenomenon for which there were two chief explanations. On one hand, demand began to level off because the use of bituminous coal, considered as a proportion of all domestically consumed energy fuel, fell from about 67.4 percent of the total in 1929 to only 53.5 percent ten years later, principally because of a steady increase in the exploitation of oil and natural gas. On the other hand, a substantial increase in the proportion of machine-mined coal and the expansion of strip-mining accounted for an unprecedented decennial increase in the industry's overall productivity. Thus, although employment in the soft coal industry fell between 1923 and 1929 by at least 30 percent, output per unit of labor time increased during the same period by more than one-fifth, or approximately twice the average rate in each of the two preceding decades.[10]

The mechanization of coal production during the 1920s represented a business decision on the part of mining interests throughout the country to trade higher fixed costs for improved productivity and greater labor discipline,[11] a development that was encouraged initially by the highly speculative environment in American coal markets from 1919 to 1923. With the stabilization of demand toward mid-decade, however, the combination of increased operating costs and generally lower sales margins threatened the competitive fortunes of even the most efficient producer. In any given year between 1924 and 1929, the number of bituminous mining operations reporting no net income consistently exceeded those reporting profits. As a result, operating standards throughout the industry deteriorated, and the fate of the individual producer once again hinged principally on the economic and strategic determinants of the wage bill. Nothing bore better witness to this situation than a general deepening of the competitive struggle between those mining interests whose operations had at some point in the past been unionized and those that had not.[12]

Membership in the United Mine Workers, which in 1920 stood at better than half a million, may have declined by as much as 75 percent over the remainder of the decade in the wake of a marked reduction in overall employment and the capture of a progressively greater share of the market by nonunion operators. Between 1918 and 1925, the proportion of bituminous coal mined by workers under union contract declined from roughly 70 to just over 30 percent of the industry's total product.[13]

The strike of 1919 had been settled when a majority of the nation's bituminous operators, along with the UMW, agreed to submit the dispute to government-sponsored arbitration, which resulted early the following year in a substantial wage increase for the industry's unionized workers. But the agreement fell apart in the wake of the 1920–21 economic downturn, as coal operators in those districts where the union was less well established (particularly in certain regions of the South) began systematically to drive wages below the union scale.[14]

Originally, that scale had been established as part of an interstate agreement that was scheduled to expire at the end of March 1922. In December 1921, therefore, the UMW followed customary procedure and called for a joint conference with union operators in the Central Competitive Field, whom the union hoped to persuade to accept an extension of the existing two-year-old contract. The principal operators' associations in Indiana and Illinois responded positively and readily agreed to send delegations.[15] Most producers in southern Ohio and western Pennsylvania, however, steadfastly refused to consider the suggestion as long as their respective market positions appeared to be threatened by low-wage competition from nonunion fields in southern Appalachia. Eventually, the combined efforts of Secretary of Commerce Herbert Hoover and Secretary of Labor James J. Davis were successful in bringing the union and those operators who at one time or another had been involved with the Interstate Joint Conference together for informal discussions, but the talks failed to produce any agreement on terms for a possible renewal of the interstate compact. For their part, both the Southern Ohio Operators' Association and various interests in the region surrounding Pittsburgh insisted upon the necessity of independent district wage settlements, which would allow them to compensate for the competitive advantage ordinarily enjoyed by nonunion producers. To this proposal, as well as to the alternative of government arbitration as proposed by Secretary Hoover, John L. Lewis and the UMW would not consent. With the expiration of the current collective agreement on 31 March, therefore, the stage was set for what was to become the largest single strike yet in the troubled history of the American soft coal industry.[16]

The coal strike of 1922 involved some 460,000 bituminous miners who stayed off the job for an average of four months. It was a massive work stoppage, the most serious ever to hit the industry, and it caused a good deal of concern not only among the coal operators against whom the miners had struck but among various members of the Harding administration. It was widely anticipated, on the basis of past experience, that the net effect of strike-related coal shortages and price inflation would be to create ideal conditions for the wholesale entry of yet new nonunion capacity, which would likely leave the industry in a less predictable state than ever, regardless of the outcome of the strike. Officials in Washington, therefore, wanted to see the dispute terminated as quickly as possible. The administration's position seemed to alternate between encouraging an accommodation that would clear the way for an extension of the 1920 interstate agreement and, in more desperate moments, advocacy of strikebreaking with a view to weakening UMW resistance to a compromise on the question of separate district contracts. The situation was further complicated by the fact that even after the strike had been under way for several weeks, most coal operators still generally opposed any settlement patterned after the experiment of two years earlier,[17] and strikebreaking seemed not to have a substantial effect in the central districts because virtually all experienced miners in these areas belonged to the union. Moreover, many states required the licensing of coal miners so that such statutes would have to be repealed before a scab labor force could be recruited. And, last but not least, many would-be strikebreakers were lured away from the commercial districts by the relatively high wages being offered in independent wagon mines, a vast number of which began production as soon as the strike com-

menced, operating on an extremely narrow or nonexistent margin of investment risk, in pursuit solely of short-term profit from the high spot price for
coal.

According to data compiled by the federal government, the number of
active bituminous mines in the United States increased from 8,038 at the close
of 1921 to 9,299 just one year later. Indeed, although the miners' strike idled
better than 60 percent of the industry's productive capacity from April through
July 1922, total output that year reached a level more than six million tons
greater than in 1921, which had been free of any similar interruption. Production declined substantially during 1922 in every state but Indiana within the
Central Competitive Field. Production in West Virginia and Kentucky increased that year by about 10 and 25 percent, respectively, enabling producers
in those states to sweep into the coal markets of the North. In anticipation of
such an opportunity, nonunion interests in West Virginia, who normally did
not ship an appreciable quantity of coal to the industrial markets of the
Chicago-Gary region, secured a number of lucrative contracts from buyers in
that area before the strike disrupted coal supplies. When the strike began,
approximately 70 percent of the nation's estimated nonunion capacity already
had come under contract, much of it to purchasers who ordinarily were
serviced by UMW-covered operations in the Central Competitive Field.

It was the unwelcome prospect of a potential long-term loss of markets by
coal interests in the north-central districts, along with the union's unwavering
position on the issue of marketwide as opposed to district wage agreements,
that finally forced a settlement of the 1922 miners' strike. As coal prices
soared and anxiety mounted over the steadily accelerating intrusion of nonunion competition, a progressively larger number of producers in the Central
Competitive Field were inclined to agree to a settlement on essentially the
union's terms. On the basis of this apprehension producers representing approximately 20 percent of Central Competitive Field capacity, along with
several operators from other regions of the country, finally agreed formally at a
meeting in Cleveland in mid-August to extend for a period of two years all
contractual arrangements with the miners' union according to the terms in
force immediately before the expiration of the 1920–22 interstate agreement.
Other, somewhat more reluctant, producers fell into line over the course of the
next several days, particularly after it became evident that the railway shop-
craftsmen, also on strike that summer, were rapidly weakening under the
pressure of federal court injunctions. The possibility that normal rail traffic
might be resumed threatened to increase the vulnerability of unionized coal
markets to inroads by nonunion competition. The first to break under the
pressure was the Pittsburgh Coal Company, which decided on 30 August to
sign the Cleveland agreement. And because Pittsburgh Coal was the largest

single producer in the country, most of the remainder of the organized sector of the industry, and particularly all previously unionized producers in the Central Competitive Field, ultimately had very little choice but to conform.[18]

The structure of forces and interests that finally brought the 1922 crisis to an end was almost as compelling in the long run as it had been following the "great strike" of 1919. In February 1924, a meeting between the original signatories to the Cleveland agreement was held in Jacksonville, Florida, whereupon the 1922 pact was renegotiated and extended until 31 March 1927, all with a minimum of the usual acrimonious dissension between the parties concerned. To be sure, coal operators in the Central Competitive Field continued to be troubled by, and to articulate their concern over, the relative inflexibility of production costs as affected by union wage agreements. In particular, they anticipated that lower-cost nonunion competition would likely pose a permanent, perhaps undiminishing, threat to the stability of the industry's product market. In the spring of 1924, however, the primary concern of producers in the central districts was to avoid a strike by union miners upon termination of the existing collective agreement. It was widely feared that any such disruption, or even the mere public anticipation of one, once again would precipitate a displacement in market shares to the advantage of nonunion competition in the South, just when coal operators in the Central Competitive Field had begun to recover at least some of the losses incurred during the strike of 1922. The real issue to be resolved among the interests in attendance at Jacksonville, therefore, was not whether to extend the current agreement with the union but over what period of time a new arrangement might be held in force.[19]

And yet the relatively tranquil business environment in which the new interstate compact was adopted should not be taken as an indication that the soft coal industry in the United States had somehow finally transcended its earlier contradictions. On the contrary, the accomplishments at Jacksonville were tested almost immediately by the first in a series of profound economic shocks that the coal industry was destined to endure periodically for the next decade and a half. With strikes and railway car shortages eliminated, the pressure of surplus capacity and shrinking demand now came down on the bituminous industry with crushing weight. These latest difficulties, moreover, were sorely aggravated by the necessity of liquidating large coal reserves that consumers had accumulated in the expectation of another strike, which was removed as a threat by the 1924 Jacksonville agreement.[20]

As usual, the burden of market shrinkage in bituminous mining was heaviest in the union states, which operated under a fixed wage scale, whereas the southern fields were essentially free to readjust wages in such a way as to afford the best opportunity for competitive gain. After the Jacksonville agreement was signed, most nonunion operators reduced wages, first to the 1919 and later the 1917 level. Some made even more drastic cuts. By the end of 1925, coal operators in practically all of Alabama, Virginia, southern West Virginia, eastern Kentucky, and most of Tennessee were paying their employees an average of one-third less than the current union rate. The effect on the relative cost of production is illustrated by the ability of nonunion interests in western Kentucky, for example, to sell coal in 1925 at an average of $1.44 per ton f.o.b. mine, whereas the average sales realization in Indiana, Kentucky's nearest union competitor, was $2.02. This disparity was not unusual. According to one contemporary student of mining economics, "A like difference, sometimes more and sometimes less, existed between the average prices of other union and nonunion states" as well.[21]

The chief consequence of all this was an eventual collapse of union power within the industry, as every producer's survival in such wild deflationary conditions ultimately came to depend above all on business maneuverability and the avoidance of as many economic strictures as possible, especially uncompetitive wage rates.[22] The process of erosion began among various marginal companies in districts that technically were not part of the Central Competitive Field but whose operations had nevertheless been unionized, and which now proceeded to abandon the terms of their negotiated contracts and reduce wages. Producers most commonly closed down temporarily and then later attempted to resume operations with nonunion labor hired at a radically reduced basic wage.[23] This strategy frequently required the eviction of entire families from company-owned housing along with various other displays of outright repression. In the denunciatory rhetoric of John L. Lewis, the operators not only had "torn up their wage contracts," they had "manned their properties with armed mine guards, searchlights, barbed wire fences, stockades and [other] such paraphernalia of war." They had also resorted, he charged, "to the use of unfriendly courts and . . . sought to bind the workers hand and foot by the issuance of court injunctions, stripping the worker of nearly every right guaranteed him under the Constitution." They had, "in substance and effect, conducted a campaign of community terrorism in the isolated mining villages."[24]

The union-smashing competitive scramble, the most brutal features of which resembled Lewis's poignant description, gained momentum in all of the nation's soft coal markets throughout 1925. Late the previous year, Commerce Secretary Hoover compared what he had seen of the process thus far to a "surgical operation" from which the entire industry no doubt would emerge better off economically.[25] One observer in Illinois, however, viewed anticipated developments there from a somewhat less sanguine perspective. He pointed out that mine entrepreneurs had to worry not only about the impact of subnormal industrial activity but also about extensive and growing economies in coal consumption, the substitution of other fuels, a marked increase in the use by smaller industrial establishments of purchased power from public utility companies, and the ceaseless proliferation of noncommercial "captive" or "industrial out-put" mines. All of these changes, which had come "in rapid succession within a comparatively brief period" and had thus "borne very heavily on the independent commercial producer," he noted, were bound "to make continuing operation for many mines impossible under the present wage scale." He then went on to predict "a further and substantial number" of Illinois mine closings by the following spring and that, "as Tantalus died of thirst with water just barely out of reach, so will a growing number of union miners sit disconsolate alongside of an idle tipple with a non-competitive wage scale as their sole and only comfort."[26]

By the first of the year, the situation facing bituminous operators in Ohio was reported to be "critical" because of the competition of low-cost nonunion mines in West Virginia and Kentucky. Under the circumstances, some of the Ohio interests traditionally tied to the miners' union decided that it would be worth their while at least to explore the possibility of a negotiated suspension of the Jacksonville agreement, "until such time as conditions . . . become normal."[27] On 11 February 1925, a subcommittee of District 8 operators from Ohio met with John L. Lewis in Indianapolis to discuss the issue, but the UMW president flatly rejected the idea with a blunt reaffirmation of his determination to resist any downward revision of the union scale. The Ohioans subsequently tried to persuade union operators in Pennsylvania, Indiana, and Illinois to join them in an effort to force Lewis back to the bargaining table.[28] The representative parties gathered in Cleveland and conferred on the matter in mid-March, but they were unable to reach any agreement on how far they might be able to push the union. All of the operators had agreed beforehand that wages should be reduced, but most of them also thought that the better part of wisdom would be to adopt "Fabian tactics" and "avoid a fight" because nonunion operations would immediately move to take commercial advantage of any interruption of production in the central districts.[29] A strategy of greater patience and caution was favored especially by delegates from Indiana and Illinois, who had been punished by the pressures of competition since Jacksonville somewhat less severely than operators in Ohio and western Pennsylvania. Despite Lewis's earlier rejection of the idea, the latter "were of the opinion that the miners had had enough and might listen to a proposal for a reduction." Indiana and Illinois, however, felt that the proper moment had not yet arrived, sensing that "the period of slack times and unemployment must drag itself out still further" before the miners in their districts would be in "a mood to consider a revision downward."[30]

In the meantime, reports that the disruptive challenge of nonunion coal was "bearing down more heavily than ever," or similar messages, were being heard with increasing frequency throughout the industry. In the same summary of events that carried the details of the operators' conference in Cleveland, the Washington correspondent for *Coal Age* commented on what he perceived to be a rapidly deteriorating situation in virtually every aspect of the trade, with almost all nonunion tonnage shaking down to the 1917 scale or something lower, more and more capacity going nonunion, an ever greater number of miners shifting to nonunion territory, and the promise of increasingly intense competition among nonunion operators. A new wave of wage reductions also appeared imminent, led by one of the big Rockefeller interests, the Consolidation Coal Company, which had recently forced the miners employed in its Somerset properties to take a 25 percent cut in pay.[31] Later in the spring, this trend assumed ominous proportions with respect to the future stability of interdistrict relations in the Central Competitive Field. The critical month was May 1925, when the Pittsburgh Coal Company, still the largest producer in the industry, but which in the management's words now had "its back to the wall," closed the last of fifty-four of its mines operating on the Jacksonville scale and then the following August began reopening them on the basis of the 1917 rate. To remain competitive, other producers in western Pennsylvania were immediately forced to employ the same tactic, which henceforth became known in the business as the "Pittsburgh Plan." By the end of the year, any previous commitment to the idea of even limited regional unity among the operators had vanished, as witnessed by the formal dissolution of the Pittsburgh Coal Producers' Association.[32]

Coal prices and wage rates climbed marginally upward during 1926 in response to a temporary increase in export demand, resulting from another strike by British coal miners. The nonunion districts still retained a clear competitive advantage, however, and business continued to be diverted from the North to the South. Between 1923 and 1926, production in Ohio fell by 31 percent, in Illinois, 13 percent, and in Indiana, 12 percent. Production in Virginia, however, increased by 20 percent, in West Virginia, 33 percent, and in Kentucky, 41 percent. These and similar adjustments in the output of individual states had a profound impact on the regional distribution of market power within the industry, as revealed by data collected in 1927, which indicated that the combined annual output of eight southern states had become the source of supply for nearly half the nation's soft coal requirements, compared to only about 38 percent in 1924.[33]

The Jacksonville agreement was scheduled to expire early in 1927, but not since the turn of the century had the miners' union occupied such a poor bargaining position with regard to its ability to demand and receive a satisfactory contract. Yet in mid-February, when negotiations with the Central Competitive Field's union operators opened in Miami, Lewis and the rest of the UMW bargaining council arrived for the meeting prepared to resist any general wage reduction. They adopted this position knowing full well that acceptance of lower rates in the central districts inevitably would be followed by new competitive reductions in the outlying fields and hence the completion of but one more phase in the perpetuation of a seemingly endless deflationary spiral.[34]

The management representatives of unionized mining operations in Ohio and western Pennsylvania, who were acting with the general approval of the major producers' associations in Indiana and Illinois as well, arrived in Miami determined to hold out for nothing less favorable to their own immediate interests than a sliding wage scale, which presumably would allow the necessary maneuverability for effective competition against nonunion operators.[35] Thus confronted with two fundamentally irreconcilable positions, the Miami conference quickly deadlocked and adjourned *sine die* after only a week of negotiations.

In desperation, the union now moved to concentrate its critically diminished coercive capabilities with an announcement that union producers in various outlying districts would be permitted to continue operations according to the terms of the Jacksonville agreement after the 31 March expiration date, pending a final settlement with producers in the Central Competitive Field. The same offer was subsequently extended to various operators in reasonably secure areas of Indiana and Illinois. But management showed very little interest in the proposal, and on 1 April 1927, the UMW, already in an unprecedented state of organizational collapse, was forced to call yet another industrywide coal strike.[36]

This time only about 176,000 miners participated in the work stoppage, compared to somewhat more than twice that number in 1922. But even the disadvantaged position of the union did not prevent the strike of 1927 from considerably reducing output in fields north of the Ohio River. As in the past, coal mined in nonunion districts farther south immediately began to move into markets ordinarily serviced by northern producers. Unlike the situation during earlier work stoppages, however, nonunion output, together with the effect of considerable consumer stockpiling in anticipation of the strike, was now adequate to meet all current domestic requirements. To be sure, in the wake of the temporary disruption in union fields, overall production during 1927 was down slightly from the year before. But it was about the same as in 1925, a relatively normal year for the industry. Even during the strike, therefore, coal prices generally continued to fall, greatly increasing the pressure on producers still operating within the competitively disadvantaged constraints of the last interstate joint agreement finally to break with the miners' union.

By mid-1927, the demise of the UMW was anxiously anticipated by virtually everyone with a competitive interest in the cost of mining bituminous coal. Several of the country's major railroads closed their captive properties and began buying coal from southern producers with a view to resuming operations eventually on a nonunion basis. Many other large consumers of commercially mined soft coal adopted buying practices designed specifically to help their suppliers defeat the miners' union. Recognizing an opportunity to reduce their fuel costs in the long term, scores of purchasers now refused to buy any union coal, regardless of its sale price. Even those producers who initially were less anxious to press for destruction of the UMW and who could have easily continued to pay union scale if the issue had involved only non-union competition in the outlying districts now also were placed in jeopardy by the rapidly growing volume of nonunion production within their own sales region and thus were forced to adopt a more aggressive bargaining position.[37]

The coal strike of 1927 seems to have stimulated relatively little interest among public officials in Washington in resolving the dispute through federal intervention. In 1922 the miners' union had been in a position to create critical shortages in the nationwide supply of soft coal. This time, however, because supplies were generally sufficient, industries and public utilities that were vitally dependent upon the availability of large quantities of the mineral remained essentially unaffected by the interruption of production in union mines. The reason was the steadily diminishing importance of union capacity in recent years relative to the proportion of the industry's overall product for which the union capacity was accountable. With the strike still in progress, Secretary of Labor Davis commented unapprovingly on this point late in 1927, when he explained that in the absence of any real shortages there was "no force of public opinion to compel action from without." More troubling, according to Davis, was the lack of support within the industry for even a voluntary settlement, in pursuit of which he imagined the government might serve in a reasonably inconspicuous mediatory capacity.[38] The labor secretary's concerns in this respect, however, were exceptional. Most members of the Coolidge administration appeared to be perfectly comfortable with the current ability of the bituminous coal industry to adapt to a competitive situation characterized by an ever more pronounced displacement of the union from a position of strategic significance. Their disinterest encouraged a general attitude on government involvement more or less in line with Hoover's assessment of the issue in testimony before a congressional committee approximately a year earlier. On that occasion the commerce secretary had suggested that as long as nonunion production assured "the continuity of essential services," it was likely that "sufficient protection" would be afforded "to make [wholly] unnecessary [the invocation of] any extraordinary powers" to deal with the situation.[39]

Still, the Coolidge administration felt constrained to make at least a modest political gesture to the union. In December 1927, apparently after repeatedly being urged to do so by Lewis, Secretary of Labor Davis sought to arrange a conference between union officials and industry representatives from western

Pennsylvania, northern West Virginia, and southern Ohio. But the futility of the effort was almost predictable. Most of the producers immediately rejected Davis's invitation, stating that they were "not interested" in any change of their "present arrangements" and that they would seriously consider attending such a conference only if it were called "specifically for the purpose of revising the [wage] scale to meet nonunion competition." This suggestion, of course, Lewis and the union rejected categorically in favor of extending the terms of the Jacksonville agreement. Other operators who might have attended the proposed conference had there been reasonable assurance of reaching a consensus on the issue refused to do so "unless all others in their district would [also] attend." A handful of some of the less hostile producers finally did meet in Washington with representatives of the union from 13 to 15 December. As expected, however, the gathering proved to be of no practical consequence to the resolution of any of the problems then confronting the industry, including the issues that had precipitated the strike.[40]

Both the industry and the union had clearly fallen on extremely hard times. UMW membership by the end of 1927 stood at barely a quarter of what it had been in 1922; and yet, for the time being, the miners' union continued to function more or less as usual. Indeed, in the fall of 1927 the UMW still held an important, if rapidly diminishing, segment of the industry at bay. It even won a temporary extension of the Jacksonville scale in several northern districts whose markets were less vulnerable to inroads by nonunion competition to the south than was typically the case in either western Pennsylvania or southern Ohio. The governing achievement here (commencing 1 October 1927) was a six-month continuation of the preferred $7.50 per day rate in Illinois, the only state in which virtually all production had been halted by the 1927 strike. The extent of the work stoppage in Illinois resulted in a good deal of business being lost to southern competition—a situation that was partially relieved by the eventual resumption of full-capacity operations in the North, but only partially. An expected reversal of the negative trend never did materialize, and when the temporary agreement with the union expired early the following spring, the Coal Operators Association of Illinois firmly rejected any subsequent arrangement, except on terms that would enable the northern producer to recapture lost markets.[41]

Now, finally, because Illinois had been the union's last real stronghold, Lewis and the UMW International Policy Committee had no alternative but to reconsider the organization's fundamental strategic orientation to the industry, which could involve little more than a formal, essentially impotent, adjustment to the objective conditions of the trade. In the end, the Central Competitive Field bargaining unit was dismantled and for the first time individual union districts were authorized by the national leadership to negotiate their own separate collective agreements, an "opportunity" that rapidly resulted in their collective demise. By the end of 1928, only a few producers in northern Illinois, central Ohio, and widely scattered parts of Indiana were still operating under union contracts, and these invariably provided for wages substantially below the Jacksonville scale.[42]

In the bituminous coal industry, one competitor's gain is another's loss. This was the inescapable logic of the market, and the current downward adjustment of wages in the coal fields of the North would not become the first exception.

During the last quarter of 1928, lower prevailing wages and the consequent reduction of regional coal prices enabled many producers in both Ohio and Illinois to regain some of their recent losses in business volume. The recovery accelerated over the course of the next several months, and by the end of 1929 producers in each of these states attained a market standing approximately equal to that which they had held in 1926.

Coal producers in western Pennsylvania and Indiana did not fare nearly as well, at least in part because of a significant increase in strip-mining in areas immediately adjacent to those states' preferred markets. Still, by the end of the decade the so-called Central Competitive Field had recovered essentially all of the market losses originally attributable to the intrusion of cheaper coal from West Virginia, Kentucky, and other points south since 1926. As a result, the entire industry once again, if only briefly, took on the appearance of a reasonably well-integrated commercial organism.[43]

Thus the collapse of union power in the northern districts after 1927 had the effect of equalizing competitive conditions throughout the industry. The commercial benefits, however, were not long-lived. By the beginning of the following decade, the process of "equalization" would guarantee only uncertainty on the part of coal producers everywhere as to whether they could ultimately survive the most serious crisis the industry had ever faced. Even before the nationwide economic collapse, bituminous operators almost without exception found themselves unable to reduce wages and other operating expenses quickly enough to keep pace with falling coal prices and thus frequently were forced to clear their stocks at a net loss.[44] A general concern quickly emerged throughout the industry that the current deflationary plunge could all too easily become a never-ending downward spiral. This fear was reflected as early as the summer of 1929, when certain elements of the trade began to voice their displeasure with the practices of what the president of one large midwestern company referred to as "coal guerillas," who were "cutting the wages of thousands of miners below a sound economic basis."[45]

The situation was soon complicated by a disturbingly "undisciplined" reassertion of economic self-interest on the part of the miners. They were motivated by the appearance in 1930 and 1931 of several new independent unions whose origins were rooted in the inability of the UMW to hold the line on competitive wage reductions after 1928. These organizations generally tended to take a more militant position than the UMW when making representations on behalf of their membership. Indeed, not only were the leaders of groups such as the National and Progressive miners' unions frequently noted for their radical political affiliations, they also were known to harbor a general disregard for the principles of pure and simple "business unionism." All of this was highly unsettling to the coal operators who had to contend with the situation directly as an added disadvantage in the calculation of their own short-term competitive prospects, regardless of how marginal that disadvantage may actually have been.[46]

In an open letter circulated among mine operators throughout the industry in June 1931, Frank E. Taplin, president of the Cleveland-based North American Coal Corporation, candidly expressed his opinion that "the time has come when operators will have to seriously consider whether it is better to operate with a well-regulated Union which has a legitimate right to exist," or to continue competing "with a lot of price-cutting, wage-cutting operators," the demonstrated effect of which "fills the mines with Communists." Taplin, whose company controlled extensive properties throughout the Central Competitive Field, then observed that "operators who have dispensed with Union agreements have had plenty of time [since 1927–28] to view the experience of running without any fixed wage scale." Surely, he thought, all such interests would admit "that the situation is even worse [now] than when we dealt with the Union." Obviously more troubled by the deepening competitive anarchy among producers in the Central Competitive Field than the prospect of returning to a business situation characterized by a reasonably predictable North-South wage differential, Taplin declared that he "would much prefer to deal with the United Mine Workers" than with those wage- and price-chiseling operators who, in every respect, were "a detriment to the industry." He was thoroughly convinced, therefore, that because most operators would "not stick to any decent fixed wage scale . . . if left to their own devices," the only conceivable means by which to "solve" the wage problem—and thereby the price problem as well—would be "to put all competitive fields under a well-managed union."[47]

Taplin's admonition was received remarkably well in various quarters of the industry, even among certain interests as far south as West Virginia.[48] And within a matter of weeks the editors of *Coal Age* concurred that, alas, "a reestablishment of the United Mine Workers to the position of dominance it held prior to 1920 would [indeed] offer tangible promise of genuine economic betterment to the industry." Early in the fall, the same trade journal published a preliminary outline for a "stabilization program," which according to its authors immediately attracted "widespread" and "distinctly favorable" interest from key operators throughout the industry. Basically, the plan called for modification of the Sherman Act in such a way as "to permit joint agreements among operators" on production and pricing policies, as well as "recognition" and "acceptance of an outside labor organization by a sufficiently large percentage of the operators to give the wages and working conditions so established a controlling influence in the districts where direct recognition is withheld."[49]

In 1931, of course, the UMW was still far too weak for most coal producers to anticipate the point at which they might become obliged to accept the unionization of their employees as the key to the restoration of competitive order within the industry. Nevertheless, Lewis and a handful of union operators in the Central Competitive Field urged the White House to support their cause. And it was as a direct result of their request that President Hoover, no doubt suspecting that any response from the industry as a whole would be unenthusiastic at best, finally instructed Secretary of Commerce Robert P. Lamont and Secretary of Labor William N. Doak in the early summer of that year to poll a representative list of operators on the feasibility of convening a joint conference between themselves and officials of the UMW to consider stabilizing the industry's wage and price structure.[50] As expected, most of the operators consulted were convinced that any such meeting would be useless.[51] Thus the conference that Lewis and the union favored most was never held, although Secretary Lamont did meet informally with a group of about twenty-five operators early in July to discuss various problems confronting the industry and the difficulty of settling upon a mutually agreeable range of solutions. Although they squabbled among themselves about their relative responsibility as competitors for the deflationary pressure on coal prices, those in attendance at the gathering generally shared the opinion that unless the market coverage and bargaining power of the miners' union were to improve radically, short of substantial and unprecedented government intervention, little or nothing could be accomplished in the foreseeable future to regularize the industry's competitive affairs.[52]

By this time, certain key producers, although still a distinct minority in the trade, had begun to indicate that they wished to enlist the federal government's direct participation in a systematic effort to stabilize the market price of soft coal.[53] Secretary Lamont responded late in the year to increasingly frequent queries on this issue from some of the more actively concerned lobbyists in the industry. He was unable, however, to offer anything more encouraging than the suggestion that coal operators would for the time being have to be content in seeking, to the extent allowable under the nation's antitrust laws, a more "cooperative spirit" among themselves, based on what he called "mutual confidence and fair dealing."[54]

In this vein, the National Coal Association, representing bituminous interests in at least ten different states, eventually decided to encourage the formation of what amounted to independent district sales cartels, with a view to the establishment of coordinated merchandising and pricing policies between coal producers on a regional basis. This proposal, which was commended by *Coal Age* for its "usefulness" if not mistakenly construed as "a panacea for the basic ills of the . . . industry,"[55] received immediate consideration in all of the major mining districts east of the Mississippi.

The first tangible indication of the proposal's genuine appeal came with the formation of Appalachian Coals, Inc., early in January 1932. Basically, Appalachian Coals was conceived as a kind of marketing agency, whose jurisdiction was to extend throughout West Virginia, Kentucky, and Tennessee. Its function was not really to sell coal—that would be performed by a number of subagents—but to maintain minimum selling prices among producers who were associated as shareholders in the new organization. The agency also sought to inaugurate a form of production control by apportioning available coal orders among the associated producers.[56] The originators of the scheme found the initial response of the operators reasonably encouraging. Within a month of the date on which Appalachian Coals was officially chartered, producers of more than 20 percent of the commercial tonnage in the district had agreed in writing to participate in the plan and companies controlling another 27 percent had indicated they would sign in the near future.[57] In the meantime, however, according to the terms of a prior agreement between representatives of the new marketing agency and the U.S. Department of Justice, activation of the cartel arrangement would have to await an official ruling on the legality of the southern Appalachian plan under the federal antitrust statutes. This hurdle was not easily overcome. An early but unfavorable decision in the United States Circuit Court of Appeals ultimately postponed implementation of the scheme until the spring of 1933.

Throughout the 1920s, any suggestion of federal legislation affecting more than the retail aspects of bituminous mining failed to be taken very seriously either inside or outside the industry. The ineffectual U.S. Coal Commission was the only substantive product of a legislative initiative sparked by Senator William Kenyon's proposed "coal code," which had first been offered in connection with the perceived necessity of an effective response to the crisis of 1922. Then, once again, some six years later, James E. Watson, an Indiana Republican and chairman of the Senate Committee on Interstate Commerce, held hearings on a measure that he and a handful of other Washington legislators believed would stabilize market relations in the disordered bituminous industry. Had it been accepted, the Watson bill would have established a standard code of operation, which in addition to reinvigorating the miners' union would have provided for government regulation of wages, prices, and profits. As a special enticement to the operators, the measure would have relaxed the antitrust provisions of the Sherman Act as well, thus permitting cooperative production and marketing arrangements subject to the retention of a license from a new federal bituminous coal commission, charged with enforcing industrywide compliance with the various provisions of the code. The UMW was strongly in favor of the measure, but the operators were virtually unanimous in their opposition, in part because of the lingering attraction of an opportunity to exploit the current powerlessness of the union, and in part because of the generally unappealing nature of the federal licensing provision. Moreover, neither President Calvin Coolidge nor Secretary Hoover showed any interest in the measure, and as the Senate hearings drew to a close everyone assumed that the bill was destined to go no further.[58]

Four years later, however, both the material fortunes of the trade and the mood of many of the operators had undergone a considerable change. By 1932, with no end to the deflationary spiral in sight, unprecedented numbers of mine owners in desperate straits were acknowledging their willingness to support not only a renewal of bargaining relations with the UMW, as had been urged by Frank Taplin and a few others a year or so earlier, but also more far-reaching regulatory schemes, such as that introduced by Senator James J. Davis, the former Republican secretary of labor, and Congressman Clyde Kelly, both of Pennsylvania.[59] The Davis-Kelly bill, which resembled the Watson bill in nearly every detail, was also given an unqualified vote of approval by the traditionally cautious U.S. Chamber of Commerce.[60] That support, however, was still easily counterbalanced by the opposition of consumer interests and an overwhelming majority of the coal operators, who steadfastly refused to agree to a legislated response to the industry's problems. Attitudes and positions on such matters within the industry were increasingly fluid and subject to change. But this phase of developments was clearly governed by an inclination to withhold final judgment on the question of federal regulation, at least until the uncertain legality of voluntary production and marketing pools was finally resolved. That issue was still in the hands of the courts. Yet as long as there was any chance that regional sales cartels or some other form of self-imposed rationalization might become a realistic option, most of the nation's bituminous coal operators remained less than enthusiastic about submitting either to the restoration of bargaining relations with the UMW or to the imposition of federally supervised trade practices.[61]

In the meantime, Washington lawmakers were quick to react to the hesitancy of the operators on the Davis-Kelly bill as the attention of both Congress and the coal producers suddenly shifted to a substitute measure introduced in the House of Representatives by David J. Lewis of Maryland. The Lewis bill followed closely the outlines of the British Coal Mines Act of 1930. It designated the producing district as the fundamental unit of organization and provided for the formation of a coal operators' national council, which was to serve as a representative policy-coordinating body in the implementation of an intricately devised system of production controls. Individual quotas were to be determined on the basis of any given mine's average annual capacity since 1919. Each producer would be allotted a proportionate level of production based on his "standard tonnage" calculated as a percentage of current market demand. The bill also provided for the creation of an independent coal commission that would be authorized to fix both maximum prices and freight rates, the latter subject to review by the Interstate Commerce Commission.

The Lewis bill had wide appeal within the industry, as much for its ambiguous and contradictory character as because it conferred organizational autonomy at the district or regional level.[62] The bill was worded in such a way as to make production an inalienable right, in observance of which the operator would be allowed to increase his overall output merely by "purchasing" additional quota allotments. In short, even as late as mid-1932, there had yet to appear any indication of a consensus within the industry as to the type or level of commitment necessary for a truly effective response to the ever-widening crisis.[63]

Actually, none of the proposed solutions to the soft coal industry's economic ills could have suited the competitive goals of every entrepreneurial element in the trade. The idea of regional exclusivity was appealing to many producers in the outlying and southern Appalachian districts. This segment of the industry was still potentially capable of expanding its commercial penetration of northern markets and thus had every reason to be gratified when the U.S. Supreme Court finally handed down a favorable decision in the *Appalachian Coals* case. That ruling, issued in March 1933, found Appalachian Coals, Inc., innocent of the charge that its activities as a cooperative sales agency would be detrimental to the interests of "free competition" or in any way constitute a violation of the antitrust laws.

As pleasing as this decision was to some coal mine operators, the district-by-district approach was not regarded uniformly within the industry as the most suitable means of handling a problem that was ummistakably interregional in character.[64] Producers in the northern fields in particular objected that marketing cartels—in competition with one another—obviously would be insufficient in reducing wage differentials between widely separated mining districts, especially if the southern regions continued to enjoy relative immunity from the influence of unions. Indeed, it was with this concern in mind that key producers in the Central Competitive Field, led by longtime union operators in Indiana and Illinois, ultimately confronted the new Democratic administration with their unequivocal preference for a government-sponsored regulatory program dedicated to the stabilization of production, prices, and wages on an industrywide basis.[65] Most of these were the same operators who as much as two years earlier had professed their willingness, in principle, to support revitalization of the UMW as the only readily apparent means of reducing excessive wage competition within the industry. This was a highly controversial position. Yet it, too, was about to be resurrected with unprecedented force as the major producer coalitions in the bituminous mining industry struggled to attain economically divergent ends by the manipulation of new political opportunities attendant upon Congress's adoption of the National Industrial Recovery Act early in the summer of 1933. The outcome of this struggle and the closely related experiences of key management groups in the cotton textile and garment manufacturing industries, several of which also hoped that a more active government industrial policy would bring an end to capitalist anarchy in their own immediate sphere of interest, is the subject of the chapters in Part II of this book.

# Part Two

---

# Labor and the NIRA: A Concert of Interests

# 4 Legislative Odyssey

The economy was in its fourth year of depression when Franklin Delano Roosevelt was inaugurated as president in March 1933. The number of unemployed had reached thirteen million, or about one-quarter of the civilian labor force, and the country's real net product had declined by approximately 33 percent and national income by more than 50 percent since the beginning of the downward slide in 1929. Popular expectations of an effective political response to the steadily deteriorating economic situation had become increasingly apparent during 1932 coincident with the largest annual decline in output and employment since the onset of the crisis. Confidently expressed preferences for various emergency measures were emanating from organized business groups who had a clear, if often extremely narrow, vision of what might be accomplished in their own best interest, as well as from those who professed to be aware of the increasingly profound sense of political frustration and economic despair among all Americans. Yet in the spring of 1933, business and political leaders were still nearly as far from agreement on the organizational requirements of a thoroughgoing response to the national economic calamity as they had been three years earlier.

Born essentially of the unprecedented breadth of the Depression and the initial rush by legislators to meet the often conflicting protectionist expectations of nervous constituencies, an irresolute political atmosphere in Congress between 1929 and 1932 precluded any agreement on central economic issues. Legislative chaos and the extremely cautious attitude of most businessmen during this period toward any suggestion of a political solution to their economic problems, moreover, served only to encourage Herbert Hoover's unremitting and outspoken confidence in what Ellis W. Hawley has described as a highly personalized version of "associationist" capitalism.[1] Thus, although control of the political situation after 1929 escaped him, Hoover pursued, with considerable self-assurance, a course of action toward which he was naturally inclined and steadfastly advocated a policy of voluntarism. For even though the wisdom of that doctrine had come under growing suspicion in view of an apparent contradiction between its basic precepts and the practical require-

73

ments of the moment, its firm rejection was prevented before 1932 by the absence of a clearly articulated and politically salable alternative.

Meanwhile, by 1930, precisely because of the pervasive sense of political insecurity engendered by the Depression, the conservative consensus of the 1920s was nearing collapse. Sustained economic and political uncertainty gave rise to the delineation of widening fractures among the GOP hierarchy and the alienation of an ever greater body of Republican congressional sentiment from President Hoover's almost maverick disregard of political realities.[2] The seriousness of the situation was revealed plainly in the midterm elections, when, after a decade of overwhelming Republican dominance, the Democrats captured 105 seats and the balance of power in the House of Representatives by a margin of 5 and reduced the Republican plurality in the Senate from 11 to 1, leaving the potential of a deadlocked body in the hands of a solitary Farmer-Laborite.[3]

The practical effect of the political rout was not immediately apparent. With the aid of conservative southern Democrats and a few remaining party loyalists, Hoover was still able to defeat all but the most ineffectual of an assortment of federal relief measures which Senate liberals, led by Robert F. Wagner of New York, had begun to push in earnest several months before the congressional elections. Ironically, however, Hoover was forced almost simultaneously to compromise his preference for voluntary economic controls by the persuasive efforts of his own appointed functionaries. The grandest occasion on which such an effort occurred was when Eugene Meyer, governor of the Federal Reserve Board, joined with Treasury Secretary Andrew Mellon and some of the nation's most influential bankers to declare the necessity of establishing a mechanism similar to the recently liquidated War Finance Corporation as a means of relieving hard-pressed private institutions from the suffocating constrictions of the domestic financial crisis. Hoover wanted the bankers to set up cooperative credit pools, which the latter thought would be inadequate to the restorative task at hand.[4] In the end, amid increasingly enthusiastic backing in Congress for federal support of the domestic credit structure, the widely perceived need for a government agency empowered to function essentially along the lines recommended by the banking interests became too compelling politically for even President Hoover to resist. Thus, finally, late in 1931, he too proffered a reluctant endorsement of that goal.[5]

Indeed, by this time, any tangible influence Hoover may have once had over the fragile balance of the nation's political and economic affairs had been almost completely neutralized by the cumulative effects of the current crisis.[6] Ultimately, in one final breach of faith, even the few remaining adherents to the Republican administration's two-year-old wage maintenance policy in the durable and capital goods industries also gave way under the prolonged strain of the Depression and began reducing their rate scales in what conservative financial interests had long insisted would be an "inevitable step in the process of economic readjustment."[7] The wage maintenance agreement was the cornerstone of Hoover's attempt to construct a voluntary barrier against the deflationary spiral. But now, obviously in anticipation of the approaching demise of this and similar arrangements, U.S. Steel president James A. Farrell acknowledged the unassailable logic of an opinion already shared by most businessmen when he quipped at a meeting of the American Iron and Steel Association in May 1931 that those who imagined that purely cooperative restraint among employers might any longer mitigate the harsh economic realities of the competitive struggle to survive were "living in a fool's paradise."[8]

## The Norris-LaGuardia Act

As the economic crisis deepened and distressed constituencies grew increasingly impatient for capable political leadership to take charge, desire in the dilatory Seventy-second Congress to create at least the appearance of movement finally overcame even the most sympathetic of Hoover's erstwhile allies. In the spring of 1932, the editors of *Business Week* described an "almost hysterical condition . . . a state of fear on Capitol Hill which the oldest inhabitants regard as a high water mark,"[9] as conservative Republicans and heretofore hesitant Democrats alike hastily lined up behind one federal relief proposal after another in anticipation of the inevitable popular retribution they would face at the polls in the fall.

It was in this atmosphere of political desperation that Congress finally passed the Norris-LaGuardia anti-injunction bill early in 1932 by an overwhelming margin of 75 to 5 in the Senate and 363 to 13 in the House. Court injunctions and restraining orders were widely employed during the 1920s as strikebreaking devices. Organized labor, in search of relief, argued its case in numerous state legislatures with moderately favorable results toward the end of the decade. By 1928 the jurisdiction of federal courts in labor disputes, and especially the legally sanctioned prohibitions of the "yellow dog contract," had become a prominent national election issue.[10] In that year, and again in 1930, Senator George W. Norris, a progressive Nebraska Republican, proposed federal anti-injunction legislation. In both instances, the Judiciary Committee, dominated by arch-conservatives, failed to report the bill for consideration by the full Senate. For this Norris later decided he should have been grateful because even had the measure won the support of a majority in each house, before 1931 Congress almost certainly would have sustained a presidential veto, in which event he thought the issue probably could not have later been successfully raised in the more receptive Seventy-second Congress.[11] By 1932 the political sensibilities of the members of both parties in the national legislature were so totally at odds with those of Hoover that a presidential veto of the anti-injunction bill would have been futile. Of this Hoover was aware, although it apparently did not prevent him from continuing to work behind the scenes to forestall legislation, or, failing that, to anticipate various ways in which the executive branch might diminish the impact of the measure once it had become law.[12]

Liberal and civil libertarian opinion continued the campaign for anti-injunction legislation after the failure of the Norris bill in 1930. The local leaders of many trade unions, however, remained content to pursue the issue in their state legislatures, where some tangible gains had already been realized. Indeed, because congressional proponents of the measure repeatedly declined to accept certain amendments requested by the AFL which would have strengthened it, sentiment within the federation hierarchy in favor of the Norris bill was, almost from the outset, frankly reserved. It was not until December 1931, when its congressional backers were confident of victory and thus apparently anxious to report the legislation even in the absence of firm support from the AFL, that William Green and the federation executive council finally were authorized in convention formally to endorse the bill without the preferred amendments.[13]

The only real barrier to the legislative success of the anti-injunction law had been removed by the results of the congressional elections in 1930 and the consequent decline of the conservative majority on the Senate Judiciary Committee. In the spring of 1932, therefore, it was almost foreordained that Congress would pass the measure once given a clear opportunity to do so. Yet it would be a mistake to suppose that the adoption of the Norris-LaGuardia Act suddenly made Congress the uncompromising protector of labor's rights as against the traditional prerogatives of business power. Most members of both the House and the Senate, and certainly the conservative Republicans who voted in favor of the measure, were unalterably opposed to anything that smacked of "class legislation," of which some businessmen who testified against the anti-injunction bill described it as being a common variety. Congress was predisposed to approve the Norris bill, not because many members in either house cared deeply about the implications of their vote vis-à-vis abstract principles of social justice, but rather because, and in spite of the protestations of business spokesmen, the measure appeared at the time to be a fundamentally unmomentous and uncomplicated piece of legislation.[14]

In substance, the Norris bill had been conceived in the best tradition of laissez-faire. According to Philip Selznick's characterization of the two basic functions of public law in modern capitalist democracies, it was essentially "facilitative" as opposed to "prescriptive" in intent.[15] The measure went little further than to reaffirm before the law labor's right to organize and bargain in its own collective self-interest, free from the imposition of political and legal restraints as had been guaranteed previously, at least in principle, by Section 20 of the Clayton Act and other federal statutes.[16] Indeed, there is every indication that the specific provisions of the anti-injunction law were not among the dominant concerns of a great many of its congressional supporters. Nevertheless, in early 1932 the Norris bill provided the only real occasion for the legislative unanimity by which it was universally hoped that threatened political futures might yet be redeemed, but which, as far as more fundamental national economic issues were concerned, had been so thoroughly frustrated by the pervasiveness of the economic crisis.

## The Legislative Vortex: March–June 1933

Some historians have suggested that early New Deal labor policy had important institutional roots in the principles and mechanisms of Woodrow Wilson's War Labor Administration, which was instituted as part of the domestic mobilization apparatus during World War I.[17] It is true that there were certain bureaucratic and functional similarities between the first National War Labor Board,[18] federal intervention in railroad labor disputes during the 1920s, and various New Deal predecessors of the National Labor Relations Board as finally established in 1935. It is also true that Franklin Roosevelt, in his capacity as assistant secretary of the navy from 1913 to 1920, had become personally acquainted with the work of the Shipbuilding Labor Adjustment Board.[19] In cause and effect, however, the politics of industrial relations during the New Deal differed considerably from the politics of mediation common to numerous instances of government intervention in labor disputes before 1933. During World War I, the federal government and business alike were primarily concerned with controlling the deleterious effects of labor's temporarily enhanced market power on the industrial economy and the national war effort. The direction taken by federal labor policy during the 1930s, by contrast, was essentially a manifestation of a more positively conceived response to the interindustrial convergence of rampant deflationary pressures, including the culmination of disintegrative tendencies that had been operative during the previous decade in several key industrial product markets and the diminished relative market power of labor. Ultimately, the Wilson administration's wartime labor policy, and that of the Roosevelt administration during the Depression of the 1930s, evolved under, and in response to, fundamentally different economic and political circumstances, involving substantially different motives and expectations on the part of those directly concerned with the formulation and implementation of policy.

Roosevelt had never been a partisan of organized labor. Both personally and officially, as a New York state senator from 1910 to 1912, then as assistant secretary of the navy during World War I, and finally as governor of New York from 1928 to 1932, FDR's attitude toward labor had been, in the frequently quoted words of one moderately critical biographer, at best, "benevolently paternalistic."[20] His election to the presidency in 1932 owed little or nothing to trade union support. Indeed, several important national union leaders, including United Mine Workers president John L. Lewis, remained loyal to Herbert Hoover and the Republicans throughout the contest. Moreover, if Roosevelt's sensitivity to the legitimate aspirations of organized labor gradually increased during his first term in office as a great many historians seem to believe, this was very likely the result of a long-term political education and not the belated flowering of some innate progressive impulse. Thus, although throughout his political career FDR customarily supported the adoption of various measures traditionally recognized as the legislative building blocks of New Deal labor policy, he most certainly was not their relentless advocate.[21] Any such advocacy, one may reasonably assume, would have contrasted too sharply with his personally ambitious but profoundly cautious approach to politics. For this reason, therefore, as one observer has written of Roosevelt, "labor found him helpful when its political artillery was loaded and well-aimed, but merely friendly when it seemed outgunned in the battle for votes."[22] Such pragmatism was entirely in character for FDR. For despite what Arthur Schlesinger, Jr., has identified as the man's occasional "moments of concreteness,"[23] Roosevelt was not in the habit of making boldly independent policy commitments, for fear of the political risks that might entail. His deliberately reserved behavior in this respect was manifest repeatedly as a fundamental aversion to programmatic politics of any sort, an aversion that has been identified by innumerable commentators as the basic source of Roosevelt's typically expedient (some would say "flexible") approach not only to the problems of labor but to most of the critical policy issues with which he was forced to contend, beginning with his candidacy in opposition to Hoover and ultimately as the newly elected head of state.[24]

As a result of his routinely accommodating political style, Franklin Roosevelt entered the White House under the burden of a long list of vaguely worded, frequently conflicting campaign promises, symbolized by the offer of an ill-defined "new deal" for the American electorate. On the strength of this slogan alone, public anticipation ran extraordinarily high. But for combating the economic depression, the Roosevelt government clearly had come to power without any overall plan. "There were," according to Raymond Moley, "only pieces of a program and ideas that still lacked formulation."[25]

At least five main currents of thought or policy orientations adrift during the spring of 1933 eventually combined to mold the defining features of the National Industrial Recovery Act (NIRA).[26] First, there was the concept of national industrial planning, a moderately statist solution to overproduction and underconsumption, in which the federal government would assume primary responsibility for keeping the economy on a smooth and even keel. Perhaps the most forceful advocate of this approach among Roosevelt's top advisers was Rexford Tugwell, a professor of economics at Columbia University, whose counsel probably had less direct impact on the president's thinking than the relatively restrained, more nearly traditional advice of two other Columbia academics, Raymond Moley and Adolf Berle. Together these three men made up FDR's election strategy group, the so-called Brains Trust. Moley and Berle were inclined to preserve a somewhat more generously liberal participatory role for business in the planning concept than would likely have been recommended by Tugwell, who, by his own account, found Roosevelt almost instinctively resistant to anything even remotely resembling a "collectivist" approach to the problem of economic recovery.[27]

Second, there was the public works concept, which would involve vast government expenditures designed to "prime the pump" of business recovery and thus provide for the immediate reemployment of labor. Most of the pressure in this direction came from key political figures in Congress, particularly Senators Wagner, Robert La Follette, Jr., and Edward P. Costigan, all of whom seem to have been genuinely impressed with the growing need for direct federal assistance to the unemployed. Both as progressives and as responsible public officials, they felt compelled to address the completely unacceptable implications of unrelieved joblessness for the long-term prospects of economic recovery and the general security of the national political order.[28] Roosevelt, however, had never indicated much support, from the time he received the Democratic nomination to the inauguration ceremony, for the public-spending route to recovery. He consistently attempted to present himself as being even more committed to a balanced budget than his predecessor, and with the full support and encouragement of his own administration's fiscal conservatives, FDR continued to resist the spending approach throughout the first critical weeks after his assumption of office on 4 March 1933.[29]

Third, there were the so-called business planners. Representatives of this group advocated at least a temporary suspension of the federal antitrust laws with a view to limiting price-cutting and generally "rationalizing" industrial operations through the organizational efforts of trade associations or other autonomous groups of entrepreneurs interested in seeking the benefits of economic regulation, industry by industry, without the imposition of rigidly inflexible government controls. By the spring of 1933 dozens of proposals and endorsements of proposals for self-government in industry had been received by the Roosevelt administration and aired for public consideration, most of which were patterned fairly closely after either the famous "Swope Plan," authored in 1931 by Gerard Swope, president of the General Electric Company, or the similar measure prepared and published by Henry I. Harriman for the U.S. Chamber of Commerce early in 1932. Both the Swope and Harriman proposals urged that trade associations or their equivalents in industry be given every necessary legal sanction so that they might put into effect their own independently determined controls on levels of output, certain variable costs of production (including wages), and, when it was deemed appropriate, the retail price of goods as well. They also accepted some responsibility for the sponsorship of such generally worthy goals as more stable employment and the adoption of compulsory social insurance for workers.[30]

Within the Brains Trust, Adolf Berle appears to have been the most determined advocate of the business planning concept. One of the clearest displays of his influence in this regard was contained in Roosevelt's famous campaign address at the Commonwealth Club in San Francisco on 23 September 1932. This document, which had been drafted by Berle with only minor revisions by the candidate, was formulated around the position that industrial production must be regulated to fit stable market conditions, all perfectly consistent with the business planners' concept of controlled competition. Just a few days after the election, Berle drew up a memo for Moley enumerating his recommendations for legislation to be proposed at a special session of Congress, which he expected Roosevelt to convene early in the spring. Second among these, next to a "domestic allotment plan or some other plan designed to increase [the] purchasing power of the farmer," was "industrial stabilization—limited permission to industries to get together under suitable supervision or stabilization plans, *provided* they afford reasonable probability of greater employment, protection to the consumer, and are kept under control."[31]

Berle's ruminations in this connection closely prefigured the essence of the National Industrial Recovery Act.[32] His, and to a lesser extent Moley's, receptivity to the business planning approach set the stage in March 1933 for the submission that month of a number of detailed stabilization proposals from the likes of Harriman of the Chamber of Commerce and similarly inclined individuals affiliated with the National Association of Manufacturers (NAM), the Cotton Textile Institute, and other trade groups. Yet, as of early April, all of this activity had succeeded in moving Roosevelt only marginally closer to the position of those who favored antitrust liberalization. With the possible exception of its immediate acceptability for resolving chaotic conditions in the oil, bituminous coal, and other natural resource industries, the "trustification" of industry was still one of several competing policy options theoretically available to the new administration. In the last analysis, however, FDR was frightfully wary of any departure from traditional American ideals of competitive enterprise so bold as that being advocated by the business revisionists without some reasonable assurance as to its political acceptability. Lacking that, he finally rejected any thought of proposing an across-the-board moderation of the nation's antitrust laws, at least in the current session of Congress, and so informed business lobbyists personally on 11 April.[33]

A fourth policy orientation evolved during the winter of 1932–33 and the first few weeks following Roosevelt's inauguration in the hands of what Robert F. Himmelberg has identified as the "start-up planners."[34] This group included such influential figures as James P. Warburg, Meyer Jacobstein, Fred I. Kent, and Harold G. Moulton, whose goals were quick recovery and reemployment. These goals were to be accomplished largely through the extension of loans to industry, in addition perhaps to financial guarantees against business losses, measures that were presented as alternatives to the deficit-spending, public-relief approach. The so-called start-up proposals clearly had their greatest appeal among the administration's fiscal conservatives, including Roosevelt himself, because they offered a potential escape from the mounting pressure to spend. Raymond Moley, however, who received and appended his criticisms to all such plans before they ever reached the president, still was not convinced that public works or other potentially costly stimulative programs could be ruled out as viable and appropriate policy options. This, at least, was his position at the end of March. Accordingly, when he and Roosevelt met on 4 April with the various start-up measures in hand to discuss the feasibility of choosing and implementing a recovery plan, they readily agreed to defer any final decision on the basis of their shared concern that, as Moley later put it, "thinking in business and government circles on the subject had not yet crystallized sufficiently to justify any further moves at that time."[35]

Sometimes referred to as the "share the work movement," the fifth and seemingly most popular policy orientation adrift during the winter of 1932–33 eventually materialized as a preference for the standardized limitation of work periods in industry, a strategy tailored to facilitate the widest possible distribution of existing employment. The familiar and uncomplicated premises that underlay this approach gave it its appeal. On one level, the idea appears to have emanated directly from traditional progressive concerns about the chronic maldistribution of wealth in the United States. More or less parallel, however, was the equally "progressive" desire to buttress and enhance the purchasing power of the working citizenry, with the expectation that that alone would go a long way toward restoring the nation and American business to economic good health, thus obviating the need for any deeper adjustment of the basic institutional structures of society.[36]

Adopted and popularized by the likes of Sidney Hillman, Edward Filene, Hugo L. Black, Robert Wagner, Felix Frankfurter, and Marriner Eccles, the purchasing power thesis was also rooted firmly in what might best be characterized as a proto-Keynesian, "underconsumptionist" interpretation of the Depression.[37] In the words of one particularly perceptive student of the ideological patterns of New Deal thought, "it ran like an iron rod" through the intellectual life of the era,[38] defining in certain critical respects the range of politically acceptable policy options available to the recovery strategists. The purchasing power thesis seems to have been the economic argument that eventually allowed the New Deal progressives to reach a consensus on the broad outlines of a recovery plan. Although the New Dealers were not inveterate optimists, the purchasing power thesis was derived from an essentially hopeful, if by no means perfectly benign, prognosis of the Depression. It implied the existence of serious but nonetheless remediable shortcomings in the system, not fundamental contradictions, and it was on this basis that it could be advanced so widely, with almost universal appeal, not only as an analysis of the causes of the Depression but as the guiding light to those who would achieve its cure as well.[39]

Roosevelt's understanding of the Depression's subtler technicalities was informed by a basic familiarity with the purchasing power thesis. It was in response to this generally shared sense of things gone awry that FDR and his industrial commissioner, Frances Perkins, had combined their efforts (albeit with very little success) in an attempt to bring about wage-and-hour legislation during Roosevelt's term as governor of New York. After she became FDR's secretary of labor in March 1933, Perkins forcefully pursued her belief that wage-and-hour controls were urgently needed to shore up workers' income, arrest the deflationary spiral, and create jobs. Before the inauguration, she and Felix Frankfurter persuaded Roosevelt to include state regulation of hours and wages as one of the topics to be raised at the national Governors Conference scheduled to convene on 6 March. To the labor secretary, however, this was a limited accomplishment, which she seems to have taken as merely an opening wedge in a strategy designed eventually to achieve the adoption of a comprehensive program of federally regulated employment standards, a goal that Roosevelt apparently endorsed, at least in principle, when Perkins initially broached the subject as a condition of her agreement to accept the cabinet post.[40]

Yet during his first few weeks in office, wage-and-hour legislation seems not to have been one of FDR's chief concerns. He was more preoccupied with the need for emergency banking reforms, propping up the agricultural sector, and initiating a general relief program for the unemployed. This is not to deny that Roosevelt was at least vaguely aware of the continuing and deepening need for an overall economic recovery plan, although initially he declined to devote much time to the details of the issue. In mid-March, FDR instructed Moley to sift through various legislative proposals that had been brought to his attention in recent weeks to determine which of them might be worthy of serious consideration. At the same time, Senator Wagner and Undersecretary of Commerce John Dickinson were working independently along similar lines. Still, when Roosevelt and Moley met once again on 4 April to consider specific legislation, they concluded that the time had not yet arrived for a firm presidential commitment. The basis of that decision, Moley later explained, had to do with their feeling that the nation's business leaders were still too far from agreement among themselves as to precisely what level of political intervention the economic situation required. In addition, a troublesome and directly related question was whether Congress was ready to allow business interests and those working on their behalf a role in the policy-making process that would enable them to guarantee the acceptability of whatever legislation eventually might be enacted.

In the latter respect especially, the antitrust revisionists had very little cause for optimism. Just two weeks before Roosevelt's inaugural, the Washington correspondent for *Business Week* reported that "most members of the House and Senate [currently] regard with suspicion any suggestion to relax the laws regulating business." The same commentator attributed this "suspicion" to the widely held belief "that the real purpose of nearly all such suggestions, no matter how carefully limited in scope they appear to be, is to nullify some general principle." This attitude must change, he predicted, or "no one of the many proposals to permit restriction of production or joint selling agencies or the like is going to pass."[41]

At the same time, however, Congress seemed favorably impressed with the general concept of the Thirty-Hour Week bill. This measure was introduced in the Senate on 21 December 1932 by Hugo L. Black, Democrat of Alabama, followed early in January 1933 by a counterpart in the House of Representatives sponsored by William P. Connery of Massachusetts.[42] The reasoning behind the Black bill derived from the underconsumption/purchasing power interpretation of the Depression. Along with its unique functional simplicity and the absence of any soundly formulated alternative, that intimate association with the purchasing power rationale largely explains the measure's unusually rapid rise to popularity as a potentially significant contribution to the goal of economic recovery. In deference to long-standing opposition from both the Supreme Court and the AFL, the bill had no provision for a minimum wage. But Senator Black argued that a maximum thirty-hour workweek would spread jobs, halt the expanding attack on labor standards, and increase the purchasing power of workers. Specifically, the measure would prohibit shipment in interstate commerce of goods produced by establishments in which any person was employed more than six hours a day, five days a week.

Congress held hearings on the Black-Connery bills during January and February 1933. Spokesmen for organized labor generally supported the measure,[43] but representatives of organized business groups such as the U.S. Chamber of Commerce and the National Association of Manufacturers tended to cloak an array of substantive objections to the "inflexibility" of a mandatory thirty-hour workweek by expressing concern for the probable "unconstitutionality" of the proposed legislation. At least one significant group of business leaders, however, did not oppose the bill. Both northern and southern textile interests seemed intrigued by the prospect of legislation that would enforce a reduction of spindle running time throughout their industry, particularly if it could be coupled with greater tariff protection for domestic producers.[44] The Black bill's popularity in Congress presented textile manufacturers with a unique opportunity to impose effective production controls on the industry after the frustration of a patently unsuccessful campaign to line up support within the trade for a program of voluntarily restricted output. Producers in New England in particular were attracted to the idea of federal legislation, some of them arguing that it might dissuade them from eventually pressing for a "moratorium" on state labor restrictions that placed them at a competitive disadvantage with their southern counterparts, whose operations were subject to less rigorous employment standards.[45]

At this point, however, the politicians were still undecided about what to do. At the hearings on the Black bill, suggestions were entertained regarding a variety of measures that could be construed as collateral to the thirty-hour week proposal yet applicable to a somewhat more comprehensive recovery program. Much of the inspiration for these tentative approaches to the recovery problem came from the regulatory precepts embodied in such measures as the Davis-Kelly coal stabilization bill, upon which Congress also had deliberated recently.[46] The president-elect was preoccupied with a number of other Depression issues at the time. But there is evidence that he was sufficiently aware of these evolving legislative crosscurrents to investigate (briefly) the possibility of striking a balance between the advocates of the increasingly popular work-sharing approach, on one hand, and the business associationists, on the other, many of whom favored suspension of the antitrust laws so they might legally "conspire" to restrict competition, generally rationalize their commercial operations, and increase profits. Thus, in mid-February, reports appeared in the press to the effect that Roosevelt had recently "suggested to business leaders a trade whereby the anti-trust laws would be modified in return for a 6-hour day, 5-day week agreement." This idea reportedly followed from the president's belief that "Progressives in the Senate . . . heretofore unalterably opposed to any relaxation of the restrictions on 'Big Business,' would yield to get the shorter working day and week."[47] No action was taken, however, as the Seventy-second Congress languished passively through the few remaining days of the lame duck session. The House Committee on Labor reported the Connery bill favorably, but otherwise Congress declined at this time to move any further on the recovery front.

The newly installed Seventy-third Congress was much more anxious to demonstrate a capacity for decisive action. The legislative climate was receptive, therefore, when the Black-Connery bills were reintroduced on 10 March

1933. They were reported favorably by the Senate Judiciary Committee on 30 March and by the House Committee on Labor on 4 April. Two days later, to almost everyone's astonishment, the Senate passed the Black bill by a vote of 53 to 30 after rejecting an administration-backed amendment that would have changed the prescribed maximum workweek from thirty to thirty-six hours.[48]

The Senate's hasty, if not altogether unexpected, approval of the Thirty-Hour Week bill shocked the administration out of its habitual state of profound indecision, which most recently had been exemplified by Roosevelt and Moley in their refusal on 4 April to move ahead with the formulation of a recovery proposal. Thus the administration's almost studied inaction finally enabled Congress to assume the legislative initiative, and Roosevelt, with a certain amount of discomfort, would have to respond.

FDR's first concern was the likelihood that Representative Connery, in an exercise of power as chairman of the House Labor Committee, would immediately call up his version of the thirty-hour bill, rush it through Congress, and confront the administration with the uncomfortable necessity of passing judgment publicly on a measure that was rapidly gaining popularity among some constituencies but which most business interests denounced vociferously as bad economics and therefore unacceptable. Roosevelt's position was made doubly difficult because he essentially agreed with the business argument that an across-the-board thirty-hour workweek was unnecessarily restrictive, not to mention his suspicion that such a measure by itself ultimately would be inadequate to the task of ending unemployment and the Depression. This view is attested to by Moley, who has written that his notebook contained FDR's "reaction to the Black bill under the category of 'Threats.' " Indeed, the president "was quick to realize that, should it pass the House, it could only paralyze industry, not revive it, and [on that basis] immediately appointed a Cabinet committee under Secretary Perkins to work out a substitute."[49]

In the end, House Speaker Henry Rainey and other Roosevelt allies on the House Rules Committee managed to stall any further consideration of the thirty-hour bill until the administration was able to come forth with its own legislation, or at least an amended version of the Black bill. Frances Perkins appeared before an executive session of the House Committee on Labor on 12 April with the findings of her cabinet group, which along with the Black bill became the subject of a new round of hearings beginning on 25 April. At this juncture, Secretary Perkins openly joined the ranks of the underconsumptionists, taking the position that the key to economic recovery was the systematic expansion of mass purchasing power. She urged the adoption of a thirty-hour workweek for most industries, with the exception of certain atypical situations for which a somewhat more flexible application of the law might be considered. She also proposed the creation of a system of independently functioning minimum-wage boards to be supervised by the Department of

Labor, in conjunction with new authority vested in the secretary of labor to restrict production and rationalize competition through a partial relaxation of the federal antitrust statutes and government oversight of binding trade agreements.[50]

With the exception of Sidney Hillman, president of the Amalgamated Clothing Workers, union leaders were opposed to the so-called Perkins modifications, largely on the basis of traditional AFL objections to a legislated minimum wage, except when applied to the employment of women and minors.[51] Labor opposition to Secretary Perkins's substitute proposals ultimately was assuaged only upon the inclusion of a clause specifically in recognition of AFL president William Green's insistence that any such legislation must also guarantee labor's collective bargaining rights against the interference or coercion of unscrupulous employers.[52] But by far the most controversial feature of the House Labor Committee's final recommendations (obviously inspired by the Perkins proposal) was the creation for a period of two years of a tripartite federal trade regulation board to be headed by the secretary of labor. Firms trafficking in interstate commerce would be required to secure a license from this proposed agency, the principal condition of which was management's agreement not to employ any worker more than six hours a day, five days a week, unless special exemption was granted by the board.[53]

Initially, most business leaders reacted at least as harshly to the Perkins amendments as they had to the original Black bill. Their principal cause for concern was the perceived rigidity of the provision for a federally licensed thirty-hour-week, and the fear that industry ultimately would have insufficient influence in determining the final specification of "fair" trade practices. The preferred alternative, represented by the position of the NAM, was that "there should be provided an appropriate executive agency to aid and encourage industries in formulating [their own] co-operative plans to arrest and remedy the destructive [economic] processes" then so much in evidence.[54] This, of course, was essentially a restatement of the old trade association concept of industrial self-regulation, with the added dimension of official government collaboration with industry majorities in a concerted effort to rationalize the competitive structure of individual product markets.

Indeed, it was possible—as the business lobbyists soon were led to believe—that self-regulation might be the general direction the Roosevelt administration would take, the president's comment on 11 April to the contrary notwithstanding. *Business Week* acknowledged early in May that the House Labor Committee hearings had "had a sobering effect . . . on those [employers] who made the first shrill protests" in opposition to the Black-Perkins proposals. But the magazine's editors also perceived certain subtle shades of opinion in the making that they felt warranted encouragement: "The Secretary's own testimony," it seems, offered reassurances which [subsequently] were strengthened by the announcement of Chairman Connery. . . that the . . . bill [in any form] is not going to be railroaded through. Industry is to get an ample hearing. . . . That the Administration is open to suggestions [in this respect] is confirmed by . . . [the labor secretary's] clarification of its position on the measure . . . which does not leave Mr. Roosevelt looking quite so adamantine on details as the first protestants pictured him. . . . [In fact], the Secretary gave the business man a clear cue for action in his endeavor to shake her proposals down to a form of control that would make him a partner in recovery instead of a yes-man. She told the House Labor Committee that they are based upon the conception that, given the opportunity and the technique, American industries could become practically self-regulating in the public interest.[55]

This statement was the opening many businessmen had been waiting for. Moreover, within a matter of days, the business press apparently was persuaded by new signs from Washington indicating that, should Congress pass "a law for controlling business recovery, it is likely to be something [much] broader and more cooperative than the Black 30-hour bill with the Perkins amendments." The editor of *Textile World* was even more specific when revealing his assumption that industry soon was "to be given another chance to find its way out of the maze into which war, technological advance, unbridled individualism, and the lack of control power have led it." This new opportunity, he indicated to his readers rejoicefully, almost certainly would "take the form of [an] organized cooperative effort within individual industries, whereby the will of the majority will be imposed upon the minority, with of course proper provision for protection of the public interest."[56]

Actually, the Perkins substitute for the Black bill was never identified specifically as an administration measure. Roosevelt had become increasingly sensitive to business opposition, which was being voiced in no uncertain terms during the days and hours immediately preceding Secretary Perkins's appearance before the House Committee on Labor. Both at the executive session on 12 April and in her statement before the full committee on 25 April Perkins seemed to be operating under an undeclared, semiofficial constraint as to how firmly committed to her approach she might indicate the president was.[57] In addition to encouraging Perkins in her endeavors after the Senate's approval of the Black bill on 6 April, Roosevelt apparently had asked Raymond Moley to reexplore the entire question of industrial rehabilitation. Hence the administration's support for the labor secretary's wage-and-hour proposals was tentative and intentionally qualified. On the same day that Perkins appeared before the House Labor Committee, Moley charged General Hugh Johnson, who had worked closely with the Democratic campaign organization and the Brains

Trust as an expert on farm and business policy, with the task of drafting a cooperative recovery plan for business and government. Accomplishing such a draft was Moley's second major initiative in the aftermath of 6 April. On 17 April he had asked New York financier James P. Warburg to persuade Senator Wagner, whom the administration recognized as one of the most influential members of Congress, also to participate in the formulation of a general recovery proposal. Wagner was known to be favorably disposed to some of the more ambitious industrial rehabilitation schemes offered by the likes of Harriman and Swope. Among these, however, Wagner was particularly attracted to a proposed National Economic Recovery Act drawn up jointly by Harold Moulton of the Brookings Institution and Meyer Jacobstein, a former New York state congressman and now a prominent Rochester banker, whose preferred approach the senator apparently saw as a logical complement to the public relief strategy that he personally had championed for so long.[58]

On 22 April, presumably in response to Warburg's recommendation that he do so, Wagner invited several individuals with an interest in recovery planning to a series of conferences on the subject, the first of which took place three days later, once again coincident with Secretary Perkins's testimony before the House Labor Committee. The Wagner group included, in addition to Moulton and Jacobstein, Fred I. Kent of the Bankers Trust Company in New York; Virgil D. Jordon of the National Industrial Conference Board; James H. Rand, Jr., of Remington Rand; trade association attorney David L. Podell; industrial economist Malcolm C. Rorty; Senator Robert La Follette, Jr.; Representative Clyde Kelly, coauthor of the Davis-Kelly coal stabilization bill; and last but not least, Congressman Kelly's longtime collaborator and consultant to John L. Lewis and the United Mine Workers, W. Jett Lauck.

Lauck, who at one point during the 1920s had worked as an economist for the railway brotherhoods, was an astute analyst of the great advances in productive efficiency that had occurred in recent years in American industry. He understood many of the underlying frailties of capitalism in the modern social process. And he was particularly sensitive in the context of the Depression and the pursuit of recovery to what he perceived as an interdependent relationship between the maintenance of mass purchasing power, the need to temporize excessive business competition, and the protection of labor's collective bargaining rights.[59] Lauck had taken every opportunity since the beginning of the Depression to persuade UMW president Lewis to take the lead in any movement to revive and stabilize the soft coal industry, and he did not stop there. The desperate situation in bituminous mining was initially the problem that concerned him most, but by 1931 his focus had expanded to include the desirability of industrial stabilization in general, which he also thought Lewis might be able to influence via his channels to the White House and other repositories of effective political power. Lewis was not confident that he "could undertake with propriety to act as a spokesman for industries other than coal," but Lauck still felt that great opportunities for industrial reform lay just ahead.[60] To further their position on coal stabilization, Lauck and Clyde Kelly were making plans in the summer of 1932 to take advantage of "the psychological state of candidates for re-election," which they believed would play a decisive role in the adoption of remedial legislation.[61]

Jett Lauck's greatest opportunity to influence American industrial history obviously came with his appointment to the Wagner group. Indeed, it was to a subcommittee composed of Lauck and Harold Moulton that the senator finally delegated the task of drafting a formal proposal for recovery legislation. In the deliberations that followed, which more often than not took place with the participation of Congressman Kelly as well, Lauck recommended as a model of what might best be done "the specific provisions of the Davis-Kelly [coal] stabilization bill," including those sections pertaining to "suspension of the anti-trust laws" and the assurance of "safeguards" for labor, in response to which he claims to have encountered "no opposition." Moulton readily "agreed" to everything that Lauck felt was necessary. As Lauck recounted the outcome in his personal record of activities for 27 April, the subcommittee had "fixed the bill up in very satisfactory form."[62]

In addition to the exploratory activity of Johnson and Wagner, there was a third important influence at work that eventually drew Roosevelt and Moley away from the Perkins substitute for the Black bill. Robert F. Himmelberg, in the most thoroughly researched and closely argued account of the NIRA drafting process to date, writes that this influence took the form of "pressure from business and its spokesmen within the Administration, especially John Dickinson, Assistant Secretary of Commerce." The business groups involved consisted of the same interests that had appealed to Roosevelt for antitrust revision during March and early April. The difference now was that "they had absorbed fully the lesson that their objective had to be cloaked in the rhetoric of recovery planning to attain success," and they "converged upon Dickinson and his superior, Daniel Roper, when they realized how fully these two sympathized with the business objectives."[63]

Himmelberg indicates correctly that "the immediate reason for the rallying of the business leaders behind Dickinson was to secure defeat of the Black bill." He also points out—again correctly—that their "aim was not merely to defeat federal regulation of wages and hours, but to use the prevailing concern with the issue as an opening to secure the long-sought goal of 'industrial self-regulation,' which now was emphasized as offering the best means of reviving the economy." The National Association of Manufacturers appears to have taken the lead in this direction. "Roosevelt's [blunt] rejection of antitrust relief [on 11 April], as James Emery explained to an NAM member, had forced the association to approach the goal 'through another angle . . . out of the Black bill.' The strategy was to show that 'inability to make cooperative agreements with respect to hours of production' had resulted in 'cutthroat competition, under-payment of wages and demoralization of industry.' Industry regulation of hours of work would, in other words, be substituted for the direct control of prices and production [that] Roosevelt apparently would not [yet] concede."[64]

When the first detailed knowledge was gained of what soon would materialize as the Perkins substitute for the Black bill on or about 12 April, the NAM and other business lobbyists immediately intensified their effort to gain control of the course of legislative events. When the House Labor Committee hearings began on 25 April, the industrialists and their political supporters closed ranks as never before and overwhelmed the Capitol with the force of their argument for industry control of all major regulatory decisions. Dickinson opened an attack on the labor secretary's proposals from within the administration, writing to both Moley and Perkins of the potentially disastrous economic and political consequences should such a measure ever actually become law.[65] He recommended instead that industry be given an opportunity "to agree upon and propose . . . [its own general] code of labor standards covering maximum hours . . . and minimum wages," in lieu of their imposition by government.[66]

On 2 and 3 May, Dickinson and Wagner combined their efforts to arrive at what each might have described, on the basis of very similar criteria, as a "workable" recovery plan.[67] The result was acceptable to Jett Lauck, who immediately assured John L. Lewis that "the labor standards are still in the bill and are mandatory upon any one coming under its provisions."[68] The plan, interestingly enough, was also acceptable to the industrial lobbyists, who fully expected that it would satisfy their predilection for a loosely regulated "associative" response to the problems of profitless enterprise. Once again, Himmelberg summarizes the evidence expertly:

> On May 4 most of the key business leaders who were active in the negotiations with the Wagner-Dickinson committee[s] assembled for a self-congratulatory and self-laudatory session before a large group of conventioneers attending the Chamber of Commerce annual meeting and anxious for a word on the shape of the coming recovery bill. The confidence and assurance displayed were complete. It was clear the speakers felt that the main features of the bill had taken form and that business had triumphed. Recent events had opened, Emery said, "an opportunity which many have long sought to find a chance to determine whether or not industry can organize itself to set up a form of self-government." Somewhat incautiously perhaps, in view of the NAM's long history of moderation in this respect, Emery vented his contempt for "irrational minorities" who now would be controlled. "I personally am rather sick of living under organized minorities in industry or in

politics," he said of the non-cooperators of every industry. J. Harvey Williams, Goldthwaite Dorr, and others who spoke all echoed Emery's confident assertion that "self-government was within the business community's grasp."[69]

That evening President Roosevelt addressed the Chamber of Commerce in terms that could only have reinforced Emery and company's profound confidence that the recovery bill in preparation would indeed be everything business had hoped for.[70]

These expectations appeared to be shaken temporarily when it was learned that Hugh Johnson had also prepared a recovery proposal. The problem was that Johnson had done so in collaboration with Donald Richberg, attorney for the railway brotherhoods, who was known to be critical of the recovery program advocated by the business lobbyists. With Richberg involved, it was feared that a specifically prounion clause might yet be written into the final bill, although this may well have been of less concern than the suspicion that Johnson was inclined to permit the extension of greater regulatory power to the federal government than many businessmen would comfortably accept.

Roosevelt received both the Wagner and Johnson proposals on 10 May, whereupon he appointed a new committee consisting of Wagner, Johnson, Richberg, Dickinson, Perkins, and Budget Director Lewis Douglas to work out as quickly as possible the details of a single recovery bill. The business lobbyists immediately demanded access to the new drafting committee so that they might represent as effectively as possible their preference for the Wagner-Dickinson proposal, or at least a similar version of the regulatory principles embodied therein. FDR responded approvingly by authorizing the formation of an ad hoc Business Advisory Council (BAC). Consisting most prominently of Robert L. Lund, president of the NAM, as well as Emery, Harriman, Lamont DuPont, Charles R. Hook of American Rolling Mills, and one or two less well-known personalities whom Boston newspaper publisher John H. Fahey described as being "more in step with modern business developments than the average," the BAC immediately became a party to the drafting committee's deliberations.[71] One week later, an omnibus compromise—the National Industrial Recovery Act—had emerged and was promptly put before Congress.

Title I of the proposed legislation declared a national state of emergency so as to justify a limited two-year suspension of the federal antitrust laws. Under the auspices of a newly created National Recovery Administration, the legislation authorized the various competitive units of any given industry to draw up a "code of fair competition." Each code so devised would be applicable to the entire industry and would bear the force of law when approved by the president, whose powers in this regard were enhanced by the terms of a special licensing provision also contained in the act. The controversial realm of industrial-labor relations was to be covered by Sections 7a, b, and c, which accorded employees "the right to organize and bargain collectively through representatives of their own choosing" and required employer compliance with duly established maximum working hours, minimum rates of pay, and other standards of labor subject to the approval of the president.[72]

During the final stages of the drafting process, the NAM mounted a last-ditch effort to soften the collective bargaining provisions of the recovery bill along with a request for stronger import controls and other relatively minor alterations of the proposed legislation. These objections, however, seem not to have been pursued very doggedly,[73] and, in any event, the Business Advisory Council appears to have approved the bill before it was submitted to Congress on 17 May. By the end of the month, however, NAM spokesmen once again were involved in an effort to secure certain amendments to the labor provisions of the bill, which had undergone what some employer representatives chose to regard as a critical transformation during the earliest phase of Congress's deliberations on the measure.

As originally submitted, Section 7a was phrased in such a way that even the adamantly antiunion NAM had interpreted it as basically an open-shop provision. On the opening day of hearings before the House Committee on Ways and Means, however, William Green insisted upon—and was granted—certain changes in the wording of 7a, which when applied would not only bar employers from interfering with the freedom of workers to organize and engage in collective bargaining but also afford them protection against being required to join a "company union" as a prior condition to employment.[74] Lund and Emery, in particular, gave the impression that they considered Congress's acceptance of Green's amendment a betrayal of their initial generosity in agreeing to the labor provisions in their original form. The NAM raised these objections directly with the White House and promptly set out to mobilize the business lobby in support of its position in a manner reminiscent of the tactics employed several weeks earlier in response to the Black bill.

It is safe to assume that most businessmen did not share these feelings, that is, that their basic trust had been seriously violated in the course of recent legislative events. The amended Section 7a typically was considered as little more than a fairly minor defect, not of enough significance to warrant defeat of the entire measure. To be sure, employer opposition was forthcoming; but it frequently occurred in connection with bargaining over the details of other, equally controversial issues, such as the steel industry's interest in better import controls, and more general reservations about the licensing and tax features of the NIRA. Even Robert Lund, in a personal communication to Commerce Secretary Roper, dispatched while the business leaders' optimal expectations on all matters of substance including the labor provisions still were being argued in hearings before the Senate Finance Committee, alluded only to the existence of certain "imperfections" in an otherwise commendable piece of legislation, which he acknowledged generally had been "received by industry with the highest enthusiasm."[75]

One of the principal interpretive issues at stake here is the question whether Section 7a in its final form constituted a political concession to organized labor of truly historic proportions insofar as the perceived needs and interests of the industrial employer were concerned. Historians traditionally have believed that it was. Even Himmelberg, whose generally superb rendition of the legislative history of the NIRA bears the obvious imprint of the revisionist thrust of most of the work published on the New Deal during the past several years, counts the labor provisions of the recovery bill as an exception to the otherwise probusiness character of the measure.[76]

It is undeniable that 7a constituted a rhetorical concession to the trade unions. It is true also that the NAM and other business groups were offended by this concession, particularly after the adoption of the Green amendments, which were interpreted by some, especially the representatives of the automobile and steel industries, as constituting a possible threat to the legal status of company unions. It soon became clear to all concerned, however, if it had not been all the while, that any such possibility was contingent on the nature of certain decisions yet to be taken in the administration of the recovery act. On 10 July, therefore, the NAM's steering committee on recovery legislation appealed directly to chief NRA administrator Hugh Johnson for official assurance that NRA policy would not upset existing collective bargaining arrangements. It is even possible that private guarantees to this effect had already been given, which may account for Lund's curious expression of confidence in an exchange with Johnson as early as 3 July that, in actuality, 7a appeared "not" to give "labor any rights which it did not have before the act was passed."[77] In any event, even if Lund was being a bit premature—and it is by no means certain that he was—all the necessary "official" assurances had been received by at least the third week of August in the form of an NRA policy statement, issued jointly by Richberg and Johnson in connection with deadlocked negotiations over the details of the automobile industry code. In specifying the allowable range of collective bargaining arrangements under the recovery act, the Richberg-Johnson policy clarification appeared to uphold the principle of "proportional representation" as opposed to that of "majority rule" and thus, if only by implication, to sustain the propriety of company unions as well.

The elimination of this and a number of other nagging political uncertainties in the end seemed to allay the greater part of any lingering concern among businessmen that the bureaucratic and interest-laden complexity of the NRA might yet turn out to be more than they could contend with. The fear engendered by the terms of the President's Reemployment Agreement (PRA)[78] that the administration might permit the inflation of production costs through increased wages and shortened hours without compensatory price adjustments, for example, eventually proved baseless. So did most of the apprehension that preceded William Green's promise that he personally would attempt to restrain the more impatient elements of the AFL from engaging in overzealous or otherwise ill-considered strike activity pending settlement of the permanent codes.[79] An adequate defense of the open shop and company union was still the vital concern of an identifiable element in American industry, of course, and that concern was manifest repeatedly during the late summer of 1933 and well into the following year in the form of a bitter and ongoing controversy over competing interpretations of the NIRA collective bargaining provisions. This preoccupation, however, was mostly confined to the heavy mass-production industries—automobiles, steel, rubber, electrical manufacturing, and the like—in which trade unions had not previously attained a firm strategic foothold. This was essentially uncharted territory for organized labor, all the more forbidding because the Roosevelt administration turned out to be an ambivalent ally in the effort to overcome what traditionally was one of the most jealously guarded prerogatives of industrial management: the largely unencumbered freedom to set the terms of employee engagement.[80]

An entirely different situation prevailed in numerous older, generally less heavily capitalized industries all across the country. In such industries, labor costs typically constituted an essential factor in the competitive equation, in which case trade unions, industrywide collective bargaining, and thus the labor provisions of the NRA codes as well not infrequently were looked upon by management as perhaps the only available means by which at least a modicum of order might eventually be restored to a depressed and chaotic product market. Such a choice was almost always born of necessity, with a definite correlation between prior subjection to union power or otherwise rigorously enforced employment standards on one hand and management's willingness to advance the idea of universal adherence to such standards on the other.[81] According to this formulation, the principal assumption was that some combination of union power and the regulatory potential of the NRA code apparatus might be exploited to achieve industrial stabilization, which in plainer language simply meant driving the operating costs of the so-called "price chiselers" up to some minimally acceptable competitive norm.

This strategy struck an especially concordant note in the general context of what I have already described as the underconsumption/purchasing power interpretation of the Depression, wherein the regulation of employment standards became the key not only to the immediate problem of industrial control but to dealing with the very roots of the economic calamity.[82] The overall interpretive significance of this historical linkage, I believe, cannot be overemphasized. For it is basically in terms of these intimately bound policy objectives that one can explain both the initial popularity of the Black bill (outside of business circles) and the virtual duplication of several key facets of that measure in the more complex but generally less controversial NIRA. Both legislative proposals were fundamentally conservative in intent. That is why Senator Wagner could ultimately insist (apparently contrary to the opinion of some) that the thirty-hour bill had not been so much "sidetracked" for the recovery act as blended with a somewhat more patiently devised, and in his view economically sound, plan of action—an "integrated whole," as Hugh Johnson described it in his New Deal memoir.[83] The result was a measure designed to do virtually everything that was understood to be necessary to end the Depression: foster reemployment, halt wage deflation, and generally restore labor's purchasing power, on one hand, and rationalize the competitive structure of the industrial economy by suspending the antitrust laws and encouraging cooperative trade agreements, on the other. All of this, it was supposed, if pursued in a reasonably balanced fashion, would contribute to the basic goal of business revival. Indeed, the NIRA traversed the traditionally cumbersome federal legislative process with remarkable speed in large part because Title I of the act effectively combined what originally appeared to some contemporaries as at least two distinct policy objectives, without apparent prejudice to the realization of the essential elements of either. Congressional advocates of the work-sharing approach were assured of a concerted effort to bring about reduced working hours and protected wage floors, eventually to be specified in each of more than 550 separate industrial codes. At the same time, the trade unions were given by the terms of Section 7 what appeared to be new safeguards and even enhanced opportunities in the realm of collective bargaining, the practical limitations of which were not immediately appreciated by the intended beneficiary. Organized business was given the opportunity to determine, on the basis of its own estimate of what the commercial traffic would bear, the details of the code provisions, industry by industry, including, in most instances, the terms of employment as well. Although sometimes this would be done in collaboration with the unions, depending upon their strategic position in the competitive structure of the particular industrial product market in question.

One final consideration should be mentioned in reference to the question of precisely what labor was "conceded" with the adoption of the NIRA and why, although the substance of the issue is implicit in much of the factual detail already provided in this chapter. Ultimately the antitrust revisionists and their political allies found a certain advantage in combining a policy that sought to guarantee certain minimum labor standards with a policy tailored to achieve the greater cartelization of American industry. In addition to the simple economic rationale that accounts for this coupling of goals in a number of instances, as a political strategy it also had the effect of pacifying some of those "antitrusters" in Congress who otherwise had indicated reluctance to accept nullification of the traditional hierarchy of legalities protective of the competitive spirit in American enterprise—depression emergency or not. On 9 May, a group of House Democrats attempted to preempt the administration on this issue by circulating a petition that called for the formation of a party caucus dedicated to the preservation of the antitrust laws. Very little came of the threatened revolt, however, because the supporters of the NIRA finally presented the recovery bill as a measure that proposed nothing more harmful than allowing business, under proper government supervision, to mobilize its own resources against the evils of "cutthroat" competition, which of course issued primarily from excessive wage-cutting and the unscrupulous exploitation of labor—or so the argument ran.[84] The strategy worked, and on 26 May the NIRA was passed in the House by a vote of 323 to 76.

In the Senate, the administration and other supporters of the recovery bill had a more difficult time. In the floor debates that took place during the second week of June, the drama begun in the House of Representatives resumed with even greater intensity. An unlikely coalition of conservative Democrats and progressive Republicans, characteristically inspired by the forceful arguments of veteran GOP insurgent William E. Borah, mounted a relentless attack on the measure for its apparent bestowal of legitimacy on heretofore outlawed "monopolistic" business practices. These objections never were entirely appeased,[85] resulting finally in Senate approval of the NIRA by the surprisingly narrow margin of 46 to 39. Even Hugo Black, whose legislative proposal for the thirty-hour week played a prominent role in triggering the burst of political activity that ultimately produced the recovery bill, denounced the NIRA as a "sellout" to those who, wittingly or not, would destroy the American free-market system.[86]

# 5 Codified Capitalism, I

A brief upturn in production and employment during July and August 1933 led some contemporaries to the premature conclusion that a more optimistic business outlook engendered by the adoption of the National Industrial Recovery Act and allied New Deal programs had actually reversed the course of recent economic history. To be sure, this sudden increase in economic activity was no illusion. But it was based on little more than a temporary stimulus occasioned by a sudden rush in the manufacturing sector to build up inventories as a hedge against the anticipated impact of NRA-supported price increases in the weeks and months to come. By the end of September, the economic indexes had again turned sharply downward, setting the stage for the first serious wave of apprehension about the alleged merits of the federal government's unprecedented recovery scheme.

The charges and countercharges in this respect were varied and multidimensional, encompassing many different facets of the New Deal's particular brand of "political capitalism."[1] But clearly the most pervasive source of difficulty for the NRA arose in connection with the apparent inability of the codes adequately to fulfill their intended regulatory function in many of the nation's most highly competitive industries. This was the sector in which the rationalization of standard capitalist behavior promised the greatest potential return in terms of the desire to restore balance and order throughout the economy. These usually were labor-intensive industries, and the hope of achieving industrial control in them was linked directly to the effective enforcement of the labor provisions of the code and the prospective stabilization of the cost structure of competitively overdeveloped product markets. It was soon recognized, moreover, not least by the NRA administrators, that the difference between moderate success and complete failure in the quest for stabilization more often than not turned on the ability of labor unions to limit the ease with which the individual entrepreneur might avoid full and uninterrupted compliance with the prescribed standards of employment in a given branch of industry. In fact, however, organized labor during the early 1930s— in spite of Section 7a—was so seldom in possession of the countervailing power with which to effect such a binding constraint on business affairs that the contradictory imperatives of competitive enterprise seemed almost always to reign supreme.[2] Here, once again, the record of economic developments in the bituminous mining and clothing industries provide two especially clear cases.

## The NRA and the Garment Trades

"The sweatshop," announced the *Christian Science Monitor* on 6 July 1933,

> has returned to American industry in its worst form, and groups combatting the exploitation of workers are following with intense concern Washington proceedings on the fair practices code to be drawn up under provisions of the National Industrial Recovery Act, hoping that this code will make the present $4-a-week wage for 70 hours work impossible.
>
> Proof of the situation in the garment industry may be seen on every hand in fly-by-night stores of the bargain or receiver's sale variety throughout the United States.
>
> While the jobber is the key to the era of cutthroat competition, the contractor alone knows the hardships endured by the workers, who have practically no escape from his decisions. Such a situation not only oppresses the workers, but exerts a powerful influence to depress the general conditions of the industry. And in the wake of the sweatshop, with its mismanagement of the common welfare and ignorant wastage of human effort, is an inevitable train of child dependence and delinquency and old age for which, on debased wages, no provision can be made. . . .
>
> The merchant demands rush delivery. Plenty of workers are to be had, and the manufacturer mans his plant for night and day work. The huge machines roar endlessly; the workers are pressed to the limit of their endurance, and in a week it is all over. The whole force is laid off and the factory shut down until the wasteful process begins again with another rush order.
>
> On terms, then, of racketeering, cutthroat competition and sweated labor, Seventh Avenue, main stem of New York's biggest industry— garment making—has been able to remain a teeming thoroughfare throughout the slump. With prices the lowest in memory, this industry has stayed at the top of the city's production list.
>
> The gypsy contractor does business on a shoestring, choosing for his location places outside the inspection rounds or in a state where labor

laws are laxly enforced. In New York State he prefers Long Island, Staten Island and Westchester County, or he goes to Pennsylvania, Massachusetts, Connecticut, New Jersey, trucking his stuff into the retail center at night. . . .

In their desperate need for work and wages, girls and women jump at the invitation to "sit down right now at a machine and go to work"; they do not venture to inquire about wages and, indeed, some are told they must work a week, or even two, as learners. Even experienced workers are having to accept this invitation. At the end of the "learning period" they are told their work won't do and they are dismissed for a new group. By this trick a contractor can get several thousands of dresses sewn for almost nothing. Thus is the plight of the women and girls of the needle trades being added to the saga of the southern textile operatives, the Kentucky miners and the jobless wanderers.[3]

On the basis of this and similar reports, it appeared that the recovery program would have to work miracles if the clothing industry were to be spared the competitive disorder that traditionally resulted from the acute vulnerability of the trade to even the slightest recession in market demand.[4] In the spring and early summer of 1933, that vulnerability seemed limitless.

In a sense, it might be said that the first "code of fair competition" had been conceived at the Brandeis conferences of 1910, which resulted in the adoption of the Protocol of Peace for the women's coat and suit trade. It will be recalled from Chapter 2 that perhaps the most outstanding feature of the protocol system was the absence of any differentiation between trade functions and labor functions in their mutual relationship to the competitive structure of the clothing industry. The reason for this melding of functions was that labor costs in garment manufacturing had always been the governing variable in the economic fortunes of the trade. Accordingly, as one leading student of the subject has observed, "Even after the National Industrial Recovery Act opened the door to restrictive trade practices that would otherwise have been illegal, the needle trades did not forsake the basic issue of equal labor costs for the more tempting fields of regulating sales, limiting production, or fixing prices."[5]

Within a month after the adoption of the NIRA, a key group of garment employers willingly assumed the role of contemporary counterpart to the New York manufacturers in the women's coat and suit trade who had initiated the protocol movement in 1910. Their task was the same as the preceding generation's: the preparation of a code of fair competition devoted almost entirely to the establishment of uniform labor standards. Actually, a special manufacturers' Joint Control Committee had been working since 1929 on the persistent problem of nonunion competition, which many of the previously most uncooperative employers in the trade now also wished to see eliminated. By mid-1930, according to Raymond V. Ingersoll, retiring chairman of the Brooklyn Ladies' Garment Manufacturers' Association, the majority of the producers in "all branches of the industry were unanimous in their diagnosis of the ills that beset it. Even the jobbers' representatives who, up to that time, had clung to the theory that the jobbers were not interested in labor standards because they did not directly employ labor, were now willing to join in an arrangement to combat the growing menace of the sweat shop."[6]

By the late 1920s, the garment unions were no longer capable of policing the competitive practices of the trade as closely as the associated manufacturers would have liked. To do so, the unions required direct assistance, which was forthcoming only with the approval on 4 August 1933 of NRA Code No. 5. Indeed, all the key labor provisions of the cloak and suit code simply reiterated the terms of the collective agreement then in force between the International Ladies' Garment Workers' Union and those employers in the New York market who elected to restore their ties with the manufacturers' association, which may have represented as much as 75 percent of the trade's total productive capacity by the time the code was submitted for approval.[7] Specifically, the code for the cloak trade provided that "whenever in this industry agreements between employers arrived at by collective bargaining shall exist or shall come into existence hereafter, all the provisions of such agreements with reference to labor standards not prohibited by law and not inconsistent with [the] NIRA shall be administered as though a part of this Code."[8] The NRA codes adopted by the other branches of the women's wear industry followed essentially the same pattern: in each case, the terms of the union contract provided the basis for the definition of fair trade practices in general.[9]

In the men's clothing industry, originally two separate draft codes were proposed—one by each of the two rival manufacturers' associations. The larger of the two employers' groups, the Clothing Manufacturers' Association of the United States, whose members ordinarily operated under contract with the Amalgamated Clothing Workers of America, represented about 75 percent of the total productive capacity of the industry. The other employers' group in the men's industry, the Industrial Recovery Association of Clothing Manufacturers, had been formed especially for the occasion in June 1933 and claimed to represent the interests of only 111 or so nonunion shops in various markets and localities around the country. From the very beginning, these two organizations were unable to reconcile basic differences of opinion on the more important details of code administration. In particular, the Industrial Recovery Association insisted upon coequal administrative status and would not be satisfied with minority representation on any board of control. And on the question of wages above the minimum, the minority group suggested a flat increase of 20 percent above the prevailing rate on 1 July 1933, whereas the

Clothing Manufacturers' Association, with union support, took the position that all current differentials to the advantage of more highly skilled workers (up to a maximum of $30 per week) should be preserved. Ultimately, on both counts, the issue was decided by NRA Deputy Administrator Lindsay Rogers according to the preference of the union manufacturers.[10]

The code formulation process in each of the needle trades was similarly dominated by an associated majority of producers. Invariably, those dominant factions were located in the New York City region, the undisputed center of the trade, where the garment unions were able to play a key role in drafting various code proposals. The New York manufacturers, usually with the collaboration of the unions, set their sights on two basic objectives. Their first concern was the establishment of minimum wage rates for each craft or skill as opposed to a flat minimum applicable to all jobs within a given trade. Their second aim was to eliminate, as much as possible, geographic differentials in specified minima so as to protect their own position in the national market. In either case, however, contrasting points of view based on geographic location were always less important than distinctions about competitive interest between manufacturers bound by collective agreements with the garment unions and those that were not. In the millinery industry, for example, previously unorganized shops in production centers outside of New York City changed their general attitude as soon as they were brought under collective labor agreements by the union. Thus, according to one NRA staff report, "Unionization not only removed the objections of these markets to occupational minima but made them vigorous proponents thereof." Certain representatives of the Chicago millinery market had been among the leaders of an anticlassification faction within the industry during the summer of 1933. But then immediately upon the settlement of a strike in favor of the union, "these same representatives unblushingly swung to the other side and became outstanding advocates of classification." These employers should not be accused of "unwarranted perfidy," the author of the NRA staff report notes. "Their position merely changed with changing circumstances. The union agreements to which they became bound called for the payment of minimum wages graded according to occupation. They were naturally anxious [therefore] that similar burdens be borne by all their competitors."[11]

Yet these "burdens" were not distributed equally throughout the industry, despite recent impressive organizational gains by the union. The primary function of the NRA, of course, was to regulate the costs and rewards of business in general. Just as in the case of the cotton textile industry, however, the garment codes never produced as great a return in eliminating excessive competition as their most committed patrons had hoped. Moreover, if the associated manufacturers appeared to be genuinely disappointed, it was only because they would not readily admit that their ideal expectations for economic stability and order were contradictory with the compelling desire to maintain control of the code machinery so as to protect their own competitive position in the trade. The garment codes (like the NRA code system as a whole) represented not the embodiment of a disinterested scheme for the rationalization of American industry as some contemporaries may have preferred to imagine but rather a political contrivance that in a capitalist economy could easily be exploited for purposes of domination and power. The business "rationalizers," after all, would have interpreted any sacrifice of their own essential economic interests as the ultimate irrationality. Hence various groups of manufacturers frequently sought special exemption from the standards applied by the codes, which they themselves may not have had a hand in formulating, or that may not have adequately reflected the imperatives of their own immediate entrepreneurial well-being vis-à-vis the overall competitive structure of the industry.[12]

Union membership in virtually every branch of the garment industry increased markedly during the first few months of operation under the code system. ILGWU membership climbed from a low of about forty thousand in mid-1933 to almost two hundred thousand by the end of 1934.[13] In numbers there was strength; and where the union in the garment trades was strong, employer compliance with the labor provisions of the code was more likely to be uniform. The potential benefits of compliance were widely recognized by those who longed for an end to excessive wage and price competition, but adequate evidence had yet to appear that the industry was about to embark upon a period of perfect economic harmony. Among those engaged in the manufacture of cotton garments, for example, there were immediate objections that a forty-hour-week limitation, which had been written into the code,[14] was not having the desired effect of reducing overall output. This failure was clearly indicated in the case of one New York City shirt manufacturer who complained directly to NRA officials in October 1933 that production throughout the industry was perhaps "95 to 100 percent" of the precode average, with the result that markets were still glutted with goods and competition was still exceedingly fierce.[15] Indeed, the total number of competing establishments engaged throughout the country in the manufacture of both women's and men's wear increased markedly subsequent to the implementation of the code apparatus: by 33 and 31 percent, respectively, between 1933 and 1935. In New York State alone, the number of men's, youths', and boys' establishments nearly doubled, increasing from approximately seven hundred firms in 1933 to more than thirteen hundred by 1935. There was a comparable increase in the number of women's establishments in New York as well—from about thirty-seven hundred in 1933 to almost fifty-seven hundred in 1935.[16]

Moreover, especially in the manufacture of women's wear, the relative weakness of the garment unions in several major outlying districts continued to pose a competitive challenge to the majority of the industry's producers located in New York City. In the cloak and suit trade, by mid-1934, perhaps 90 percent of the manufacturing units in New York had been signed to a union contract, according to data compiled for an NRA staff study. Three important Pacific Coast markets—Los Angeles, San Francisco, and Portland—also had a high proportion of establishments in the cloak industry under union contract: 85, 96, and 97 percent, respectively. Chicago was the next highest with 84 percent. The suburban communities adjacent to all of these cities, however, had a much less impressive record of union penetration, ranging as low as 10 percent in the areas surrounding Chicago. Moreover, Boston was only about 72 percent organized (21 percent in the suburbs); Philadelphia and Cleveland, 69 percent; Kansas City, 40 percent; and Baltimore, 35 percent. In the dollar value of sales, however, between the spring of 1933 and the spring of 1934, Baltimore enjoyed an increase of almost 77 percent, and New York City came out slightly below the national average of 20 percent. Indeed, several markets across the country experienced a substantially more pronounced rate of increase in sales revenue than New York, including Kansas City with 35 percent; Chicago, 34 percent; Cleveland, 25 percent; and Portland, 24 percent. Four cities usually classified as outlying districts of the larger Chicago market—St. Paul and Minneapolis, Minnesota, and Aurora and Batavia, Illinois—had an average increase in the dollar value of sales of 56 percent. Any strict correlation between the relative absence of union control in some markets and the amount of increase in sales volume cannot be verified on the basis of available data, although there may indeed have been such a relationship. Rather, the point here is that New York's position in the national market (at least insofar as the coat and suit trade is concerned) had not advanced after approximately a year of operation under the code in contrast to the marked improvement in this respect of a number of other centers of production. If the race for new business is any measure of the issue, therefore, it would appear that the competitive pressures experienced by garment manufacturers in New York City, still the heart of the industry, continued to be as burdensome as ever.[17]

Nor, it seems, had the combined force of union power and the NRA codes successfully eliminated the run-of-the-mill "sweatshop" and "price chiseler" from the clothing industry. According to a study published in 1936 by the Pennsylvania Department of Labor, even production by home work continued to be conducted in that state as one readily available means by which numerous employers easily avoided the higher costs of "regulated" factory production:

> In small-town and rural newspapers throughout the state there are constantly appearing advertisements seeking to recruit [new additions to] the [already] large army of women knitting baby sacques, caps, booties, and embroidering fine dresses at incredibly low wages. Employers main-

tain no factories; the plants are the humble homes, and the usual costs of production, light, heat and rent, are borne by the women workers. Herein, also, lies an interstate industrial problem.

The enactment of a stringent homework law in New York State has resulted in a migration of homework into Pennsylvania to escape rigid regulation. Parcel post makes it easy to deliver materials to these humblest of all workers who labor long hours silently, in isolation, having no contacts with fellow workers and no voice in rates of remuneration.[18]

The NRA, in other words, had not removed the garment trades from the list of competitively overdeveloped industries in the United States. Still, a much greater proportion of the market than ever before had been brought under at least a semblance of control; competition in certain respects had been moderated, particularly insofar as the unions were able to contribute to the fashioning of a slightly more predictable business climate. Indeed, employers whose shops had been unionized were distraught at the prospect of ever having to return to the unregulated competition of the precode era. When Congress in the early spring of 1935 began to consider the question of whether the life of the NRA should be extended beyond the two-year limit specified in the original recovery bill, the garment manufacturers were among the most vociferous advocates of renewal of both the trade and employment practice aspects of the legislation. A special Apparel Industries Committee for the Renewal of NRA was formed to represent the sentiments of the clothing producers. And the chairman of the committee tried on one occasion to convey the unusual depth of their concern when he warned, perhaps a little overdramatically, that "to drop N.R.A. now would take from every intelligent manufacturer and merchant in this country his initiative and legitimate means of defense, and leave him adrift in the fog in a boat with no oars, no compass, and no port in sight."[19]

Ultimately, of course, the garment manufacturers were cast adrift from the relative security of their New Deal mooring when the U.S. Supreme Court, on 27 May 1935, effectively nullified the NIRA. Competitive conditions throughout the industry immediately began to deteriorate as nonunion producers moved to take advantage of what they saw as an irresistible opportunity to lower operating costs and expand production. One of the hardest hit was the millinery industry, in which it was reported that "all of the unorganized markets" had converted from a thirty-five- to a forty-hour week within a month of the Supreme Court's decision and that "in any number of cases the 44-hour week ha[d] been introduced."[20]

Other branches of the clothing industry experienced a similar turn of events, which quickly gave rise to the formation of a number of new cooperative associations designed to operate as a makeshift alternative to the NRA, beginning with the establishment on 15 July 1935 of the National Coat and Suit Industry Recovery Board.[21] This agency, just one of several so-called "little NRAs" that emerged in some of the more highly competitive industries across the country in the wake of the Blue Eagle's demise, derived its raison d'être from the common desire of the membership to perpetuate the minimum labor standards and fair trade practices of the NRA code. But none of these substitute arrangements ever managed to prescribe "rules of the game" as rigorous or universally binding as the now defunct government-sponsored recovery program. As a result, especially in the garment trades, responsibility for industrial control reverted once again primarily to the unions, which of course possessed limited ability to influence the competitive options of management. In the process, the industry became increasingly vulnerable to the hazards of the market, and relations between the employer associations and the unions in many cases deteriorated to the point of being dysfunctional for the purposes of industrial control. The garment unions, according to one knowledgeable student of labor relations in the clothing trades, were clearly "overburdened with responsibilities" and the employers' associations "contributed too little" to what formerly had been perceived as "a common cause." The progress that "was made in organizing the unorganized and in extending uniform labor standards to new shops during any one season" could easily "be dissipated in the following season through the added competitive pressures of business recessions or through some let-up in vigilance required to maintain the status quo. Just as in the early protocol years, labor unions and employers' associations again attacked each other for fiddling with petty grievances and for taking partisan stands where objectivity was essential."[22]

The essence of the situation was captured perfectly in a comment by Julius Hochman, general manager of the Dressmakers' Joint Board, to the effect that though the agency's special office of impartial chairman had originally been planned as a kind of "dignified Supreme Court for the dress industry," by 1935 it had been reduced to little better than a "petty criminal court daily delving into cases of plain thievery."[23] Henceforth the regulatory capacity of union power in most branches of the clothing industry became so uncertain that the very idea of an industrywide accommodation between labor and management began to seem like a fundamentally flawed proposition. Not at all unusual by 1937, for instance, were situations similar to a case in which the Millinery Stabilization Commission finally was placed in the position of having to chastise the hatters' union for making what it termed "illicit concessions" to certain manufacturers who apparently had threatened to move their shops away from the style centers and out of the union's reach if the latter posed too great an obstacle to their entrepreneurial freedom. On one hand, the union was compelled both by commitment and necessity to help preserve its members' jobs in the face of this threatened migration of factories. On the other hand, the leaders of the union knew from their experience over the years that the commission was perfectly correct in warning that an outright capitulation to management now could only further undermine the stability of the entire market, thereby increasing the likelihood that even greater concessions from labor would be required in the future.[24] Not only was this dilemma consistent with the historic disintegration of the millinery trade, it also exemplified the immensely difficult strategic position of labor at or near the end of the New Deal era in the volatile and contradictory business of garment manufacturing generally.

## Labor and the Codification of Bituminous Coal

If the New Deal experiment in the garment industry resulted in considerable disappointment for those who sought to tame the economics of that trade, the code formulation process in the bituminous coal mining industry was even more controversial and fractious. When the time came, most coal operators indicated a definite preference for local or regional codes over which they could exercise optimal influence and control. This regional perspective was entirely in keeping with the geographically oriented market rivalries of the past. It was also related to the sudden proliferation of autonomous district sales agencies in the wake of the Supreme Court's recent approval of such arrangements in the *Appalachian Coals* case.

At least one important group of operators, including certain northern interests in the Central Competitive Field, was attracted to the idea of a more uniform and geographically extensive regulatory initiative. Behind the leadership of Ben Grey of New York City and Frank Taplin of Cleveland, this group formed an organization in June 1933 known as Central Coals Associates, whose spokesmen eventually came forth with a code of fair competition designed to cover the markets of Ohio, Maryland, Pennsylvania, West Virginia, and eastern Kentucky. The sponsors of the code thus proposed to regulate trade practices throughout the better part of the Appalachian region. They also indicated their willingness to recognize the United Mine Workers of America as the official bargaining agent for all coal mine employees and recommended support of the thirty-hour workweek.

Taplin was known throughout the industry for his belief that the restoration of union power very likely constituted the only means of controlling the economics of soft coal mining. He was a Republican but had worked for FDR's election in 1932. He was also a personal friend of Raymond Moley and therefore had a direct line to the White House. Grey, for his part, had been in contact with NRA staff member Alexander Sachs, a technical adviser to the administration on the coal industry, over the details of his association's draft code at various stages of preparation. Moley, in particular, appears to have encouraged the two coalmen in their endeavors. Still, the Taplin-Grey (effectively prounion) faction of the industry was not in a position to dictate the terms of a general code. They surely would not have hesitated to do so had they been afforded the opportunity, but that was precluded by their minority status in relation to the totality of competing interests who stood to gain or lose as a direct result of the NRA "stabilization" process.

Before all was said and done, at least twenty-four draft codes (some reports place the number in excess of thirty) were presented to Hugh Johnson and the NRA staff by various operator coalitions divided by geography, unionization, and other factors related to the basic competitive structure of the industry. Indeed, this wide range of interests initially bore rather disturbing implications for the prospective achievement of any truly centralized or integrated response to the economic contradictions that plagued the market, let alone the achievement of a response designed to favor the particular needs of one operator group or another. Yet ultimately the regulatory conundrum was resolved in such a way as to enhance substantially the strategic position of those interests with coal properties in the Central Competitive Field, or immediately adjacent fields, which traditionally had been most vulnerable to the exercise of union power.

The governing factor was the recent activity and accomplishments of the miners' union. Obviously encouraged by the labor provisions of the NIRA, John L. Lewis and the UMW turned Congress's adoption of the recovery bill into the occasion for launching a major new organizing campaign throughout the industry. This time the union met with remarkable success, even in the South. By the end of September 1933 the UMW was able to sign an interdistrict contract (henceforth known as the Appalachian Agreement) that not only reestablished the union in almost all of Ohio and Pennsylvania but also penetrated a number of southern fields never before organized. This agreement, which became effective on 2 October 1933, covered operations with a combined annual output of 300–350 million tons and employing some 315, 000 mine workers in Ohio, Pennsylvania, the Virginias, Maryland, eastern Kentucky, and northern Tennessee. Since Indiana and Illinois were already almost completely controlled either by the UMW or its local rival, the Progressive Miners of America, the conclusion of the Appalachian Agreement brought the proportion of organized employees in the industry's work force up to approximately an unprecedented 90 percent. Even the steel industry's captive mines—located predominantly in western Pennsylvania and eastern Kentucky—eventually agreed to the terms of the settlement reached in the commercial districts, albeit only after the application of a good deal of pressure from Hugh Johnson and the NRA, which came in the midst of a series of bitterly fought work stoppages that lasted until early November 1933.[25]

The bituminous coal code was adopted and underwritten by the NRA simultaneously with the conclusion of the Appalachian Agreement. It established a basic wage floor for skilled and unskilled workers alike, but it also provided for the maintenance of any preexisting differentials above the specified code minima. The code also allowed for a number of regional differentials in recognition of tangible geographic disparities such as the quality and marketable value of coal available in a given area, freight rates, or the structure of the local labor market. This was accomplished by dividing the country into seventeen separate wage districts. With the exception of two relatively inconsequential western districts, a uniform minimum rate was established for each wage area. Outwardly, these standards were fixed by the NRA. In reality, however, they were the direct result of collective agreements between the operators and the miners' union, the terms of which the NRA simply incorporated into the code. Thus the basic rates set forth in the Appalachian Agreement, and in earlier unexpired contracts in fields outside of the Appalachian region (for example, Indiana and Illinois), became the basic minimum rates specified in the code. In districts where there were no union contracts by which to set uniform employment standards, the NRA negotiated minimum rates directly with the operators. The latter procedure, however, was confined to a very small proportion of the industry. By 2 October 1933, the date the bituminous coal code went into effect, basic rates of pay had been set for all producing areas in the industry and more than 90 percent of the national tonnage was operating under union contracts.[26]

The editors of *Coal Age*, the industry's leading trade journal, were generally pleased with the arrangement as they looked forward to the certainty of substantial relief from the usual "frantic scramble for tonnage at any price." They readily acknowledged that the code settlement was not without certain obvious "defects," particularly in those cases where divisional and subdivisional boundaries as established by the code did not coincide very well with the "natural lines of trade." Yet it was hoped that in time and through experience most of these problems and imperfections could be eliminated by making certain relatively inconspicuous adjustments in the details of code administration. Their final assessment, therefore, was that "the positive benefits implied in the code so far outweigh its possible minor disadvantages and hardships that every interest in the industry should work whole-heartedly to insure its successful operation."[27]

Just how many soft coal producers in the United States actually shared these optimistic sentiments is not known. But it is highly unlikely that the imperatives of successful enterprise under anything less than perfectly benign economic circumstances could sustain an entirely unambivalent frame of mind like that implied in the trade journal editorial. Certainly in the bituminous coal industry, where even under the NRA competitive interests continued to be vulnerable to every measurable fluctuation in the market, the chances for such a favorable consensus were extremely remote.

In the first place, the schedule of wages and hours that became effective with the adoption of the bituminous coal code early in October 1933 was due to expire only six months hence (on 31 March 1934), by which time another joint conference between the miners' union and the operators was to have met under the auspices of the NRA to set the terms of a new industrywide working agreement. Originally the conference was to have convened on 5 January. The meeting was postponed on this and four subsequent occasions, however, and did not actually go into session until 26 March, less than a week before the expiration of the initial Appalachian Agreement. Moreover, when the gathering finally did take place, the operators failed once again to do much more than defend their own narrow competitive interests. The operators of the northern West Virginia panhandle, for example, favored a thirty-hour week so as to enforce additional cutbacks in local production levels. Operators from western Kentucky, on the other hand, were adamantly opposed to any further reduction in working hours but insisted upon a substantial adjustment of wage differentials to shore up their position in the market relative to that of producers in competing coal fields. Most producers in states west of the Mississippi River favored maintenance of the existing code hours, but they also sought special provisions that would allow extra working time during periods of peak demand. Most operators opposed any revision upward in the wage rates established by the code. A few, such as the owners of hand-loading mines in Saline County, Illinois, requested reductions. Operators with properties in thin-seam mines in certain parts of Tennessee favored a reduction of day rates and an increase in mining and loading rates. Northern Colorado operators rejected any suggestion of a downward adjustment in working hours but pointed out that 90 percent of their tonnage paid a daily rate of $5.25 (code base was $5) and urged that southern Colorado rates be increased to at least the $5 level. In Alabama, however, a strike had been settled on 16 March with the adoption of a local wage agreement designated to run until 1 April 1935. The Alabama operators, therefore, contended that they should be exempt from the contingencies of the NRA wage conference because they had already instituted the revisions the Washington meeting was called merely to consider.[28]

In reality, the NRA wage conference was only marking time until the terms of a new Appalachian contract could be settled. Only then might a revised version of the code be finalized. Negotiations between the union and the operators had been under way since the last week of February. The negotiators failed to produce a settlement, however, until the early hours of the morning on 30 March, less than a full day before the expiration of the old contract. When finally completed, the new agreement proposed two amendments to the bituminous coal code in the form of a resolution that was endorsed not only by the operators and miners covered by the Appalachian contract but by every UMW local in the country. Taken together, these amendments would require a significant adjustment in hours and wages in the direction of greater interdistrict uniformity, leaving almost no sector of the industry untouched. Naturally, this prospect caused more than a little apprehension on the part of coal operators whose properties lay outside of the Appalachian district proper, and these interests protested vehemently the imposition of operating standards which they had no hand in formulating. Nevertheless, within a matter of hours after the conclusion of the government-sponsored wage conference on 31 March, NRA officials issued an executive order declaring the existence of an "emergency" in the industry and tentatively adopting the wage and hour proposals of the new Appalachian Agreement as effective code amendments, pending the outcome of public hearings, which were scheduled to commence on 9 April.[29]

When the coal code hearings began, the proposed wage changes rather than the question of working hours caused the greatest controversy among the mine owners. It was almost inevitable, for example, that the Alabama operators would voice particularly intemperate opposition to the wage recommendations of the joint conference in view of their recent agreement with local union leaders on a substantially more favorable contract arrangement than appeared to be attainable under the auspices of the NRA. According to one contemporary account, these operators immediately reacted by denouncing the executive order of 31 March as "invalid, arbitrary, [having been] adopted without hearing," and generally in violation of proper code procedure.[30] Indeed, the opposition in Alabama was so strong that the operators there ultimately sought a federal court injunction with the aim of preventing implementation of the code wage changes. Southern Tennessee and Georgia operators, whose properties lay in the same production district as those of the Alabama interests, were joined by various manufacturers' associations throughout the region in voicing similar objections to the "anti-Southern" bias of the proposed wage changes. Southern Appalachian operators, on the other hand, stressed that they previously had withdrawn from the NRA wage conference precisely because Alabama and Tennessee continued to enjoy a wage advantage and had not signed the UMW contract until the terms of the 31 March executive order had put them in a better competitive position. These operators, therefore, along with the northern Central Competitive Field interests, strongly favored keeping the new union settlement and the executive order intact.

Disagreement over the details of the code wage changes similar to the situation in Division III described above occurred in several other production districts across the country as well. Indeed, as a result of numerous protests registered between 9 and 11 April at the postamendment hearings in Washington, Hugh Johnson and the NRA finally were forced by the deeply embittered politics of the affair to reestablish the original code differentials retroactive to

1 April with a view to pacifying those sectors of the industry who insisted that their particular competitive situation had not received just consideration. But even the issuance of what was appropriately designated at the time as "Amendment No. 2" did not completely settle the matter. A continuation of objections and protests by particularly aggrieved interests in the southwestern coal fields resulted in the pronouncement of yet another modifying order on 4 June 1934. In the end, therefore, Amendment No. 1 was literally "amended" into oblivion. The ill-concealed effect of every subsequent remunerative adjustment was to sanction the continuation of a wage scale in southern mining districts approximately 10 percent lower than average rates in the North, contradicting the NRA's original intention of eliminating as nearly as possible all regional differentials.[31]

The failure of the NRA adequately to "rationalize" the wage structure of the bituminous coal industry necessarily held certain negative implications for the stability of the industry's price structure. As long as relatively low-wage production was allowed to compete in markets ordinarily supplied by operators in high-wage areas, the high-wage districts found it difficult to abide by the minimum price provisions of the coal code. Although it is clear that a number of other factors were involved as well,[32] it was at least partially a result of this disparity in operating costs that noncompliance with code prices had become a commonly acknowledged problem in the bituminous industry by the fall of 1934. And the result was unavoidably cumulative. To some observers almost everything connected with the code system as applied to the mining of soft coal already seemed about to collapse.[33] By the end of the winter, the prospect of ever stabilizing the most stubbornly competitive features of the coal trade with only the means immediately at hand probably could not have been judged any less likely had every effort in that regard still depended upon the notoriously enfeebled regulatory practices of the 1920s. In March 1935, when the Massachusetts state contract bids were opened, the prices actually posted ranged anywhere from thirty to fifty cents per ton below the approved list, and when bids were opened at Islip, Long Island, only six were posted at code prices compared to a total of thirty-seven that were posted below the approved floor by as much as sixty-eight cents. The average sale price of bituminous coal continued to decline, so that producers suffered a greater overall loss per ton in sales revenue during the summer of 1935 than they had in May 1933. For the entire NRA period, for that matter, producers showed a margin above cost of only about three cents per ton on all coal mined, which amounted to an average profit of less than 1 percent on total capital investment.[34]

After several months' experimentation under the recovery program, all indications were that the bituminous mining industry remained substantially unrelieved from the pressures of economic depression, and it would continue to be so burdened until such time as output and demand could be brought more nearly into balance. In this respect, however, the accomplishments of the NRA were not especially impressive. The code system did not prevent the continual entry of unregulated wagon mines and other highly marginal operations, or "snow birds" as they were sometimes called. Nor did it offer any appreciable relief from the commercial inroads of competitive fuels. Yet in spite of these and many other shortcomings, a large enough contingent of producers in attendance at an October 1934 meeting of the National Coal Association (NCA) was sufficiently impressed with the necessity of preserving at least the bare rudiments of an institutional framework within which to ply an effective policy of industrial control to vote decisively in favor of continuing the NRA approach for an additional two-year period, or until "some permanent basis of sound recovery" could be devised.[35] An official policy resolution to the same effect was adopted by the NCA board of directors on 3 January 1935.[36]

In the meantime, a special planning committee of the National Emergency Council issued a report regarding the urgent need for the development of a national minerals policy. The report was transmitted by the president to Congress early in January 1935, and the facts and recommendations it contained helped prepare the way for the introduction later that same month of a new coal stabilization bill, under the joint sponsorship of Senator Joseph F. Guffey and Representative J. Buell Snyder, both of Pennsylvania. The miners' union played a major role in drafting the measure, henceforth known as the Guffey-Snyder bill. But the UMW's efforts also appear to have had the tacit approval of a select group of Central Competitive Field operators led by Pittsburgh Coal's J. D. A. Morrow. The ostensible purpose of the legislation was to provide for the creation of a special bituminous coal commission to oversee all aspects of the industry's affairs bearing on the public interest and to administer the establishment of a national bituminous coal reserve. Of particular importance, however, at least from the point of view of those who had a financial stake in the trade, was that the proposed bill also provided for the adoption of a statutory code designed to achieve more effective minimum price regulation than had been accomplished thus far under the NRA.[37]

John L. Lewis and the UMW decided to push for the enactment of a new coal stabilization bill for the simple but compelling reason that the NRA code had begun to show all the signs of irremediable inadequacy, with the notable effect that, as the union president expressed it, the industry seemed once again "headed toward the old competition for tonnage contracts at any price."[38] Lewis, of course, understood at least as well as anyone else that the staying power of the miners' union was entirely dependent upon the avoidance of such an eventuality. This time, however, the UMW president's enthusiasm for an entirely fresh legislative initiative was not immediately shared by a clear majority of organized mine owners.[39] Rather, it appears that a significant number of customarily supportive union operators agreed with James W.

Carter, president of the Maryland-based Carter Coal Company, that it would be best to avoid any too hasty adoption of potentially controversial and untried "special legislation" as long as there was a good chance that the NIRA, for all of its faults, might still be renewed. Specifically, Carter's widely shared hope was that if the NIRA were extended, "it would become possible to experiment further with code operation and by a process of amendment seek to improve what we already have." Similarly, according to the editors of *Coal Age*, all those who "expressed approval in principle of the philosophy of the [new coal stabilizaton] bill . . . insisted that . . . [the] legislation be made temporary" and readily subject to adjustment in much the same manner as the current policy arrangement.[40] Thus it was not until after 27 May, when the unanimous decision of the Supreme Court in the *Schechter* case invalidated the NRA code system, that the National Conference of Bituminous Coal Producers (which at that point was reported to represent somewhere between 40 and 60 percent of the industry's total active capacity) came out solidly behind the Guffey-Snyder bill. The smaller, typically nonunion, producers with properties in southern Appalachia and various other outlying regions, however, generally continued to oppose the new legislation. So, too, did the noncommercial, "captive," mines owned by the railroads and steel companies, usually on the basis of specific objections to the price-control provisions of the measure, which they argued would play havoc with the highly integrated nature of their operations.[41]

Meanwhile, in compliance with the wishes of President Roosevelt, the miners had been working under a series of temporary extensions of the 1934 Appalachian Agreement, which originally was supposed to have expired on 1 April 1935. The union operators were unwilling to sign any new UMW contract until they had been given reasonable assurance that the current round of price-cutting in the industry would be discontinued, either by modification of the NIRA, or, failing that, by the adoption of acceptable substitute legislation.[42] Accordingly, following the *Schechter* decision, and because it had already been demonstrated that unassisted union power was incapable of stabilizing the industry's highly volatile price structure, a number of influential union operators finally joined the UMW and gave at least their nominal support to the Guffey-Snyder bill. That, however, was not enough. A subcommittee of the House Committee on Ways and Means held hearings on the measure from 17 to 28 June, and at least for the moment everything stopped there. The emergence in Congress of a serious difference of opinion over the question of whether this law too might ultimately fail the test of constitutionality temporarily stalled any further legislative action. In addition, and probably more central to the issue, the attention of key legislators had been captured by an increasingly visible campaign mounted not only by the bill's opponents among the operators[43] but also by two UMW rivals, the Progressive Miners of

America and the Independent Miners' Union of Western Kentucky. As a result of these concerns, the bill was not reported back to the full committee until 30 June.

In the meantime, the urgency of the entire matter was heightened by the constant threat of a nationwide strike. And, indeed, in the midst of Congress's deliberations, Roosevelt once again was forced to ask the bituminous industry's joint wage conference to extend the old 1934 contract, this time to 16 September, a request with which the conference readily complied. Then, finally, on 12 August, the congressional deadlock was broken when the Committee on Ways and Means approved a heavily amended version of the coal stabilization bill by a one-vote margin. It was narrowly adopted by the full House on 19 August, and, after further amendment, passed by the Senate on 22 August. The following day the Guffey-Snyder bill cleared a House-Senate conference, whereupon it was immediately sent to the White House and signed by FDR on 30 August 1935.[44] The way was now prepared for finalization of a new Appalachian wage agreement, which was signed by all but a small minority of operators in four traditionally uncooperative southern districts within the Appalachian conference after a short nationwide strike during the last week of September.[45] Eventually, most of the coal-producing areas outside the Appalachian and Central Competitive Field regions also accepted the contract demands of the UMW so that they, too, might resume operations and avoid the possibility of an unrecoverable loss in market shares.[46]

The Guffey-Snyder Act (also known as the Coal Conservation Act of 1935 but usually referred to simply as the Guffey Act) set up a five-member National Bituminous Coal Commission (NBCC), which was charged with the task of administering the measure partly by implementing an industrywide working agreement very similar to the NRA bituminous coal code. As had been the case under the earlier federally sponsored arrangement, coal operators who agreed to the terms of the new code were automatically exempted from the antitrust laws at the same time that they were given an opportunity to participate in the formulation of minimum price schedules on a district-by-district basis. But the new administrative apparatus had some unique characteristics as well. More or less in keeping with the enforcement practices of the past, the newly established coal commission was given the authority to revoke a producer's code membership in the event of the latter's failure to abide by the rules of the game. In addition, however, the commission was also given the power to determine an individual operator's liability for the payment of a 15 percent excise tax on the mine price of coal, or, in the case of noncommercial captive mines, on the currently established market value of the ore. This tax was to be applied to all producers whether they were subscribers to the code or not. But there was a built-in inducement designed to further the general purposes of the act in the form of a provision which specified that code members were to receive a 90 percent rebate, or 13.5 percent of the value of the coal so taxed. Regulation under the terms of the Guffey Act, in other words, was to be based not primarily on the federal government's power to regulate interstate commerce but rather on its powers of taxation. As anticipated all along by the coal producers, this issue quickly became the subject of an intense debate over the constitutional limits of congressional authority.[47]

The Guffey Act also established a new Bituminous Coal Labor Board, to consist of one employer representative, one representative of the industry's organized employees, and an impartial chairman, the joint activities of whom were to be monitored by the U.S. Department of Labor. The board was given power to adjudicate labor disputes, order operators to meet employee representatives, supervise employee elections, and investigate and determine the status of unions. Moreover, code members were compelled to accept certain provisions affecting the interests of organized labor, including several guarantees with respect to collective bargaining. The new coal stabilization bill incorporated verbatim the first clause of Section 7 of the NIRA, as well as that part of the second clause pertaining to the prohibition of "yellow dog" contracts. Of much greater significance, however, was the final mandatory provision of the code, which sought to apply the principle of majority rule in relation to the general issue of employee representation. Specifically, union agreements negotiated in any district or group of districts between representatives of more than half the mine workers and the agents of producer interests whose combined operations accounted for at least two-thirds of the area's annual tonnage were to be accepted as the basic regional standard for the calculation of both minimum wages and maximum working hours or anything else having to do with the terms of mine employment in the affected market area. Upon evidence of failure or refusal of a code member to abide by the operating standards so established, the NBCC could revoke the producer's membership in the code arrangement.

Unfortunately for the miners' union and those coal operators who had favored such a measure all along, the Guffey Act never became operational. Its opponents within the industry immediately took their case to court. Continuing opposition from several large coal producers along with widespread uncertainty about the constitutionality of the new coal stabilization measure finally resulted in the registration of producers controlling only about 70 percent of the industry's tonnage with the commission.[48] Certain districts, primarily in the Southwest and West, did establish minimum prices according to the terms of the act. In such cases, producers controlling about 90 percent of a district's active capacity typically subscribed to the code. For the most part, these were smaller, commercially isolated market areas, with sufficiently few competitive units that the chance to flatten out excessive intraregional price variations generally was very appealing to local operators. From the point of view of most of the producers in the industry, however, this was not a realistic prospect—at least not in the fall of 1935. In these more numerous, commercially integrated market areas, where producers controlling up to 30 percent of the local tonnage failed to subscribe to the code, its initial adherents generally suffered such heavy sales losses to outsiders as virtually to assure their eventual estrangement from the new coal commission's regulatory mandate.[49]

Ultimately, of course, the fate of the Guffey Act rested in the hands of the courts. By the end of 1935 more than eighty cases were on the docket, most of which had resulted in the issuance of temporary restraining orders against the collection of the 15 percent excise tax. Then, on 18 May 1936, all was seemingly resolved by a U.S. Supreme Court decision that invalidated the entire measure.[50] But those producers in the industry who, along with Lewis and the rest of the UMW leadership, still favored the adoption of an effective price-control law remained undeterred. Indeed, it was largely at the behest of these interests that Joseph Guffey and Representative Fred Vinson of Kentucky introduced substitute legislation just two days after the Coal Conservation Act of 1935 had been declared unconstitutional. There was an initial setback in 1936 when Senator Rush Holt of West Virginia temporarily delayed the legislative process by a threatened filibuster, but in the end yet a new coal stabilization bill was adopted by large majorities in both houses of Congress.[51]

The Guffey-Vinson Act of 1937 staunchly upheld the basic regulatory principles embodied in the earlier law, albeit with certain modifications intended to reduce the risk of any further interference by the courts. The two most noteworthy changes in this respect were the omission of the labor provisions of the original Guffey Act and the reformulation of the tax provisions so as to obviate the objection that they functioned in such a way as to penalize operators who did not adhere to the employment and wage guidelines prescribed by the National Bituminous Coal Commission.

Opinion within the industry for and against the new price stabilization bill tended to divide along traditional competitive lines. Charles O'Neill, chairman of the legislative committee of the National Conference of Bituminous Coal Producers, which claimed to represent the interests of at least eight hundred mine owners in twenty-two states producing more than 125 million tons annually, declared his organization's unqualified support of the measure. Coal operators in central Pennsylvania generally favored adoption of the Guffey-Vinson bill, and producers in the western portion of the state were split. Ohio also was divided, although sentiment in Illinois and Indiana was almost unanimously favorable. The UMW hierarchy was similarly committed in favor of the bill, even though the labor provisions of the original coal stabilization act had been removed. Because price stability and union wage security in the industry had always been closely interrelated, it was generally assumed that the latter would now automatically be enhanced by attainment of the former.[52] Indeed, the highest concentration of unfavorable opinion appeared once again in the largely nonunion southern Appalachian fields, although the bill had some supporters even in that region. Certainly the most outspoken opposition to the measure came from Alabama, where one producer went so far as to charge that the bill was being sponsored by "an organized minority [sic] of coal producers and allied labor leaders for their own selfish purposes and [that it undoubtedly] would be controlled by them at the expense of [the] smaller competitive fields."[53]

After receiving a characteristically mixed response from the coal producers, the Guffey-Vinson Coal Conservation Act of 1937 managed to survive the duration of the Depression era, albeit not without considerable difficulty. A multitude of petty administrative and technical problems, along with the industry's still largely unresolved economic state, provided the measure's enemies with more than enough ammunition for their relentless obstructionism. This led to serious concern on the part of a number of interested observers that the outcome was, as Donald Richberg lamented early in 1938, "likely to parallel the undermining and final destruction of the NRA."[54] Richberg's worst fears were never realized, but his general apprehension about the industry's future nonetheless was well placed.

In the end, neither the miners' union nor the regulation of coal prices as provided in the 1937 legislation was able to shield coal producers adequately against the normal fluctuations of the market. Wage and price stability in bituminous mining was essentially a dead letter if considered in isolation from the more fundamental and continuing context of overdeveloped capacity and stagnant or declining demand. With this problem in mind, the editors of *Coal Age* drew their readers' attention to the valuable lesson to be learned from the post–World War I experience of the nation's railroads. The record there left little doubt that, although the federal government might guarantee the maintenance of prices without a great deal of difficulty, it did not have the power to guarantee the maintenance of volume and demand. This, of course, was the root of the issue in a competitively overdeveloped industry such as bituminous coal mining. It was widely agreed that as "a curb upon unfair and ruinous [business] practices within the industry," the Guffey-Vinson Act held "excellent promise." A similarly hopeful view had already been expressed by the owners of unionized mines with respect to the UMW's generally improved market coverage and the beneficial aspects of closely controlled wage competition. But this, too, had only limited serviceability in view of the need to cope with other, more fundamental, aspects of the industry's largely self-inflicted plight.

The upper limits of price and wage stabilization in bituminous mining had just about been reached by 1937. Once this reality was acknowledged, it began to occur to many operators that greater efficiency in production was probably the only practicable means by which to cope with the seemingly permanent constraints of stagnant demand, particularly because of the growing availability of substitute fuels. The business choices the coalmen now seemed to confront were conveyed succinctly by one commentator who warned that those who wished simply to "survive" would hereafter be "compelled either to dip into their surpluses or borrow for new investments in cost-reducing machinery."[55] Even at this late date, there was almost as much concern as ever that the unrelieved problem of overdeveloped capacity ultimately could lead an indeterminate number of producer interests to utter ruin. Against such an eventuality the New Deal provided no firm guarantees. Indeed, as most contemporary observers plainly recognized, the industry's continuing vulnerability to every slump in market demand was at least partially attributable to the "stabilizing" effect of the NRA code arrangement—that is, in roughly the same proportion that it worked to shield mine properties exhibiting relatively poor marginal efficiency from the natural hazards of unregulated price competition. A measurable improvement in the ability of the miners' union to hold geographically far-flung components of the industry to a standard scale,[56] along with the increasingly mandatory nature of expensive capital improvements, contributed no less significantly to a major upward thrust in fixed operating costs. These steadily mounting financial liabilities, moreover, were only partially offset after 1937 by a corresponding increase in mine productivity.[57] The fortunes of the trade were obviously saved in the short run by the stimulus of heightened wartime demand. But with the return of peace in 1945, the bituminous industry almost immediately entered yet another period of profound demoralization and economic disintegration, a manifestly recurrent condition for which a politically acceptable remedy appeared to be no less elusive than it had after World War I.

The history of the bituminous coal mining and garment manufacturing industries during the first forty years of this century is, in many ways, the shared history of an experiment in social control. The Protocol movement in the women's clothing industry and the organizational strategies that were pursued by the Central Competitive Field operators in the soft coal industry before the 1930s provided a training ground for the theory and practice of federal policy during the reign of the National Recovery Administration. In neither phase, however, was the record of accomplishments outstanding. After more than three decades of sporadic collaboration with organized labor aimed at the achievement of a more stable business environment in the bituminous mining and garment industries, not even the highly supportive policy orientation of the New Deal was enough to vindicate an optimistic view of the long-term prospects for success.

# 6 | Codified Capitalism, II

As we have seen, it was not unusual for trade unions to be viewed by a certain managerial element in the bituminous coal mining and garment manufacturing industries as an agency through which to stabilize labor costs and limit business competition. Efforts on the part of some mine owners and clothing manufacturers to employ this regulatory strategy reached their peak during the Great Depression. It must be recalled in this connection, however, that a strong union presence had been an economic fact of life in both of these industries long before the coming of the New Deal. The aim of gaining effective control over the competitive realm with the help of organized labor was seldom a purely elective option for management during the 1930s. As I pointed out initially in Chapter 4, the adoption of such a strategy almost always was a choice born of necessity, with an unmistakable correlation between prior subjection to union power or otherwise rigorously enforced rules of employment on one hand and management's willingness to advance the idea of universal adherence to such standards on the other. This clearly was the pattern in the garment trades and the mining of bituminous coal, the particular circumstances of which can be contrasted with the virtual absence of any such constraint on management in the cotton textile industry. In cotton textiles, the politics of industrial stabilization were unique because the economics of interregional competition bore a comparatively weak legacy of institutionalized union power.

## Labor and the Cotton Textile Code

The leaders of the cotton textile industry had worked behind the scenes during the weeks immediately preceding the adoption of the NIRA at least as diligently as any other business group to bring about a new "partnership" between government and business dedicated to the alleviation of economic difficulties which had crippled that industry for the better part of a decade. Accordingly, when it became known—certainly no later than the beginning of the second week in May—that the Roosevelt administration was in the process of drafting a comprehensive recovery plan, representatives of the Cotton Textile Institute immediately sought to demonstrate their enthusiasm for such a prospect. They tried to indicate the controls they preferred to see sanctioned by launching yet another voluntary production-curtailment program, which henceforth would require the nation's cotton mills to operate no more than two forty-hour shifts a week. The response from the membership was distinctly favorable, and on 10 May CTI president George A. Sloan wired FDR that fully one-third of the industry, including an impressive number of southern interests, endorsed the plan. By 19 May, once again according to CTI officials, the proportion of the industry in favor of the plan had risen to two-thirds.[1]

The cotton textile industry was the first to get on the NRA bandwagon, with a committee consisting of six northeastern producers, nine southern manufacturers, and four representatives of the New York mercantile interests busily at work on the details of a code by the beginning of June, more than two weeks before the NIRA finally emerged from Congress. "The industry's leaders," Louis Galambos has written, "had a clear concept of what their goal was. The members of the [Code] Committee knew exactly what they wanted. In May, 1933, they were striving to achieve the same goal that had brought about the formation of CTI in 1926: stability of prices and profits."[2]

When the committee began its work near the end of May, two of the major provisions eventually to be included in the code had already been drafted. By this time about 80 percent of the industry had agreed to accept the "40-40" weekly work and production schedule. That left only the issue of minimum wages, the general principle of which was supported by most of the producers in the industry. With respect to the question of how high the minimum should be, however, or what might constitute an acceptable North-South differential, the extent of disagreement was considerably greater. Nonetheless, by the beginning of the second week in June, even that controversial point seems to have been settled to everyone's satisfaction, apparently including Thomas F. McMahon, president of the United Textile Workers of America (UTW). The arrangement finally settled upon provided for a $10 minimum weekly wage in southern establishments and an $11 minimum in the North. According to Galambos, both this and CTI's 40-40 production-curtailment formula were "accepted by the government with hardly any resistance." Alexander Sachs and other members of the NRA staff may have been a "bit suspicious" of the production limitation, "but the industry's arguments were persuasive, particularly the argument that 40-40 would stabilize production and employment at the level that had been reached in 1929. Stability at that level looked good from the perspective of 1933." The Roosevelt administration, moreover, had abandoned the principle of antitrust in the recovery bill that it submitted to

Congress, which seemed to imply the admissibility of a provision like 40-40, so the industry's representatives "never budged from their strong position on limiting production."[3]

By the time the recovery bill emerged from Congress on 16 June, key representatives of the cotton textile industry and Hugh Johnson's staff had completed the first NRA code. It consisted of five basic provisions: the minimum wage and forty-hour workweek proposals as outlined above; the two-shift, limited-production operating schedule; a provision for the control of entry and expansion; and Section 7a of the NIRA, which was incorporated in the cotton textile code unchanged.[4]

Public hearings on Code No. 1 opened on 27 June, and according to the editors of *Textile World*, the most noteworthy aspect of the three-day event was the nearly "unanimous approval" of the "principles" underlying the proposal in question. "Witnesses made no attempt toward excursions into academic discussion of the [basic] premise. They seemed in agreement that, in essence, the code represented an honest attempt to apply the new law equitably to all engaged in . . . [the] industry."[5]

There were, of course, some (not insignificant) differences of opinion on detail. The representatives of labor argued for a shorter workweek than the forty-hour maximum prescribed in the original version of the code. AFL president William Green recommended a thirty- or thirty-two-hour week, while McMahon of the UTW, whose earlier agreement to the code committee's preference had since been rejected by the union's membership, now urged no more than a thirty-five-hour week.

The union representatives also objected to the proposed minimum wage. Green suggested a weekly minimum of from $14 to $16, whereas McMahon thought $14 would be adequate, if the employers would agree to abolish the regional differential. The northern manufacturers, represented at the hearings by Robert Amory of Spring Mills in Massachusetts, were not particularly pleased with the wage differential either but ultimately dropped any thought of serious opposition out of the knowledge that no substantive agreement could be accomplished without conceding at least that much to the southern branch of the industry.

The child labor issue, however, caused no difficulty whatsoever. On the second day of hearings, the manufacturers' code committee reported its willingness and desire to add a clause prohibiting the employment of children under the age of sixteen. Henry P. Kendall, president of the interregionally based Kendall Company, even suggested the inclusion of a provision designed to prevent the employment of women and children at night, all of which seemed to be taken in stride by the southerners. Indeed, the only sustained divergence of opinion occurred between the representatives of management and labor, which ultimately accounted for a relatively modest adjustment in the terms of the code as originally presented. In the end, the 40-40 production schedule remained intact, and the minimum wage was increased from $10 and $11 to $12 and $13 for the North and South, respectively. The revised code also prohibited the employment of children under the age of sixteen as recommended virtually without dissent by the manufacturers.[6]

Contrary to the express purpose of the cotton textile code, its immediate effect was to stimulate a speculative boom in the trade, as producers—North and South—sought to get as much as possible out of current operating expenditures before the expected increase in costs from application of the code began to take hold. Moreover, in addition to the prospect of higher wages under the terms of the code, soon the industry would be burdened by a new tax levied by the Agricultural Adjustment Administration on the processors of farm goods. The tax on cotton was heavy: 4.2 cents per pound, or about 50 percent of the prevailing price of raw cotton. The tax was to become effective on 1 August 1933 and would apply not only to purchases of cotton intended for processing after that date but to any quantity held in inventory as well. As a result, the eagerness of buyers to secure finished goods before 1 August led to an unprecedented surge in demand during May, June, and July, which textile manufacturers naturally were anxious to fill. The height of activity came in July, when production ran 22 percent above the six-year average from 1922 to 1927. At the same time, producers' inventories reached their lowest level in eight years and overall employment its highest ever.

The boom continued even after the code went into effect, and, all in all, 1933 was the most profitable year for the cotton textile industry since 1927. By late fall, however, demand once again had begun to slacken. Prices stabilized and in some cases fell, which in turn triggered a rash of complaints from producers about the increased burden of operating costs. One survey of the southern branch of the industry found that by October 1933 the minimum-wage provision of the textile code had already resulted in an increase of over 100 percent in the wage bill of many mills and the average expenditure per unit of product for the industry as a whole for wages was estimated to have increased by approximately 70 percent. The manufacturers, moreover, were quick to observe that these increased liabilities generally were not being compensated by a corresponding increase in prices and that they could not continue indefinitely to absorb such costs.

If higher labor costs provided one pervasive source of discontent among textile manufacturers, the bitterest complaints were reserved for the processing tax, which was estimated to have increased the operating overhead of individual mills by anywhere from 8 to 13 percent. Many producers claimed that they could not readily pass these added costs along to the consumer because to do so would put them at a competitive disadvantage with less expensive cotton imports, as well as with a large variety of other domestically produced fibers, each of which was rapidly growing in availability. In the face of these unmistakable economic realities, therefore, even someone as enthusiastically supportive of the NRA as George Sloan found himself in the position by February 1934 of having to acknowledge that the performance of the cotton textile code thus far had proven to be a mixed blessing for the industry.[7]

Southern textile manufacturers generally expressed greater dissatisfaction with the operation of the code than their New England counterparts, particularly insofar as the wage and hour provisions had a greater relative impact on the cost structure of the southern branch of the industry. Most northern operations freely expanded production in response to heightened overall demand during the summer of 1933, whereas many southern mills were already operating on a two-shift, 110-hour-week basis and thus were forced to curtail their weekly running time to the eighty-hour NRA maximum once the code went into effect. It was the southern producer, therefore, who bore the brunt of the reduction in capacity stipulated by the code. In addition, the code had the effect of raising wages in the southern branch of the industry enough to reduce the regional differential to the lowest point ever. Down significantly already, from 39 percent in 1924 to 26 percent or so immediately before the code went into effect, by early 1934 the differential had fallen to about 18 percent. Barely had the recovery apparatus gotten off the ground, therefore, when textile manufacturers in the South began to express their concern that the northern branch of the industry soon would be in a position to exploit the narrowing wage gap with much greater competitive impact than the southern representatives on the code committee had anticipated.[8]

In reality, of course, it was to be expected that a perfectly equitable adjustment of a long-standing interregional conflict such as that which plagued the cotton textile industry probably never could be achieved. This simple truth, however, did not alter the need for some means of sorting out the industry's worst difficulties if the logic of economic regulation was to be vindicated. Accordingly, in December 1933, the code authority for the industry recommended yet another limitation of output by reducing the allowable weekly running time by 25 percent of the current maximum permitted under the code. This recommendation, which was approved by Hugh Johnson on 2 December 1933, reduced machine hours from eighty to sixty per week and the normal workweek from forty hours to thirty, with the principal object being to reduce production so as to eliminate excessive inventories.

At first, the new curtailment formula seemed to work satisfactorily, and production and sales began gradually to balance out. By January 1934, however, the industry's economic situation once again had begun to deteriorate. Higher cotton goods prices caused by the new 25 percent curtailment, the continuing burden of the processing tax, and the increased price of raw cotton all combined to weaken demand while production remained at the very upper limit of the allowable restricted output. Indeed, by the spring of 1934, it was clear that the textile code was not doing all that it had been designed to do, for the industry was still plagued by tremendous competitive instability. And yet this realization seemed to be tempered by a general feeling that matters almost certainly would be much worse had it not been for the adoption of the NIRA, which in spite of its obvious inadequacies seemed to afford a far more promising opportunity to grasp and control the economics of the industry than any of the pitifully ineffectual voluntary efforts sponsored by the Cotton Textile Institute before 1933. In 1934, then, few textile manufacturers were prepared to scrap the code, their many frustrations and disappointments with its performance thus far notwithstanding.[9]

One area in which cotton textile manufacturers were able to exploit the NRA mechanism reasonably well was in the field of labor relations. Here, the power of the employers was left almost wholly unrestrained, although this had certain serious drawbacks with regard to the more general problem of industrial control.

During the initial hearings on the cotton textile code, Hugh Johnson was persuaded by certain interested manufacturers to appoint a special committee to monitor the problem of the so-called stretch-out. This term referred to individual producers' attempts to circumvent the restrictions of the limited workweek by forcing employees to tend more machinery than normal, thereby "stretching out" the productive capacity of the plant during a specified period of operation. The committee named by Johnson for this purpose consisted of industrial relations expert Robert W. Bruere as chairman, Benjamin Greer as the manufacturers' representative, and George L. Berry, president of the International Pressmen's Union, as the spokesman for labor. The committee was biased in favor of management from the outset in that it never pursued its designated task in more than a superficial manner. Indeed, Bruere and his two associates generally were so tolerant of the employers' typically libertarian creed that the manufacturers soon moved to transform the triumvirate into a permanent Cotton Textile National Industrial Relations Board with authority to handle all labor problems that might arise under the code. The formal establishment of the board in August 1933 enabled the manufacturers and their trade association to wield virtually uncontested power over labor. Its first major decision was voluntarily to divest itself of any claim to administrative autonomy. It sought and ultimately received NRA approval of its wish (apparently dictated by Bruere) to make the code authority for the industry the final arbiter of all complaints and accusations related to the maintenance of labor standards in the cotton textile industry. This meant that neither the individual worker nor the textile workers' union had any recourse other than to submit its grievances to an agency in which there was no effective labor representation.[10]

This arrangement gave rise to monumental difficulties. The response of the code authority to the legitimate interests of labor was callous in the extreme, and the extensive conciliation apparatus connected with the Bruere board repeatedly demonstrated an incapacity to act independently of the whims of management.[11] As a result, throughout the spring of 1934, wildcat strikes— particularly in the southern branch of the industry—became ever more frequent and violent as groups of ordinary mill workers sought to register their objections to management's increasing use of the stretch-out, as well as to an overall loss of pay because of the shortened workweek. Data compiled by the U.S. Bureau of Labor Statistics indicate that the hourly earnings of cotton textile workers increased between July 1933 and July 1934 on an industrywide basis by an average of 65.4 percent—more than in any other industry except men's furnishings. The real weeky earnings of these workers, however, were substantially lower in July 1934 than they were when the code had gone into effect the previous summer. In no week since the adoption of the code had the industry averaged more than 36.5 hours per employed worker, though 40 hours were required to attain the specified minimum weekly earnings of $13 in the North and $12 in the South. The average reduction in working hours below the forty-hour maximum, therefore, combined with a simultaneous increase in the general cost of living, accounted for an actual reduction of 25 percent in the real earnings of cotton mill employees during the course of the code's first full year in operation.[12]

In May 1934 the code authority pushed the textile workers to the brink of rebellion by requesting an additional industrywide machine-hour curtailment of 25 percent for a limited twelve-week period during the summer. After some initial hesitation, Hugh Johnson and the NRA bureaucracy finally approved the code authority's request on the basis of the manufacturers' argument that such a move was necessary to offset rapidly increasing overcapacity throughout the industry. The decisive factor here was data supplied by CTI, which showed that sales amounted to only about 49 percent of production during the last two weeks in April. Any new curtailment, of course, would reduce labor's overall earnings once again, and on 28 May, UTW vice-president Francis J. Gorman threatened a general strike if the planned cutback in operations was put into effect on 4 June as scheduled. Johnson, wanting desperately to avert a major strike, finally worked out a compromise between the manufacturers and the union wherein the UTW agreed to countermand its current strike order without relinquishing the right to strike in the future. In addition, provision was made for more labor representation on the Bruere board, and the NRA was given a series of questions to study concerning the wage and employment policies of the industry, which it was assumed would result in fundamental changes in the code.[13] These expectations, however, were premature. According to Galambos, "Although the Authority was angry over Johnson's decision to alter the code by changing the membership of the Industrial Relations

Board, the settlement was recognized as a victory for management." The union did not receive any concessions from Johnson that were not considered "absolutely essential." The NRA studies of conditions in the industry were not likely to be conclusive in prompting the administration to action. Although the settlement included a provision for the temporary curtailment of production beyond the 40-40 regulation in deference to the interests of management, it did not recognize the UTW as the legitimate bargaining agent for the industry's work force. Nothing was said about trying to hold wage levels up while production curtailment was in effect, which meant that the Cotton Textile Institute's officers had every reason to "celebrate when they saw the final settlement."[14]

Within a matter of weeks, the threat of a general strike once again hung over the industry. The NRA staff ultimately sided with the manufacturers by supporting their claim that the current state of the market would not allow them to make any upward adjustment in wages. Moreover, on 22 August, the NRA approved an indefinite continuation of the machine-hour curtailment as originally ordered three months earlier, apparently on the basis of evidence which showed that "production continued to exceed sales during most of the time the curtailment was in effect, with the result that unsold stocks were [actually] higher at the end of the curtailment period than at the beginning."[15]

Early in September 1934, the UTW, joined now by its leftist rival, the National Textile Workers Union, called an industrywide work stoppage. Neither of these unions was well situated strategically for such an ambitious undertaking, particularly because very few mills in the southern branch of the industry had been effectively organized. The violence and general bitterness with which the 1934 cotton textile strike got under way was so intense, however, that the Roosevelt administration came under immediate pressure to do something to relieve the situation. FDR responded by appointing a special mediation board under the chairmanship of John G. Winant, former Republican governor of New Hampshire, whose job essentially was to defuse the controversy before it spilled over into other similarly troubled industries.

Despite the manufacturers' initial distaste for the idea of government arbitration, which they feared might entail de facto recognition of the union, the Winant board soon proved that it intended no harm to the established prerogatives of management. With respect to the issue of collective bargaining, for instance, the board decided that the only legitimate way to determine union jurisdiction would be on a plant-by-plant basis, thus assuring defeat of the UTW's organizing campaign in the South. Nor could the board find any evidence to justify a change in the hours and wages of labor, although on this matter it attempted to preserve some claim to impartiality by recommending further government study of the issue. Finally, Winant and his collaborators on the special mediation board found that fully to protect the workers' rights under Section 7a of the National Industrial Recovery Act, a new, genuinely independent textile labor relations board would have to be established to take responsibility for this admittedly delicate matter out of the hands of the trade association. Ultimately, the strike was settled on this distinctly unimpressive note, a settlement that bore obvious testimony to the desperately weakened state of employee organization throughout the industry at the conclusion of labor's ill-fated struggle with the cotton textile manufacturers in the fall of 1934.[16]

The union's defeat in 1934 meant that the material condition of the work force in the textile industry would continue to be highly vulnerable to the whims of management, which in turn were governed by the characteristically unstable competitive structure of the product market. This equation worked just as easily the other way around, however, in that labor's characteristic vulnerability to the whims of management was one of the primary sources of the cotton textile industry's traditionally unstable market structure. Indeed, there was a direct and unmistakable relationship within the industry between the generally unrelieved chaos of labor-management relations on one hand and the chronic ill health of ordinary business prospects on the other. It was for this reason that the Winant board, in the midst of all the turmoil surrounding the strike of 1934, determined to examine the situation as objectively as possible. As part of its formal report to the president, the board issued a clearly stated warning that the stretch-out had become a major problem in the industry in two obviously interrelated respects: first, it provoked unnecessary discontent among the workers; and, second, it tended to defeat the essential purposes of the machine-hour limitations, which in turn contributed to the renewed atmosphere of economic gloom in evidence by the end of 1934.[17]

The first year of operation under the code had been relatively profitable for American cotton textile producers. The industry's total before-tax revenue in 1933 amounted to almost $32 million. During 1934, however, there was a general decline in profits as net income fell to about $8.5 million and the number of establishments reporting no income jumped from 288 to 481, or 52 percent of the companies filing federal tax returns. Between the fall of 1934 and April 1935, at least 71 companies stopped production entirely because the prospects for any near-term improvement in the market were so poor.[18]

For the most part, the manufacturers were prepared to recognize—and in some cases even praise—certain limited accomplishments made possible by the NRA textile code. By the fall of 1934, however, the competitive structure of the industry was just about as difficult to live with as ever and the producers were never very hard-pressed to specify exactly which problems were of greatest concern to them. For some it was the overabundance of small, "inefficient" competitive units, which the "socially responsible" producers preferred not to have to accommodate. All of the manufacturers resented the imposition of the processing tax, against which they constantly agitated, even suggesting that its elimination would enable them to be somewhat less resistant to the wage demands of labor. The problem of foreign imports (primarily Japanese) was also frequently mentioned as an increasingly significant source of the industry's difficulties.[19] And, finally, there still was the traditional North-South market rivalry, which was exacerbated by every economic downturn experienced by the industry.

The descent into profitlessness during the last six months of 1934 stimulated old regional resentments, which had been at least partially submerged by the false sense of economic security initially engendered by the code. Now, however, the North-South wage differential once again became a point of intense controversy between those interests traditionally most affected by the geography of competition, and major fractures reappeared within the ranks of the Cotton Textile Institute. Indeed, the general deterioration of economic fortunes throughout the industry revealed just how fragile and superficial the cooperative consensus had been, as adherence to the regulatory principles embodied in the textile code, and particularly the labor provisions, became more seriously compromised. The predominant tendency now was to cut corners for competitive advantage. Late in December, for instance, John Winant voiced his concern that "textile employers in the South, while paying the code minimum . . . [increasingly were] not observing differentials for persons of higher skills."[20] The stretch-out, as well as a variety of related means of evading the code, seemed suddenly to pervade the industry, and the response of a few of the more deeply concerned producers began to be reflected in the uncharacteristically desperate lengths to which they indicated they might be willing to go in an effort to remedy their plight.

Most cotton textile manufacturers, of course, including Donald Comer, one of the leaders of the southern branch of the industry, still adamantly opposed the idea of industrywide bargaining with the UTW or any other textile workers' union. Assistant Secretary of Labor Turner W. Battle got a sharply contrasting view of the situation, however, from a group of "reputable manufacturers" in the South during the midst of the 1934 strike. In a confidential memorandum to Frances Perkins, Battle reported that the group of producers with whom he had recently met "feel," first, "that the strike is being fostered and engineered by [the] New England manufacturers." Second, they were not inclined, "as they express it, [to] sign a 'blank check' for the Winant Board to fill in. They feel that . . . the [former] Governor of a New England state would be inclined to make decisions affecting the cost of production that would work to the detriment of southern mills." The interminable difficulties of code enforcement, moreover, appeared to be exemplified by the case of "the old Atlantic Mills at Macon, Georgia, who have openly refused to comply with the code and nothing has been done about it." Deeply disturbed by this and other displays of official laxity, Battle's informants told him that "unless some effective compliance is initiated, [they] would now like to see the industry 100% organized in preference to reverting to the unfair competition of two years ago."[21]

This position, to be sure, was not widely held among cotton textile manufacturers in the United States, least of all those attached to the southern branch of the industry. Nor was there much hope that the union as presently constituted could bring the industry to heel, a fact that the producers with whom Battle conferred apparently imagined would be beneficial to their own competitive interests. It is also clear, however, that such sentiments were indicative of a much more basic and commonly shared predisposition among various elements of the trade to view the enforcement of minimum labor standards as the key to industrial stabilization. This perception, moreover, was dictated by the lingering effects of economic disintegration during and subsequent to the demise of the NRA. It was only natural, therefore, that the legislative debate over the Fair Labor Standards Act of 1938 should provide the next occasion for the unrestrained politicization of the cotton textile industry's most persistent structural dilemma. In that debate, too, the governing issue would continue to be the North-South wage differential and related inconsistencies in the terms of employment, which contributed to the perpetuation of sharply defined regional disparities in operating costs and hence in the fortunes of the trade.

## The Associationists and the Law

Ultimately the NRA code system was no match for the intensely competitive nature of the cotton textile industry in the United States. The dual problem of overcapacity and shrinking demand seemed to be just as great a burden to the industry in the spring of 1935 as it had been in the spring of 1933. Actually, the industry as a whole managed to stay in the black during 1933, the year the textile code first became operational. In both 1934 and 1935, however, net losses were recorded by substantially more than half the firms in the trade, a highly disproportionate number of which were located in the northeastern region of the country. Indeed, it was the widely publicized plight of this branch of the industry that prompted FDR in April 1935 to call a special White House conference with the governors of the most seriously affected New England states. This gathering led to the formation of a Cabinet Committee on the Cotton Textile Industry, which Roosevelt placed under the direction of Commerce Secretary Daniel Roper.

The committee's investigation began almost immediately, and by August 1935 it was ready with a comprehensive list of findings and recommendations. In the meantime, the NRA had been demolished by the Supreme Court's decision in the *Schechter* case, which made the search for a broad new policy initiative on textiles a matter of greater urgency than ever. When the committee's report was finally issued, therefore, it contained a complicated mixture of both old and new approaches to the problem, including the continuation of machine-hour limitations, the establishment of a leasing system for the retirement of surplus or obsolete equipment, additional restrictions on Japanese imports, the promotion of research to find new uses and new markets for textiles, and, last but not least, some provision for the enforcement of minimum labor standards throughout the industry. These recommendations, however, were very tentative—a wide-ranging list of administrative and policy options suitable for further study. The committee did not offer a specific proposal for legislation.[22]

The first post-NRA proposal for a legislative response to the problems of the textile industry appeared in the form of a bill drafted late in 1935 by the United Textile Workers and introduced in Congress by Representative Henry Ellenbogen of Pennsylvania. The Ellenbogen bill would have outlawed certain unfair trade practices, provided for the enforcement of uniform labor standards throughout the industry, and required the formation of a national textile commission, whose responsibility it would be to determine minimum wage scales, guarantee collective bargaining, regulate job classifications and assignments, and prescribe the number of permissible work shifts per day, or any other controls and restrictions necessary to prevent overproduction.

A subcommittee of the House Committee on Labor held hearings on the Ellenbogen bill in January and February 1936. During the course of those hearings the measure received its most enthusiastic support from representatives of the UTW, the Textile Converters' Association, the silk mills, and, generally, the same cotton manufacturing interests who a year earlier had been among the industry's more committed advocates of NIRA renewal. Most cotton textile producers, however, and especially the southerners, strongly disapproved of the bill, with the labor provisions, the licensing powers of the proposed textile commission, and the possible imposition of a retroactive excise tax on cotton goods receiving the harshest criticism. The bill never had much of a chance for success. In addition to the discouraging opposition of an apparently large majority of the nation's cotton textile interests, by May 1936 even the vaguest reservations about the measure in Congress had been greatly reinforced by the Supreme Court's invalidation of the similarly designed Guffey Coal Act.[23] Moreover, a general upswing in business and profits during 1936 had the effect of eliminating any sense of urgency about the need for special legislation. Ellenbogen reintroduced his bill early the following spring, but once again the measure failed to attract enough interest to carry it beyond a series of inconclusive committee hearings.[24]

Cotton mill activity in 1936 increased by 26 percent over that of 1935. This was roughly 20 percent over the 1923–25 average and about 10 percent over 1929. The temporarily improved business outlook in 1936 sustained a modest surge of optimism in the industry well into 1937.[25] An expansive mood was particularly apparent in the South, where the value of the industry's product increased by nearly 30 percent between 1935 and 1937. The cotton-producing states witnessed the appearance of fifty-seven new mills during this period, although the total number of active spindles in the southern branch of the industry was about the same in 1937 (18.2 million) as it had been in 1935. The total number of active spindles in the Northeast was reduced by about 1.4 million between 1935 and 1937 and spindles in place by about 2.5 million. The general improvement in business and the industry's continuing shift southward took a heavy toll on a new, post-NRA, round of production-curtailment programs sponsored by the Cotton Textile Institute, as the irresistible attractions of a partially revitalized product market led once again to the proliferation of extended double-shift operations and the eventual collapse of voluntary regulatory programs throughout the industry. These developments tended to weaken the competitive position of textile producers in the Northeast, whose labor costs as of July 1937 averaged about 20 percent above those of their southern counterparts.[26]

In March 1937, the seriously faltering United Textile Workers of America relinquished control over its few remaining locals to the newly established Textile Workers Organizing Committee (TWOC), which John L. Lewis of the CIO placed under the capable direction of garment union president Sidney Hillman. The TWOC drive in textiles opened impressively in the Northeast. Major victories were won not only in cotton textiles but in the full-fashioned hosiery, woolen, and silk and rayon industries as well. By the end of September 1937 the TWOC claimed 215,000 workers under contract, although this included only sixteen agreements covering a total of 17,500 workers in the South. Then, suddenly, the union's prospects were dashed, as for the next twelve months the textile industry—along with the rest of the economy—was racked by a major recession that forced a drastic curtailment of production and swiftly nullified most of the TWOC's hard-won gains. Wage reductions were put into effect in some southern mills as early as November 1937. Widespread decreases followed during January and February 1938 and even more extensive ones from April to July. In New England the union succeeded in staving off any serious reduction until December 1937, when the New Bedford Textile Council signed an agreement with the mill owners that not only outlawed all strikes except those called to enforce arbitration awards but also authorized a 12.5 percent wage cut in the hope of capturing more business for hard-pressed local manufacturers. This agreement took place without the consent of the union's parent organization, which eventually resulted in the New Bedford Textile Council's expulsion from the TWOC. After the New Bedford wage cut, reductions became general throughout New England, where average rates fell even more sharply than in the South. The result was a moderate narrowing of the interregional wage gap to 8 cents an hour by August 1938, which meant that southern cotton textile wages then averaged about 18 percent less than hourly rates in the North.[27]

The Roosevelt administration began to show serious interest in the idea of federal wage-and-hour legislation as a possible supplement to the NRA code system at least as early as the spring of 1934, and the promise of such a measure was subsequently adopted as one of the provisions of the 1936 Democratic platform.[28] The outcome of the *Schechter* case and similar decisions from the bench during 1935 and 1936 kept the issue temporarily off the administration's list of viable legislative options. But when the Supreme Court reversed its earlier stand on such questions in a series of major decisions beginning early in 1937, the prospect of national wage-and-hour legislation suddenly reentered the realm of possibility. Later that spring, at the request of the president, Frances Perkins reportedly took from her desk drawer a wage-and-hour bill that had been drafted several years earlier. She then turned the bill over to the legal staff of the Department of Labor, whereupon it was carefully revised and supplemented with a provision restricting the employment of child labor. The final product was introduced in the Senate by the indomitable Hugo Black and in the House of Representatives by William Connery on 24 May 1937, accompanied by a special message of support from Roosevelt.[29]

Although originally the Fair Labor Standards Act (FLSA) had not been conceived as a labor reform bill for the fabric manufacturing trades in particular, the business press was quick to point out how well suited the Black-Connery wage-and-hour bill was to "the fundamental set-up" of the textile industry, which *Business Week* characterized as "a natural-born guinea pig" for "social-economic legislation." Indeed, the connection seemed to be unique:

> Wages represent a very much higher percentage of the total cost factor in textiles than in most other industries. As such, they are the main competitive battleground. Price-cutting in textiles inevitably means wage-cutting. And when the latter becomes ruthless enough, the premium on good management, good machinery, good merchandizing is removed.
>
> Coupled with this fundamental condition is the equally basic fact that the textile industry is broken up into several thousand units, widely scattered geographically. No small group of manufacturers can determine or effect stabilization.
>
> Then there is a third reason. The textile industry has been through 15 years of depression. It had its own private slump for six years before the rest of the country followed suit. This textile depression was com-

pounded of: (1) overexpansion of plants during the war and post-war periods; (2) growth of the night shift; (3) North-to-South movement which added to over-expansion; [and] (4) revolutionary influence of new fibers, particularly synthetics and new processes.[30]

The magazine then went on briefly to review the history of earlier attempts by the industry to control competition and overproduction. The record of events began with the Cotton Textile Institute's unsuccessful voluntary production-curtailment programs of the last half of the 1920s and ended with the distinctly disappointing results of the NRA code system, which "inevitably" left the textile industry in the position of becoming the most likely "first patient" for yet another "experiment" in national industrial legislation: "The [1937–38] depression . . . hit textiles especially sharply—and the industry needs stability, particularly in maintaining its labor standards. . . . Most ethical manufacturers [therefore] want wage-hour legislation, as a protection against their unethical competitors" for strictly "selfish, not philanthropic, reasons." Moreover, because textile wages had fallen somewhat less during the current recession than they had on several other occasions in the recent past, finding a way to prevent them from falling any further now was taken to be "the important point about an established minimum wage." Thus, with wages in the textile industry still "relatively high" midway through 1938, the FLSA could be "expected to provide protection—a sort of insurance against the wage-chiseler—which will prevent a recurrence of the bitter days of 1932."[31]

Clearly, then, as a writer for the Washington office of *Textile World* was quick to confirm, the fabric trades, and particularly the cotton industry, had a very "special interest" in the Black-Connery bill.[32] In sharp contrast, however, was the near indifference displayed by employers in most major industries other than textiles.[33] A number of equally low-paying manufacturing operations in the South joined forces with their regional counterparts in the textile industry in an attempt to defeat or at least seriously weaken the proposed wage-and-hour law.[34] By 1937, however, most manufacturing interests in the United States would not have been greatly affected by a law that, in its final form, provided for an initial wage floor of only 25 cents an hour and a maximum forty-four-hour workweek. Under the FLSA, the minimum wage rate was to increase annually by only 5 cents an hour until a limit of 40 cents was reached. The length of the standard workweek was to decrease by two hours during each of the two succeeding years and then remain fixed at forty hours. This, along with a long list of exemptions from the law, pacified both the AFL, which opposed the Black-Connery bill until the specified minima had been reduced to an acceptable level below union scale, and most industrialists, who were already operating on standards considerably above FLSA requirements.[35]

The textile interests, in any event, dominated the joint House and Senate committee hearings that were held on the proposed wage-and-hour bill during June 1937. Although these interests sought—and for the most part obtained—several substantial modifications in the original version of the bill, and although there was the continual lament on behalf of an ideal preference for more nearly voluntary wage-and-hour controls, ultimately the Cotton Textile Institute, virtually every spokesman for the northeastern branch of the industry, and even a fairly significant complement of southerners supported the adoption of the FLSA. The latter group, predictably, wanted a flat regional differential written into the law, which in the end they failed to get. Not even this failure, however, caused universal disappointment in the southern branch of the industry, for the competitive position of some "high-wage" employers in the South stood to benefit as a result.[36] Indeed, as was commonly the case with such legislation, individual producer interests objected strenuously to various aspects of the FLSA, sometimes on the basis of major strategic (in this case regional) competitive considerations, and sometimes on the basis of the anticipated cost or inconvenience of adjusting to even the most minor change in standard operating procedure. Yet, as Representative Charles A. Wolverton of New Jersey observed, it was not uncommon to find among such interests those who believed that it was time the "chiselers" were driven out and the "rules of the game" regularized.[37] This premise compelled CTI president Claudius T. Murchison, in testimony before Congress on the wage-and-hour question in June 1937, to acknowledge that the proposed legislation, in spite of the loathsome administrative apparatus that it threatened to create, held "within its broad, monstrous, lugubrious form . . . the germ of economic sanity and progress."[38]

# Part Three

---

# Labor's "Second" New Deal: A Matter of Equity

# 7 Politics: The Wagner Act

When the National Industrial Recovery Act was adopted in June 1933, the nation's trade unionists believed that they had secured, via the recovery measure's controversial Section 7a, certain fairly substantial guarantees in furtherance of organized labor's interests in the American political economy. Indeed, although the NIRA had been formulated with the cooperation and guidance of some of the country's most influential corporate spokesmen, neither the business lobbyists nor the Roosevelt administration ever fully anticipated, or in any way encouraged, the inclusion of the labor provisions as they were finally interpreted by union officials. Rather, as David Brody has astutely observed, "Once it was shoved into the recovery bill [essentially] at labor's initiative, Section 7a proved impossible to dislodge—partly because it fitted so well the [elementary] logic of the Recovery Act, [and] partly because the underlying principles [of the provision] had been gaining acceptance for some years before."[1]

The fortunes of industry varied immensely under the impact of the NIRA. Some enterprises floundered helplessly between 1933 and 1935, despite the efforts of the National Recovery Administration. But several of the industrial codes instituted under the auspices of that agency, as was demonstrated in the two preceding chapters, proved at least partially successful in attaining the recovery program's primary goal: to regulate competition, put a floor under falling prices, and thereby effect an eventual restoration of business profits. By the same token, workers' wages either increased moderately or were prevented from diminishing radically in relation to profits in key industries such as bituminous coal mining and garment manufacturing, in which the extent of union penetration and the advent of near industrywide collective bargaining worked as an organizational adjunct to the general regulatory aims of the NRA code apparatus. This, naturally enough, tended to enhance the competitive position and market security of certain segments of industry at the same time that it provided a boost to the prestige of specific unions.

Nevertheless, there should be no mistake that labor's organizational gains under Section 7a were, on balance, exceedingly modest. From the point of view of the trade union movement, without distinction as to craft or particular industry, the labor provisions of the recovery act turned out to be a profound disappointment. Interpreted generally, the legislation affirmed the right of workers to organize and to designate union representatives of their own choosing, and it prevailed upon the employer merely to refrain from interfering with that right. Union leaders at first were genuinely gratified by this provision. Their initially optimistic expectations gradually changed to despair, however, as the failure to anticipate certain troublesome technicalities related to the enforcement of the measure frustrated their hopes. Labor's prospects appeared even less hopeful once the Roosevelt administration was forced to clarify its understanding of the operational limits of Section 7a, which ultimately confirmed that provision's subsidiary relationship to the clearly market-oriented priorities of the recovery program.[2] The ultimate effect was to assure that there would be very little tangible institutional resistance to systematic evasions of the law, except in a few select industries in which the unions were strategically positioned so as to be able to "punish" nonconformist employers for their transgressions.

## Strikes, Recovery Politics, and Labor Boards

When President Roosevelt signed the National Industrial Recovery Act on 16 June 1933, neither he nor anyone else anticipated the tremendous controversy that was to arise very soon afterward over the proper interpretation of Section 7a. Many employers, particularly in the heavy mass-production industries, refused to negotiate with independent trade unions and proceeded to establish or strengthen their own company-dominated organizations instead. As a result, work stoppages over the question of union recognition increased dramatically subsequent to the adoption of the NIRA. The number of employee-days lost because of strikes tripled between June and September, and the calendar year 1933 (especially the last half) witnessed the largest number of work stoppages during any twelve-month period since 1921.[3] This trend was not to be taken lightly. By the end of the summer there were the first signs of concern that the current wave of strikes and the prevailing confusion in the realm of industrial-labor relations might soon have a sufficiently negative impact upon business confidence to jeopardize the goal of economic recovery.[4]

It was on the basis of this concern and a specific recommendation from the NRA Industrial and Labor Advisory boards that a new tripartite National Labor Board (NLB) was created early in August 1933. The national board, based in Washington and presiding over the day-to-day activities of several regional boards, was to consist of seven members: three labor representatives, three industry representatives, and one public representative. In addition to the selection of Senator Robert F. Wagner as public representative and chairman, the other original NLB appointments were held by AFL president William Green; Leo Wolman, a Columbia University professor of economics and member of the Labor Advisory Board; UMW president John L. Lewis; Walter C. Teagle of Jersey Standard and chairman of the Industrial Advisory Board; Gerard Swope, president of General Electric; and Louis E. Kirstein, general manager of Filene's department stores in Boston.

The NLB was severely handicapped from the outset by numerous procedural uncertainties and its lack of any extraordinary powers of enforcement. It could ask, but not compel, the NRA to deprive an uncooperative employer of the right to display the Blue Eagle emblem. It also could recommend that the Justice Department investigate any possible violation of the law. At first, it seemed as though this approach might work. Ultimately, however, neither course of action was sufficient to sustain the credibility of the board given the extremely contentious nature of the task it was charged with performing. The compliance division of the NRA was under considerable pressure to get along with employers and thus generally reluctant to antagonize business interests by openly siding with the unions. The Department of Justice was unable to accept evidence developed by the labor board. It had to prepare its own case in detail, and its sympathy with some of the NLB's more controversial rulings was not impressive. Apparently there were enough serious doubts about the constitutionality of the NIRA that the administration in general and the Justice Department in particular were hesitant to force a test of the question in the courts. As a result, the boldest antiunion employers were able to resist the board, seriously damage its prestige, and pave the way for massive disregard of its authority by industrialists throughout the country.[5]

The NLB's first major test came in connection with a recognition strike by workers at Berkshire Knitting Mills in Reading, Pennsylvania. When the owners of the company refused to recognize the American Federation of Full-Fashioned Hosiery Workers as the legitimate bargaining agent for its employees early in July 1933, several thousand workers walked defiantly off the job. On 10 August, the newly formed NLB invited spokesmen from each party to the dispute to a conciliation meeting in Washington. This meeting provided the occasion for the birth of what henceforth was known as the "Reading Formula," the intent of which was to establish a general procedural framework for the settlement of strikes as well as the basis for a common law interpretation of Section 7a. The strike at Berkshire Mills was ended, the employees were rehired without penalty, and an election by secret ballot was scheduled in which a simple majority would determine the issue of union representation. Soon thereafter the NLB presided over the settlement of a major silkworkers' strike in Paterson, New Jersey, and, after that, several relatively minor strikes at various tool and die shops in and around Detroit. Then, in mid-October, it facilitated an end to a long and bitter work stoppage by approximately ten thousand employees of the Weirton Steel Company at its plants in West Virginia and Ohio. Here, too, the specifics of the situation led the board to apply the Reading Formula: an election was ordered for mid-December that presumably would determine once and for all the status of outside unions in the matter of employee representation.

Actually, the NLB's initial achievements assured very few substantive, long-term gains for organized labor. Industry too often refused to comply with the board's rulings, and both the president and much of the NRA bureaucracy took an ambivalent position on the question of union power, frequently accepting the direct contradiction of NLB policy. The board was frustrated at every turn. As the date of the scheduled election at Weirton Steel grew near, for instance, the president and owner of the company, Ernest T. Weir, an old-fashioned paternalist and long-standing opponent of organized labor, belatedly announced that he would permit his employees to vote only for representatives under the company union plan. This was a blatant violation of the terms of settlement approved by the NLB. The board subsequently asked the NRA to punish Weirton by withdrawing the company's right to display the Blue Eagle, but the penalty was never applied. This seemed to be the precedent many employers had been waiting for. Weir's refusal to cooperate with the board was followed only a few days later by a second major setback for Senator Wagner and the other increasingly demoralized NLB appointees when the management of the Edward G. Budd Manufacturing Company of Philadelphia summarily declined to abide by a labor board ruling on the termination of a strike and the arrangement of employee elections. Then the National Association of Manufacturers launched a concerted public attack on the board. The NLB plodded ahead with its work, but without any independent powers of enforcement its declarations all too often were ignored. By the end of the year the board had become virtually impotent.

It was at this juncture that President Roosevelt finally decided to act, hoping to restore at least a modicum of credibility to the severely crippled agency with the issuance of two executive orders, the first of which was made public on 16 December 1933 and the other on 1 February 1934.[6] Varying little in detail, each of these declarations from the White House sought to reconfirm the authority of the National Labor Board to hold employee elections and to recommend federal prosecution in cases in which some violation of Section 7a was suspected. The announcement of 1 February indicated the administration's retroactive acceptance of the Reading Formula, including the principle of majority rule, as a legitimate application of NLB authority.[7] Conservative employer interests, of course, were outraged, protesting that any such directive if actually carried out would violate the rights of minority groups, threaten the existence of company unions, and contribute to the establishment of the closed shop. These charges provoked the immediate intervention of two presidential subordinates, who sought to placate the employers by engaging in what one prominent friend of labor later derided privately as a bit of ill-conceived "horsetrading."[8] In a joint statement issued only three days after FDR's 1 February executive order, Hugh Johnson and general counsel Donald Richberg offered a detailed clarification of the NRA position on what the labor board could and could not do and thus proceeded to reject the exclusive legitimacy of majority rule as an "erroneous" interpretation of federal policy, which they announced would continue to stand behind "the right of minority groups or of individual employees to deal with their employer separately."[9] This pronouncement amounted to a much less ambiguous reassertion of the same two officials' first public statement on the question late the previous August. And there is no evidence currently available to contradict the presumption that Roosevelt himself, despite the obviously less restrictive implications of his 1 February executive order, was comfortable with the Johnson-Richberg "clarification."[10] Indeed, the terms of a settlement in the automobile industry, by which a strike was narrowly averted the following March and in which FDR and Johnson together played a decisive role, extended the most explicit official vote of approval yet to the principle of proportional representation.[11] It also imposed significant new jurisdictional limitations on the NLB by creating a separate Automobile Labor Board (ALB), whose derivative, sharply circumscribed powers clearly reflected the administration's willingness to accept the traditionally inferior status of independent unions in the heavy mass-production industries. The same was true of the national steel and textile labor relations boards, each of which was established by presidential order during the summer and fall of 1934, and each of which was unable to achieve anything but a temporary pacification of labor-management relations—a condition that resulted in few positive gains for the trade union movement.[12] Employer opposition, the proliferation of company unions, lack of support from the NRA, and, oftentimes, inert labor leadership as well combined to reduce union membership in enough instances during the tenure of the NLB greatly to moderate the overall decadal trend toward union expansion. According to one NRA staff study, the number of charters issued by national and international unions increased during 1933 and 1934 but then declined by more than 1,800 during 1935. Only 276 new federal union charters were issued between August 1934 and August 1935, and 634 unions were either disbanded, expelled, or transferred to other national or international unions. Union membership increased significantly in some basic industries during 1934 and 1935, but in several others the unions almost collapsed. In the steel industry, for example, an organization that had grown to approximately one hundred thousand members between mid-1933 and mid-1934 subsequently entered a period of contraction that resulted in the near obliteration of the entire NIRA-inspired gain. The major textile unions were practically destroyed by a disastrous industrywide strike that began in September 1934, and union membership in automobile manufacturing was still divided among several federated craft organizations that altogether represented only a very small percentage of the industry's total work force.[13]

Even though its record of victories was uneven at best and not very grand overall, industrial labor now was unmistakably on the march. The spring and summer months of 1934 witnessed one of the two or three greatest nationwide labor upheavals in American history. A strike by workers employed by the Electric Auto-Lite Company in Toledo, Ohio, ended in rioting and violence that threatened for a time to develop into a much wider conflict involving every AFL union in town. A union truck drivers' strike in Minneapolis lasted most of the summer. Early in May, the International Longshoremen's Association called for a work stoppage by dockworkers in San Francisco that culminated in a general strike supported by virtually all union labor in the city. Then, finally, early in the fall, a massive strike by more than 350,000 textile workers brought the entire eastern component of that industry to a grinding halt. These were only the most dramatic confrontations of the year. Workers went on strike, or threatened to, in dozens of other communities around the country as well, and potentially major eruptions on the scale of the textile strike were narrowly averted in the automobile, steel, and rubber products industries.[14]

If anything, hostilities between labor and management and the general strain suffered by the economy as a result of repeated work stoppages intensified after the formation of the National Labor Board in August 1933, a step the administration had taken to relieve precisely such pressures. The federal government, in other words, thus far had clearly failed to devise a coherent labor policy consistent with the objective requirements of economic recovery.[15] NRA sensitivity to the seriousness of this problem, however, had grown steadily more acute. And early in 1934 the editors of *Business Week* noted a deepening conviction "that the consumer goods industries had [already] reached the peak of whatever production could be hoped for, or was desirable, until the capital goods industries and their employees [also] could be brought back into the buying groups."[16] It was felt, not least by Hugh Johnson, that one major prerequisite was the realization of industrial peace. He believed that the prevention of labor disruptions in the heavy mass-production industries, in particular, might greatly accelerate the process of economic revival. Yet Johnson knew perfectly well that the government did not have a labor policy adequate to the task at hand, only a "welter of contradictory 'interpretations' of Section 7a," as he later described the situation in his New Deal memoir. Johnson at least as much as anyone else had contributed to the confusion and accompanying operational inadequacies of administration policy by his stubborn, incongruous adherence to two fundamentally irreconcilable principles: the unacceptability of majority rule with its distasteful implications of compulsion, on one hand, and a general displeasure with the all-too-common situation of two or more parallel unions in the same shop, on the other. But now Johnson was convinced, various personal preferences aside, that this most important of all current policy issues must be decided "beyond preadventure," as he put it, for it was causing "more bitterness and loss of time, money, and production and bad administration than any [other] single force." But he apparently also believed that the problem could not be resolved within the administration and that only the imposition of a solution by Congress might finally provide consistent policy guidelines that thus far had escaped the grasp of the NRA bureaucracy. When Johnson made these observations he was probably alluding with hindsight to certain developments that, by early spring 1934, had already begun to occur.[17]

## From Section 7a to the Wagner Act

Thoroughly frustrated by his experience as chairman of the National Labor Board, Senator Wagner was also deeply concerned that the earning power of the average American worker was not advancing rapidly enough, or, at least, at a rate comparable to a reported upswing during the second half of 1933 in industrial production and prices, corporate profits, and executive salaries.[18] He therefore soon reached the conclusion that further remedial measures would have to be taken if the economy were ever to be restored to a truly balanced and healthy state, including some reasonable assurance of an equitable share for labor. It was with this concern foremost in mind that Wagner introduced a new Labor Disputes bill in the Senate on 1 March 1934, accompanied by an identical measure offered by William P. Connery in the House of Representatives. Wagner's immediate aim was to preside over the adoption of legislation that would extend additional powers to the NLB. But his fondest hope was to give greater genuine substance to the original spirit of Section 7a, which the senator believed was being subverted by management's narrowly self-interested practices, particularly the recent proliferation of company unions and the unreasonable limitation of labor's proper countervailing role vis-à-vis capital in the affairs of the market generally.[19]

The 1934 Labor Disputes bill was recommended to Congress with a view to inhibiting precisely these tendencies by closing what was headlined in the business press on one occasion as "the loopholes in NIRA's collective bargaining section."[20] Predictably, the bill earned the immediate disapproval of the NAM and other industry lobbyists, who typically countered with the charge that the proposed legislation not only violated certain hallowed principles of the free enterprise system and American constitutional law but that if implemented it would unleash even greater industrial strife and economic disruption than the nation had already witnessed.[21] The opposition of the employers and the desire of perhaps a majority of the members of Congress to avoid the issue at least until after the fall elections ultimately turned Roosevelt away from the measure as well. This choice at the time was entirely consistent with the president's initially enthusiastic commitment to the NRA and the recovery program's basic dependence on the good-natured cooperation of business.[22] For the time being, therefore, Wagner's bill had reached a dead end. Senator David I. Walsh and Charles E. Wyzanski of the Department of Labor subsequently reshaped it into the less obtrusive substitute National Industrial Adjustment Act, but that too was unsuccessful. Organized labor was unimpressed, and the NAM was adamant in its opposition to any legislation that its constituents felt might compromise the sanctity of the open shop.

Section 7a had clearly broken down. Industrial relations were in chaos throughout the country, and Roosevelt was inspired to assume a somewhat more positive attitude toward prospective labor policy reform almost before the tempest over Wagner's Labor Disputes bill had come completely to an end. This sudden change of heart occurred in early June in connection with the administration's desire to avoid a threatened strike in the steel industry. Confronted so soon after the automobile settlement with another potential big industry work stoppage and the possibility of disastrous consequences for the entire economy, FDR finally decided to move in the direction of a clearly delineated policy more reliably suited to the resolution of labor difficulties on a case-by-case basis. This decision took the form of an intentionally neutral enabling statute, Public Resolution No. 44, that for the duration of the recovery act would allow the president to create, by executive order, a specially constituted industrywide mediation board whenever the need should arise. This was not the end of it, however. Just a few days later, on 29 June 1934, Roosevelt abolished the NLB and replaced it with a new three-member National Labor Relations Board (NLRB). Executive Order 6763 authorized the NLRB—as an agency entirely independent of the NRA—to conduct investigations, order and hold shop elections, subpoena evidence and witnesses, and invoke the jurisdiction of circuit courts to secure enforcement of its rulings.[23] But the NLRB also inherited certain substantive weaknesses of its predecessor, in that though it was charged with responsibility for judging the claims of disputants in cases coming under the purview of Section 7a, it, too, was denied the unambiguous authority by which to determine the precise terms of employee representation. The proportional representation/majority rule issue stood exactly where it had before—entirely unresolved. It would not remain so indefinitely. For now, though, with the midterm congressional elections pending, most federal legislators (including Robert Wagner and several other prominent Senate liberals) evidently were prepared to defer to the president on the question—leaving business quietly satisfied,[24] the AFL sorely disappointed, and resolution of all the truly difficult issues for a more politically opportune moment in history. There was no sustained opposition on Capitol Hill to the president's preference in the matter. It took only five days from Roosevelt's submission of Public Resolution No. 44 to both houses of Congress on 15 June to the signing of the bill on 19 June to clear the way for what amounted, ten days hence, to the replacement of one seriously deficient mechanism for the preservation of peaceful industrial relations with another such mechanism handicapped by essentially the same deficiencies.[25]

Shortly after the termination of his brief tenure as first chairman of the National Labor Relations Board, University of Wisconsin Law School dean Lloyd K. Garrison wrote that "Section 7(a) of the Recovery Act can never be thoroughly enforced with even-handed justice under the existing administrative machinery. The powers of the Board, which is the chief governmental agency dealing with 7-a cases, are quite inadequate for the proper discharge of its responsibilities."[26] Actually, this was a gross understatement. In the absence of a firm presidential commitment in support of the agency's supposedly independent authority, the NLRB faced nearly unbridled antagonism from Donald Richberg, various other NRA officials, and the courts practically from the very beginning of its existence. The board's fate seems to have been sealed, however, after it handed down a decision in the Houde Engineering Company case at the end of August 1934. In a clearly unacceptable precedent "contrary to the President's interpretation in connection with the Automobile Industry," the board erred in the manner of its predecessor by strongly endorsing the principle of majority rule. Disagreements on the subject between the NLRB and the administration multiplied from that point on, until Roosevelt finally responded to Richberg's relentless prodding and imposed severe new restrictions on the board's jurisdiction, just as he had done earlier with the NLB.[27] By the end of the following February FDR had seen to it that the NLRB was powerless to intervene in any industry operating under a National Recovery Administration code that already provided some mechanism for the resolution of labor disputes. Most notably affected were autos, steel, petroleum, coal, textiles, and newspapers.

The Roosevelt administration's ill-concealed resentment of the NLRB's emerging predisposition in favor of majority rule (like that of the National Labor Board before it) kept alive an air of confusion and general uncertainty as to just what the goals of federal labor policy really were. This indecisiveness often had a disruptive effect on the daily operational concerns of government functionaries and industrial managers alike.[28] But the latter tended to take encouragement from the intense and seemingly endless character of the debate being conducted in official circles. For it was precisely the force of this public irresolution on the question of union rights that ultimately allowed defiance of especially controversial NLRB rulings by individual employers to assume the appearance of a legitimate course of action.[29]

Francis Biddle succeeded Garrison as NLRB chairman in November 1934. Reflecting on the situation as he perceived it during the following winter, Biddle later remarked: "I was convinced that the present law was unclear and imprecise; that it could not be enforced; that a new law was needed with enforceable remedies; and that, given this opportunity and some protection, the strength of organized labor and its effectiveness to meet the corresponding power of organized capital would be greatly enhanced."[30] Robert Wagner, characteristically, was inclined to agree. He was also reasonably optimistic about the current political salability of the idea, despite his unsuccessful legislative efforts of the previous year. The midterm congressional elections had been a sweeping success for the Democrats and the New Deal with the balance of power in the Senate, in particular, now weighted heavily on the side of the progressives. This, of course, was especially encouraging from the point of view of anyone who—like Wagner and the staff of the NLRB—was convinced of the urgent need for additional, purposively more ambitious federal labor legislation.

That conviction soon materialized in the form of an entirely new National Labor Relations bill, which Wagner introduced in the Senate on 21 February 1935, followed a week later by Representative Connery's submission of a companion measure in the House. S. 1958 differed in several respects from the senator's 1934 Labor Disputes bill. But by far the most important changes were those designated to upgrade the NLRB to the status of a kind of "Supreme Court" of labor relations, whose primary responsibility would be the strict enforcement of labor's right to independent representation rather than merely the settlement of labor disputes. In particular, the legislation would empower the board not only to hold shop elections as it had been entitled to do in the past but also to certify any union or representative body selected by a majority of the employees concerned as the exclusive bargaining agent for every employee in the bargaining unit.

Hearings on Wagner's bill were held between 11 March and 12 April before the Senate Committee on Education and Labor, which reported unanimously in favor of the measure on 2 May. After the committee reported the bill, Wagner apparently secured a private agreement from Roosevelt to let events develop independently by withholding any personal encouragement the president might otherwise have given prospective opponents of the bill in the upper chamber.[31] There would, by all accounts, have been very little serious resistance in any case, but it is possible that FDR's "technical impartiality" at least hastened the legislative process somewhat. Debate on the bill in the Senate lasted only two days, culminating on 16 March with a 62 to 12 vote of approval.

Historians have never been able to account as satisfactorily as we might like for Roosevelt's willingness at this juncture to accede to Wagner. Nevertheless, a couple of factors seem relevant. First, in the aftermath of the 1934 midterm elections the political momentum in Congress was clearly on the side of additional federal labor legislation, and FDR knew it. Second, by the spring of 1935, the future of the entire recovery program was very much in doubt.[32] From March to May, almost simultaneously with the Wagner bill, the question of NIRA renewal likewise had been the subject of congressional hearings. Testimony for and against renewal was divided more or less equally. The highly competitive, nondurable goods industries—or at least certain key elements within them—frequently favored a limited extension of the act. Spokesmen attached to industries whose mode of business was governed by less competitive, oligopolistic market structures tended to be, if not opposed to renewal, at least generally unenthusiastic about it.[33] Added to this primary division of opinion were countless secondary demands for both minor and more basic—but in any case conflicting—modifications of the law by those who wished to see the recovery program survive in some form.[34] It was impossible for Roosevelt, or anyone else in the administration, to know exactly what the outcome would be. Much of the intelligence reaching the president from his own top advisers, however, was decidedly pessimistic. Donald Richberg, for example, in his capacity as newly appointed chairman of the National Industrial Recovery Board, informed FDR on several occasions of his concern that the problem of faulty code compliance and the general deterioration in recent months in both labor's and industry's attitude toward the NRA would, as he argued in one particularly gloomy assessment of the situation, "grow steadily worse during another brief period of extension." Indeed, by the end of April 1935, Richberg was so discouraged about the prospects of renewal on even minimally acceptable terms that he finally asked the president to consider the possibility that he (meaning FDR) might "suffer less and the country benefit more by killing the NRA while it is still respectable than by having it linger on, feebly trying to do the impossible, until everyone will believe that it never was any good."[35]

Under the burden of counsel such as this, coupled with the knowledge that the recovery program might eventually be endangered by the nation's courts as well,[36] it is almost inconceivable that Roosevelt could have long ignored the lure of alternative policy options if, once they materialized, such choices appeared to offer a legitimate opportunity to restore to his administration some of its former political vitality. In the meantime, growing uncertainty about the future of NRA put the entire New Deal coalition under intense strain, which, in a political atmosphere laden with troublesome rumblings of dissension from below stimulated by the likes of Huey Long, Francis Townsend, and Detroit's famous "radio priest," Father Charles Coughlin, heightened FDR's perception of his own personal vulnerability.[37] Clearly, his inclination in the face of these pressures was to follow the path of least resistance. Generally disheartened by the unpromising course of the public debate on NRA renewal, Roosevelt seems to have been increasingly prepared to accept a tactical modification of federal policy in an effort to get back more closely in step with the pace of political events.[38] In particular, he wished to avoid winding up on the wrong side of the current progressive alignment in Congress, just as some of the more moderate and conservatively inclined members of Congress wished to avoid being cast publicly as opponents of labor once the Wagner bill was forced to a vote by the sheer tenacity of its chief legislative sponsor.[39] Thus it would appear that the president was in a contrary frame of mind when Secretary of Labor Frances Perkins tried to persuade him two days after the Senate's approval of the measure that he should attempt to delay final consideration of the Wagner bill in the House for fear that the proceedings there might distract even the administration's strongest supporters from the more urgent business of saving the Recovery Act. The next day, 19 May, when he was approached by a group of Democratic House leaders who were anxious to take the bill to the floor for a vote, FDR is said to have been "privately agreeable." Thus assured of the president's "quiet" support, the Labor Committee moved ahead and reported the House counterpart to S. 1958 favorably on 20 May. On 24 May Roosevelt publicly declared his support of the underlying principles of Wagner's bill. Then, three days later, when the Supreme Court nullified the NRA in the *Schechter* case, the labor bill assumed critical importance for FDR as the only currently visible symbol of his administration's alleged commitment to the attainment of certain beneficial social and economic goals, which, in accord with the dictates of elementary political wisdom, could not be forsaken.[40] Roosevelt was extremely fortunate, therefore, that something reasonably tangible was available with which to fill the void. The full House passed the National Labor Relations Act on a voice vote later in June, and on 5 July the president signed the measure into law.

The primary intention of the Wagner Act, as stated in Section I under the heading "Findings and Policy," was to eliminate inequalities in bargaining power "between employees who do not possess full freedom of association or actual liberty of contract, and employers who are organized in the corporate or other forms of ownership association." Experience suggested, in the wording of the act, that such inequalities tend to lead to conflict in the workplace and hence to potential interruptions in the flow of commerce, or, in the worst of all circumstances, "to aggravate recurrent business depressions . . . by depressing wage rates and the purchasing power of wage earners . . . and by preventing the stabilization of competitive wage rates and working conditions within and between industries." It was the popular hope of those who drafted the labor bill that a general advance in the "stabilization" process might soon be achieved by enforcing more rigorously both labor's basic right to organize and the employer's obligation to recognize duly established employee organizations, culminating with the confirmation of an ongoing collective bargaining relationship between each of the parties concerned. Further to this end, the Wagner Act effectively outlawed the company union by making it an unfair labor practice for an employer to dominate, interfere with, or contribute financial or other support to any labor organization. And, finally, compared to the much less innovative nature of other recent developments in the realm of federal labor policy with the possible exception of legislation in 1926 and 1934 affecting the special case of steam railroads, the unique—and most significant—feature of the Wagner Act was the power it gave the NLRB to see that the results of all employee elections conducted under the auspices of that body would be honored by both labor and management in accordance with the principle of majority rule. Moreover, in anticipation of the wide variety of industrial situations in which a decision would have to be rendered, it was further specified that "the Board shall decide in each case whether . . . the unit appropriate for the purpose of collective bargaining shall be the employer unit, craft unit, plant unit, or subdivision thereof."[41]

With the exception of a handful of deeply conservative craft affiliates whose leaders were concerned that the measure might jeopardize the future independence and organizational autonomy of individual trade unions, the American Federation of Labor and its traditional allies in national politics supported the adoption of S. 1958 from beginning to end.[42] Correlatively, business opposition to the Wagner Act was probably more unified than its response—positive or negative—to any other single piece of New Deal legislation.[43] It is true, of course, as John P. Frey of the AFL Metal Trades Department seems at the time to have believed, that a generally heightened sense of the need both to rationalize "unfair" business competition and to pacify potentially threatening political currents in the United States had begun to infect at least some prominent American employers with a greater willingness to seek an accommodation with the government on the formal status of unions in industry. But the Wagner Act clearly was not representative of management's predominant inclination in this respect, or even that of a significant minority.[44] The NAM, which was dominated by some of the nation's largest industrial interests during the Roosevelt years, attacked the bill relentlessly, as did the U.S. Chamber of Commerce.[45] The Commerce Department's prestigious Business Advisory and Planning Council, which counted among its members such moderate, forward-looking "corporate liberals" as Henry S. Dennison, A. Lincoln Filene, W. Averell Harriman, Henry P. Kendall, Fred I. Kent, Louis Kirstein, Gerard

Swope, Edward R. Stettinius, Jr., Myron Taylor, and Walter Teagle, also found the measure completely unacceptable—preferring instead a two-year extension of the NIRA with its much less onerous labor provisions.[46] On the more outspokenly conservative side, and thus not necessarily within the fold of the majority, was the stance taken by General Motors president Alfred P. Sloan, Jr., whom Isadore Lubin of the U.S. Department of Labor once accused of being the perfect example of his feeling that "American business" had not "the slightest conception" of what the New Deal was all about. Sloan and two other noted conservative members of the BAC, John J. Rascob and Pierre S. Du Pont, left the council in August 1934 to found the American Liberty League, which ultimately declared its opposition to the Wagner Labor Relations bill in the most uncompromising terms imaginable.[47]

With very few exceptions, the Wagner Act was anathema to the industrial employer, large as well as small, as evidenced by business' sustained public denunciation of the measure both before and after its final passage through Congress. Even Gerard Swope—reputed dean of the liberal accommodationists in industrial management circles and one of the original appointees to the old National Labor Board but also a prominent member and first chairman of the Business Advisory Council—never felt constrained to disassociate himself, either publicly or privately, from the BAC's stern opposition to Wagner's 1935 Labor Relations bill. Actually, Swope, whom one scholar appropriately characterized as having "held trade unionism in no great awe," appears to have remained aloof from the controversy.[48]

This, however, is not the entire story, for, as those analysts who have sought to discover some tangible evidence of behind-the-scenes corporate support for the Wagner Act invariably note, some industrialists, not least Gerard Swope, had a long history of utterances in which they indicated a preference for industrial, or "vertical," unions as the logical alternative to dealing with a multitude of craft organizations—that is, if they were to be compelled to recognize independent or outside unions at all.[49] This preference, when it emerged, was based primarily on considerations of managerial efficiency and the desire to rationalize and streamline the collective bargaining process by eliminating exclusionary jurisdictional claims between two or more autonomous unions in the same plant or firm. Hence, when the editors of *Fortune* polled several corporate executives in Boston, Chicago, Pittsburgh, and Providence in 1934, they found that "most employers of labor who have considered the matter would prefer the industrial union to the craft union as the lesser of two evils and there are even a few who would accept it as no evil at all."[50] Similarly, when the automobile code was being formulated toward the end of the summer in 1933, William S. Knudsen, then vice-president in charge of General Motors's (GM) Chevrolet Division, is reported to have remarked that auto manufacturers had no objection to the formation of a single automobile workers' union covering the entire industry but that they were opposed to separate plant unions or to separate craft unions within a single factory.[51]

According to Leon C. Marshall of the NRA, Arthur H. Young, vice-president in charge of industrial relations for U.S. Steel, took almost exactly the same position as Knudsen when he indicated privately early in 1934 that he also would much prefer to deal with a single "industrial union" than with "a congeries of craft unions. He has figured out," Marshall observed, "that in the Steel Corporation with its varied enterprises he would have to deal with 29 craft unions of the A.F. of L. plus nine independent unions—and these are minimum figures. Furthermore, some . . . of these unions have overlapping jurisdictions. To a man who has devoted a large part of his activity to the semi-objective classification and definition of occupations with assignment of index numbers to them and to a man who thinks of having the operations of an entire plant move forward as a whole, the necessity of dealing with such a mess of craft unions is of course just plain anathema."[52]

A note of caution is in order, however, lest one read too much into such evidence on the politics of the Wagner Act. The material on U.S. Steel's Arthur Young is a good case in point. It would appear, in fact, that Young failed to perceive any connection between the basic intent of the National Labor Relations Act and his general disapproval of craft unions in the steel industry. Indeed, he was one of the most earnest opponents of Wagner's bill in the entire business community—telling a gathering of the American Management Association on the occasion of his receipt of its award for outstanding and creative work in the field of industrial relations that, if ever actually faced with the decision of whether to obey such an objectionable law, he would rather "go to jail or be convicted as a felon."[53] Nor is there any evidence that Jersey Standard's Walter Teagle considered the Wagner Act an acceptable indication of the prospective direction of federal labor policy. He, like Young, objected to craft unions because of their jurisdictional exclusivism. But when Teagle sat down in his capacity as chairman of the BAC's Committee on Industrial Relations to draft a report on employee representation and collective bargaining (undoubtedly sometime during the summer of 1934), the result was an elaborate latter-day defense of company, not industrial, unions—although his critique of craft unions closely followed the argument carried on by Young in the presence of Leon Marshall.[54]

In addition to industrialists such as Swope or Young, who genuinely seemed to prefer vertical over craft unions for straightforward managerial reasons, by the early 1930s a number of people in government and other areas of public life had also come to appreciate what they perceived to be certain advantages of industrial unionism. This was especially true for those who thought organized labor under the New Deal should, in the words of contemporary journalist Benjamin Stolberg, function as a socioeconomic "counterpoise to the power of capital."[55] For such a responsibility it was generally believed that the AFL, with its commitment to the preservation of more traditional, highly particularistic forms of labor organization, could not foot the bill. Moreover, the potential uses of the vertical union in policing the industrial codes seem to have been readily apparent to those charged with running the NRA. Hugh Johnson, for instance, when writing about his New Deal experiences in 1934–35, was profoundly regretful that the nearly perfect symbiotic relationship that existed between organized labor and organized capital in industries like bituminous coal mining or garment manufacturing—a relationship that he understood to be integral to the proper functioning of the code system in all highly competitive industries—was not common to the structure of the industrial economy as a whole.[56]

What bearing any of these arguments may have had on the formulation of the Wagner Act is not entirely clear. What is clear, however, is the absence of any demonstrable link between the sentiment and expectations of corporate management, on one hand, and the objective political forces that account for the legislative success of the Labor Relations bill, on the other. Indeed, even for those few employers who might not have been absolutely horrified at the prospect of such an eventuality, the Wagner bill provided no automatic guarantee that vertical unions would come to predominate. Rather, the Labor Relations bill was introduced and upon its adoption became part of an evolving legal-administrative framework within which labor unions in general, as well as industrial unions in particular, subsequently acquired greater overall institutional security within the United States.[57] But it is one thing to acknowledge this result and quite another to conclude that Senator Wagner's remarkable legislative achievement in 1935 must therefore have come about at least in part at the hands of a few unusually broad-minded industrial and corporate leaders with the capacity to shape political events miraculously to their liking. The evidence for such an idea is paltry, and what little there is has tended to obscure a more fundamental reality. Thus, not only did the most powerful corporate interests in the country steadfastly oppose the Labor Relations bill before it was adopted, but afterward most of them elected to resist both the law and organized labor on the basis of a conviction shared widely in the business community that the measure would, in view of the recent *Schechter* decision, ultimately be invalidated in the courts. In April 1937, however, the constitutionality of the Wagner Act was upheld by the Supreme Court in the *Jones & Laughlin* case, and in the meantime the industrial organizing committees of the newly formed Committee for Industrial Organization had been hard at work.

# 8 Economics: The Stakes of Power

Initially, the upstart industrial unions were seriously frustrated in their efforts during the latter half of the Depression decade because none of the corporate giants were particularly anxious to give in to union demands, sign binding contracts, or agree to the closed shop.[1] Then came two pivotal victories for the CIO early in 1937, first at General Motors and soon thereafter at the U.S. Steel Corporation—each of which occurred before the Supreme Court's validation of the Wagner Act. In both cases, certain fundamental competitive considerations at a particularly crucial juncture in the continually evolving circumstances that combine to determine a company's overall business prospects appear finally to have made "capitulation" to organized labor a much more practical, economically sound management decision than one that might have entailed a long and costly work stoppage, involving large losses in production and sales. Even so, no other major corporate figure during the period acquiesced to industrial unionism as readily as Gerard Swope of General Electric. With the possible exception of a less frequently noted display of "constructive accommodation"[2] by U.S. Rubber's similarly inclined director of industrial relations, Cyrus S. Ching, Swope's celebrated willingness to reach a quick, companywide agreement with the United Electrical Workers in April 1938 may have been the purest manifestation of management's general, if usually rather vague and uncertain, preference throughout much of the durable and capital goods sector of the economy for the vertical form of labor organization. Any effort to uncover some overall pattern amid the various forces and events that led to one or another company's recognition of "big labor" from roughly 1936 to the beginning of World War II, however, need not stand or fall solely on the basis of that tenuous explanatory link. A much more fruitful, if largely circumstantial, body of evidence points to the probable significance of a natural inclination among the managers of such establishments, once the moment of truth was reached, to accept the lesser of two evils and take the course of action that would allow them to escape the potentially disastrous effects of a major strike.

# General Motors and the UAW: A Brief Appraisal

The decade of the 1930s was a difficult one for the automobile industry. But the Depression was much harder on some auto manufacturers than it was on others. Intraindustry competition generally intensified as producers scrambled either to protect or expand their share of a substantially shrunken market. Bankruptcies were common, refinancing even more so, until by 1937 only eleven companies were still producing autos as compared to nearly one hundred in 1925. Among the survivors, the principal producers were General Motors, Ford, Chrysler, Studebaker, Hudson, Nash, Packard, and Willys. Although Chrysler and General Motors took part of Ford's sales volume, the smaller producers suffered the greatest losses. Thus, Hupmobile, Pierce Arrow, Marmon, Auburn, and Stutz all were forced out of business, and most of the smaller companies that continued to operate were left with a sharply reduced share of the market. In 1929, one-fourth of all passenger car sales in the United States were made by the smaller producers; by 1933 their share of the market had dropped to less than a tenth, and it stayed at about that level for the remainder of the decade. The smaller auto manufacturers were particularly handicapped by their limited access to capital, whereas the larger producers could usually cut costs more efficiently, dip into substantial capital reserves to tide them over the bad years, and adapt more readily to changing market conditions. General Motors, Ford, and Chrysler all experienced financial difficulties during the 1930s, but they were never threatened with extinction as were the smaller producers, or with insolvency as were many of the moderate-sized firms. The "Big Three" auto companies came out of the Depression in a stronger position within the industry than ever before.[3]

Ford's position in the industry peaked in 1921 with over 55 percent of all new passenger car sales to its credit. By 1925, however, its share of the market had fallen to 40 percent and by 1926 to slightly more than a third. Ford resumed its leadership briefly with the introduction of the Model A in the late 1920s, but by 1929 GM had advanced to the first-ranked position—if only barely—with 32 percent of the market and then moved up rapidly to nearly 44 percent by 1931. Ford's share of the market in that year was just under 25 percent, and Chrysler held the third-ranked position at a little more than 12 percent—up from 3.5 percent in 1925, the year the corporation was formed.[4]

The last full year of prosperity before the beginning of the Great Depression occurred in 1928. It was also General Motors's most profitable year to date: approximately $330 million before taxes on net sales of almost $1.5 billion in the corporation's consolidated operations and nearly $216 million (for a rate of return just under 59 percent) in its motor vehicle divisions, according to data compiled by Sidney Fine. GM in that year employed about 209,000 hourly and salaried workers to whom the corporation paid out a total in excess of $365 million.[5]

The initial shock of the Depression hit General Motors with a good deal of force. Between 1928 and 1932 sales of automobiles and trucks to dealers across the United States fell off by nearly three-quarters; after-tax profits dropped from $296 million to less than $8.5 million in the corporation's consolidated operations, which translated into a loss of nearly $7 million for the auto production end of the business. Employment at GM during these first and most traumatic years of the Depression was cut almost in half, and the corporation's payroll was reduced by approximately 60 percent.[6]

After 1932, which was the worst year of the Depression for the automobile industry as well as for many others, GM's fortunes began to improve. By 1936 the value of the corporation's net sales in its consolidated operations had tripled; its net before-tax profits had increased from $8.8 to $283.7 million, and net profits after taxes were up from $8.3 to $239.5 million. By 1936 GM's motor vehicle divisions had converted their combined $7 million loss for 1932 into a before-tax profit of about $163 million—the equivalent of a 38 percent rate of return on capital investment. The company's car and truck sales increased from fewer than 473,000 in 1932 to almost 1.7 million in 1936. The number of workers employed by GM doubled over the same four-year interval, and its payroll increased by 168 percent.[7]

GM, of course, was not the only automobile company whose business prospects improved between 1932 and 1936. It was a general phenomenon affecting the entire industry. "Depression is a forgotten word in the automobile industry, which is forging ahead in production, retail sales, and expansion of productive capacity in a manner reminiscent of the 'twenties,' " was the way *Business Week* put it in a brief review of the industry's performance as of April 1935. Ford and GM led the surge in activity with a first-quarter output of 410,933 and 388,716 units, respectively. Chrysler was third with 249,064 units (22 percent of the industry total), which was the largest three-month volume in the history of the company. Even some of the independents made substantial gains during the first quarter of 1935—Packard leading the way with a 120 percent increase in retail sales compared to the same three-month period in 1934.[8]

In April 1936 business was still booming. According to one report, automobile factories were finding it increasingly difficult to meet the requirements of a rapidly expanding market. "Dealer orders are piling up at the plants and some of the leading companies have pushed production right up to the hilt, running practically at capacity," wrote *Automotive Industries*. One "volume" producer, who was said to be "operating full tilt through March," was "already sold out for April, which is scheduled for capacity output." In another notable instance, daily retail orders were reported to be "running 25 percent ahead of production." By all appearances, there would be a significant "shortage of cars when the buying wave reache[d] its crest," which was still "some weeks off."[9]

The longer-term prospect was for a continuation of these fabulous sales opportunities, with a general expectation that consumer demand during the spring and summer of 1937 would surpass even that of 1936. In anticipation of this increase, General Motors was spending tens of millions of dollars in a vast reorganization effort involving no fewer than fifteen of the corporation's primary manufacturing and assembly operations. By the spring of 1936 a major expansion of plant capacity was under way at GM's facilities in Muncie, Indiana, and Saginaw, Michigan; a new Chevrolet assembly plant was under construction in Baltimore; three more were in the works for the Buick, Olds-mobile, and Pontiac divisions in Los Angeles; a new facility was going up in Grand Rapids, Michigan, for the production of stampings and dies; and a previously idled manufacturing operation at Syracuse, New York, had been reopened and placed on a full-capacity schedule.[10]

With sixty-nine automobile and truck factories in thirty-five cities and fourteen states representing total assets in excess of $1.5 billion, the corporation that the United Automobile Workers struck beginning in December 1936 was clearly an economic power of colossal proportions. But it was also ex-tremely vulnerable in the sense that it could not afford a prolonged battle with labor if—as one must assume to have been the case—management hoped to be in the best possible competitive position going into the 1937 spring sales season. In the course of rejuvenating and expanding its productive capacity during 1935 and 1936, therefore, GM had acquired a multimillion-dollar stake in the preservation of industrial peace. Any sustained interruption of produc-tion would cost the company dearly in lost sales not only during the auto industry's traditionally most lucrative season of the year but also during what promised to be the most financially rewarding season yet since GM and its major rivals began to find their way out of the depths of the Depression. The tremendously effective "sit-down" strikes of late 1936 and early 1937 threat-ened this potential business success.[11] As midwinter inevitably gave way to the approach of spring, *Business Week* reported that GM had already lost "considerable business" to its competitors as a result of the crippling occupa-tion of a number of the corporation's key plants by rank-and-file workers. Not knowing how long it would be before they could secure deliveries, many customers were canceling orders with GM and switching to other makes. Moreover, time appeared to be running out. If the strike could not be settled soon, General Motors would have to go into the coming sales season "with the disadvantage of being unable to stock dealers in advance." In the meantime, however, "Ford . . . [was] making V-eights at a rate of 6,600 a day, five days a week," a schedule that it expected to maintain "straight through the winter and spring." Chrysler, too, was reported to be "running all its divisions at close to capacity." Plymouth alone was turning out approximately 2,500 units a day.[12]

To argue that GM finally settled with the UAW (as it did on 11 February 1937) for eminently practical economic reasons is not to deny the probable significance of a number of other relevant factors, particularly insofar as they may have operated to constrain the corporation's tactical maneuverability during the course of its confrontation with the union. Management circles, for example, seem to have been concerned about a possible escalation of violence should the strike continue to drag on and the negative impact that this was likely to have on public opinion. Company sensitivities about this possibility were heightened considerably after the release of certain embarrassing information by the La Follette Civil Liberties Committee in late January about GM's antiunion activities, including the use of Pinkertons to "spy" on CIO president John L. Lewis. Lewis exploited every such incident for all it was worth in an effort to enhance GM's already semivillainous public image and to put Knudsen and the rest of the corporation's managers on the defensive. Lewis's ability to manipulate Roosevelt and other highly placed Democrats with an awesome personal arsenal of patiently acquired political credits also worked to his advantage in this respect, particularly in dissuading Michigan governor Frank Murphy from using state troops to enforce a court order for the arrest of the sit-downers.[13]

In the end, GM was confronted with a situation in which every conceivable avenue of escape appeared to be blocked—that is, unless management was willing to stand patiently by until the strikers' enthusiasm for the continued occupation of the company's key installations at Flint, Michigan, began to wane, or until Roosevelt and Murphy could be persuaded to force Lewis to remove them. In the meantime, of course, the corporation's competitive position—and especially the prospect of making anything at all out of the rapidly approaching spring sales season—was becoming increasingly doubtful with each passing day. Before the strike and up through January 1937 GM had been producing an average of more than 15,000 cars a week. During the first ten days of February, however (at which point negotiations between the company and the union were finally begun and a settlement reached), only 151 cars rolled off the assembly lines. GM had been shut down—a simple reality, according to Lewis, that finally forced management to settle with the union. As he explained to NLRB investigator Heber Blankenhorn just two weeks after the conclusion of the strike: "We held those key dies in Flint and we were not going to let go of them. They [the captured dies] crippled General Motors. And those boys in Flint could not have been thrown out without a pitched battle."[14]

There is very little question that GM settled with the UAW when it did because it had to.[15] The politicians, especially Governor Murphy, apparently were not going to help the company break the strike as management would have preferred. The Roosevelt administration, moreover, had been urging the corporation to negotiate all along. Theoretically, of course, the company still had the option of trying to outlast the union, patiently bide its time, and hope for a favorable turn of events accompanied by the restoration of a certain amount of tactical maneuverability. Once again, however, from management's point of view, the vital consideration almost certainly was that it was impossible to hold out much beyond mid-February without risking unacceptable losses during the coming, predictably heavy-volume, automobile sales season. When GM finally ran out of time, therefore, the cost of "doing business" with labor was deemed to be far less burdensome than the cost of doing no business at all.

## SWOC's Breakthrough in Basic Steel

Barely two weeks after the GM-UAW settlement, the United States Steel Corporation reached an agreement with the Steel Workers Organizing Committee (SWOC). Much like the GM settlement, this one, too, was the result of an expedient, business-minded decision by management to follow the path of least resistance. The only significant difference between these two momentous episodes in recent American labor history and the events that in each case produced landmark union agreements was that Myron C. Taylor, chairman of the board at U.S. Steel, managed to avoid a strike.

U.S. Steel's relative position in the industry had been declining ever since its formation in 1901, a trend that became especially pronounced during the interwar period. Several factors were responsible, but probably the most important was the overall effect of the merger movement of the 1920s, in which the industry's smaller and medium-sized producers tended to be the main participants.[16] In 1922, Bethlehem (the second largest producer in the industry) embarked on an ambitious program of expansion, first by acquiring the extensive properties of the Lackawanna Steel Company near Buffalo, New York, and then by beginning construction of a new complex at Sparrows Point, Maryland. That activity was followed in 1923 by acquisition of the Cambria Steel works at Johnstown, Pennsylvania, and in 1930 by the purchase of the assets of both the Pacific Coast and Southern California Iron and Steel companies. In the same year, another powerful independent producer appeared on the scene consisting of the consolidated operations of Republic Iron and Steel, the Central Alloy Steel Corporation, Donner Steel, and the Bourne Fuller Company. Also among the more important mergers during this period was the one consummated in 1929 with the formation of the National Steel Corporation, which involved the integration of several smaller steel plants in West Virginia, Michigan, and Ohio.[17]

By the end of the 1920s all of these companies had come to occupy a very strong competitive position vis-à-vis U.S. Steel. Not least among the reasons for their ascendance was the effect of a gradual shift in the demand for different kinds of steel from heavier products (such as rails, plates, and structural shapes) to somewhat lighter products (such as strips and sheets). U.S. Steel, which was geared up primarily for the heavier products, apparently was unable to diversify quickly enough to keep pace with its smaller but more flexible and technologically dynamic rivals. Eventually this competitive deficiency took its toll on the corporation's earning power relative to that of the rest of the industry. In each of the ten years from 1921 to 1930 U.S. Steel realized a slightly higher rate of return on net worth after taxes than the average for the industry as a whole. In this respect also, U.S. Steel suffered a little less severely during the depths of the Depression than most of the other producers. But as the industry entered the first wave of a gradual recovery in 1934 and 1935, U.S. Steel's earning power finally began to lag behind that of its competitors. The recovery in steel accelerated sharply beginning in July 1936, and the corporation's profits rose accordingly, although still at a lower rate than the average for the rest of the industry.[18]

The trend in 1936 was clear. U.S. Steel's relative position in the industry was slipping; yet for the first time since the beginning of the Depression the corporation was earning substantial profits on net income, which was nearly four times greater than that of its closest rival. Demand for steel products was up sharply, overall the industry was operating at about 80 percent of capacity, and as of the turn of the year in 1936–37 the outlook for a continuation of the boom seemed promising.[19] Naturally, none of the steel producers wanted to be left out of the running. U.S. Steel's prospects, however, were particularly uncertain because the company's huge Carnegie-Illinois complex, alas, was being targeted for a possible strike. Understandably, management's greatest fear was that any such employee action would likely be patterned after the UAW's current devastating assault on General Motors. There was a general assumption that the sit-down strategy, should it be employed, would be somewhat easier to combat in the steel plants than it was in the auto factories, but the corporation's managers appeared to take little comfort from that. They clearly wanted to avoid a strike.[20]

The unionization of basic steel in the United States was not completed until 1941, when, after a particularly bitter and violent struggle, "Little Steel" finally was brought into the fold. The real turning point for union labor in the steel industry, however, came near the end of February 1937 with a strikeless victory over the giant U.S. Steel Corporation.

In June 1936, John L. Lewis appointed the Steel Workers Organizing Committee composed of nine representatives of four different unions and headed by Philip Murray, vice-president of the United Mine Workers. The traditional steel union, the Amalgamated Association of Iron, Steel and Tin Workers, had been dwindling in significance for many years. In 1936 it was persuaded to cede jurisdiction to SWOC, although it was allowed to retain its existing contracts and membership, as well as the right to issue charters to new locals organized by the CIO.

SWOC immediately set its sights on the largest and most powerful company in the industry, U.S. Steel, which at the time employed more than 220,000 workers and controlled about 38 percent of the nation's ingot capacity. U.S. Steel was a virtual bastion of the open shop, with a long and tough reputation for hostility to outside unions. SWOC was well prepared, however, with thirty-five field offices around the country and more than 150 experienced full-time organizers drawn primarily from the ranks of the UMW, which financed most of SWOC's early organizing activities.

The first point of attack was the company unions.[21] During and after World War I, a number of steel producers had put employee representation plans (ERP) into effect—U.S. Steel as late as 1933. Even before the appearance of SWOC, however, considerable restlessness and intractability had been manifested within many of these organizations. Steel management was gradually losing control over its own company-dominated unions—particularly the more recently established ones. SWOC was able to exploit this situation with great effect by allying its organizational efforts with the day-to-day activities of ERP officials. Thus in the Chicago area, for example, by mid-October 1936 rank-and-file steelworkers were reported to be coming "into the Union en masse." Ten of the smaller mills in the district apparently had already "recognized" SWOC, with a like number of producers in Pittsburgh and vicinity reportedly having fallen in line as well. There were also reports from Pittsburgh that a new "central committee" of U.S. Steel Corporation plant organizations had been formed for the purpose of "collective bargaining." Although management had originally backed the creation of this body, rumor had it that the committee was preparing to demand a 25 percent wage increase and that about half of the workers involved with the group were already firmly "lined up with the CIO."[22] Later that fall, SWOC and the ERP central committee made a joint representation to U.S. Steel for a five-dollar-a-day common labor rate, a ten cents an hour increase for all other employees, and a standard forty-hour workweek. The corporation countered with its own, not particularly generous, contract offer. Workers in some plants accepted the offer, others did not, yet in the end management decided unilaterally to put its contract proposal into effect in all U.S. Steel plants whether or not the employees concerned had voted for it. For the corporation to proceed in this fashion so hastily, however, turned out to be a blunder. For one thing, as a particularly blatant demonstration of the company's disregard for democratic procedure, it immediately allowed SWOC to attain greater organizational momentum than ever. It also provided the union with an opportunity to supplement its organizational strategy with a petition directly to the National Labor Relations Board charging the company with unlawful domination of the entire U.S. Steel ERP apparatus, a move that ultimately exposed the corporation to the same public scrutiny that proved to be a liability to General Motors during the height of its confrontation with the UAW.[23]

Many contemporary observers were astounded when it was announced at the end of February 1937 that the U.S. Steel Corporation and SWOC officials soon would sign an agreement confirming the company's decision to recognize an "outside" union as the legitimate bargaining agent for any of its employees who were bona fide members of the organization. Others, however, seemed not to be surprised by the news. The editors of *Fortune*, for example, readily accepted the underlying logic of events in their overall analysis of the corporation's decision. Indeed, how could it have been otherwise?

> The CIO drive in . . . steel . . . was probably the most intelligently directed labor drive ever organized in the U.S., complete with a fast-footed legal staff, high political connections, and a counter espionage system that was feeding the La Follette Committee with information just as distasteful to the gentlemen of the Board of U.S. Steel as it was to their Chairman. And here Mr. Lewis's exploit at Detroit weighed heavily upon the minds entrusted with the destiny of big steel. Whether General Motors had had a right to eject the sit-downers from its plants did not seem to the gentlemen to be the question, because very obviously they could not have been ejected without bloodshed. But if this sort of thing could tie up the automobile industry, which had been hastily organized, what would prevent it from tying up steel, where the CIO was firmly and forethoughtedly entrenched?[24]

Moreover, in addition to the rapidly growing strength of SWOC in the steel plants themselves, there was also the problem of local politics and the extent to which the authorities could be trusted to back the corporation in the event of a strike. In Pennsylvania, the home of the great Carnegie-Illinois complex, the risks in this regard seemed particularly high in 1937.

> Time was when . . . [management] could have called upon the trusty Coal and Iron Police, but that faithful little band of desperadoes had been outlawed some years previously by Governor Pinchot. And time was when they could have counted on Harrisburg for the state troops, but as of February, 1937, it looked as if the resources of Harrisburg would be thrown chiefly to the other side. The rise of Governor Murphy of Michigan into the national limelight had indeed been a disturbing phenomenon to Pennsylvania's Governor [George H.] Earle, who had presidential

ambitions and would like nothing better than a chance to eclipse Governor Murphy in the headlines by refusing the economic royalists the use of the state militia. Obviously any resistance from the operators would simply make good political fodder for Mr. Earle—which was one expedient reason for not starting trouble.[25]

As a columnist for *Business Week* pointed out in a strikingly similar diagnosis of the situation confronting U.S. Steel at the time of its decision to recognize SWOC: "The corporation realized that it was picked by the CIO as the 'fall guy' for the industry, realized also that the industrial unionists had garnered considerable strength in the plants, and saw no good purpose in being tied up as General Motors was, while its competitors got the business." It looked as though "wage-and-hour changes were coming anyway, and the CIO was content to rest, for the present, on recognition for its enrolled members only." Last but not least, "the 40-hour week rule [conceded by U.S. Steel in its agreement with the union] enabled the [company's] plants to go after government orders under [the] Walsh-Healey rules."[26] For all of these reasons and more, it was clear "that the Corporation had an enormous dollars-and-cents stake in heading off an industrial war."[27]

U.S. Steel's decision to recognize SWOC was a prudent one forced by the apparently compelling nature of certain vital business considerations at a crucial juncture in the corporation's history. For the first time since 1930, U.S. Steel was earning substantial profits. Demand for steel products was on the rise, and production had reached about 90 percent of capacity. Recovery in the steel industry appeared to be in full swing, and there was every indication that the upward trend would last.[28] Moreover, in addition to the current strength of the domestic market for steel, substantial foreign armaments orders were beginning to materialize, and it was rumored that the British government was demanding guarantees of uninterrupted production before letting contracts to American suppliers.[29] Under current conditions, of course, U.S. Steel could not fulfill any such requirement. Its relations with labor were in chaos; the company's own employee organizations seemed to be causing more trouble than they were worth, and, in any event, they had clearly ceased to be a reliable defense against the intrusion of independent union activity.

Ultimately, U.S. Steel had little choice but to recognize SWOC—that is, assuming management wished to avoid the possibility of an untimely upheaval in its plants that could easily cost the corporation millions of dollars in lost sales in the midst of the first substantial upturn in business activity since the beginning of the Depression. This, in fact, is exactly what Myron Taylor had in mind when he conducted exploratory negotiations with John L. Lewis during January and February 1937. The cost of a strike, even if the corporation were victorious, would have been incalculably high. "I felt," remarked Taylor barely a year later, "that it was my duty as a trustee for our stockholders . . . to make an honorable settlement that would ensure a continuance of work, wages, and profits." Taylor readily gained the backing of the House of Morgan and the rest of the corporation's board of directors, and on 2 March a preliminary contract was signed by Benjamin Fairless for Carnegie-Illinois and by Philip Murray for SWOC.[30] Contracts between the union and all other U.S. Steel subsidiaries were concluded shortly thereafter.

Taylor, whose political outlook the editors of *Fortune* characterized as resembling that of a "British Conservative" or red Tory, was also accused by Little Steel of being untrue to his class—"a Judas in the Garden of Bessemer" and "the Benedict Arnold of the American Iron and Steel Institute," in the parodic phraseology of one reporter—when he ultimately chose not to do combat with the union.[31] This, of course, was a perfectly natural and eminently self-serving position for the smaller producers in the industry to take. They, after all, had their own competitive interests to think about, and that undoubtedly was the source of their resentment at Taylor's decision. Thus "the lesser steel companies," as Thomas W. Lamont referred to them when recalling the events of February 1937 some years later, "had apparently been desirous that . . . U.S. Steel should bear the brunt of the storm and they were perfectly willing to see the Corporation fight it out on that line even if it took all the Corporation's liquid assets." After February 1937, however, Little Steel was handed the full burden of any potential resistance to union power, and an excellent partial explanation for Taylor's decision might be his anticipation of the business advantages that would accompany that eventuality.[32]

Taylor's decision to enter into an agreement with SWOC was influenced partially also by the terms of the settlement. In this respect, U.S. Steel got off rather easily. Lewis and the rest of the union leadership were completely aware of the limits of their own power and consequently did not seek to press the corporation much beyond what management almost certainly interpreted as a comfortable accommodation of interests. On many issues, the contract essentially formalized existing company policy. The principal provision of the agreement, which involved recognition of the union, was adopted entirely on management's terms: namely, preservation of the open shop. The contract also provided for about a 14 percent increase in hourly wages, but this probably would have been implemented soon in any event because apparently even the corporation's competitors were prepared to grant at least that much just to keep the union out of their plants.[33] In this manner, the financial burden of increased labor costs attendant upon U.S. Steel's recognition of SWOC was automatically borne by the industry as a whole, which had the important auxiliary effect of allowing the corporation to maintain its customary price leadership in the domestic market for steel.

Perhaps not coincidentally, U.S. Steel's overall position in the industry, as well as its current ability to absorb somewhat higher labor costs, also was greatly enhanced by the corporation's timely acceptance into the Entente Internationale de l'Acier, or International Steel Cartel. Both Bethlehem and U.S. Steel signed an accord with the cartel on 26 February 1937, only a day or two before Taylor and Lewis finally came to terms on a union contract.[34] The principal attraction of cartel membership for American steel interests was the protection it afforded them against unrestricted penetration of the domestic market by the entente's European adherents and the necessarily unsettling effect such import competition would have had on the pricing of steel products within the United States. Under the cartel arrangement, in other words, it should have been much easier for American steel producers to cover higher operating costs simply by increasing prices. This, in fact, is exactly what took place with remarkable uniformity throughout the industry, beginning with an average 12 percent increase in product prices effective 1 April 1937. The U.S. Bureau of Labor Statistics estimated that sales revenue would increase during 1937 by approximately $386 million, based on a projected volume of business equal to that of 1936. A 20 percent industrywide wage increase paid out over the course of a year, on the other hand, would have cost the industry only about $125 million. Other factors being equal, the minimum probable increase in the industry's revenues would be at least three times greater than the maximum probable increase in its total wage payments.[35] Indeed, it was later revealed that profits in the steel industry rose from $2.50 per share during the first quarter of 1937 to $3.43 per share during the second quarter and that U.S. Steel, with almost a 97 percent increase in net profits, ultimately realized a significantly better gain for the year than the industry as a whole.[36] Moreover, additional analysis by the Federal Reserve Board indicated that although approximately 60 percent of the industry's improved profitability stemmed from a general increase in production and sales, the remaining 40 percent was clearly "attributable to the increase in price as compared to the increase in wages" that had gone into effect earlier that spring, subsequent to U.S. Steel's recognition of the Steel Workers Organizing Committee.[37]

# Conclusion

Both General Motors and the United States Steel Corporation settled with union labor early in 1937 for compelling economic reasons, not when business was bad but as it was getting better. There has been no lack of speculation since as to the possible implications of this timing, particularly among analysts for whom recognition of the UAW and SWOC by these two corporate giants appeared to signal the beginning of a more advanced phase in the routinization of conflictual behavior in the American industrial economy. But if a rough-hewn Weberian view of such developments is perhaps not completely without foundation, the actual dynamics of change to which it alludes were at best still being manifest in a radically haphazard fashion, with an outcome that in the late 1930s was entirely unpredictable. In the short run, certainly, the arguably more "rational," accommodative capitalist posture toward labor was no match for the contradictions and pitfalls of industrial economics, and especially for the tremendous setback of 1937–38, when the collapse of the trend toward recovery once again allowed the most virulent forms of antiunionism to rise to the fore. This situation eventually was relieved not by an ideological revitalization of corporatism, or even so much by the continuous reinforcement of a new legal framework more favorable to unions, as by the fortuitous circumstances of war.[1]

With the exception of U.S. Rubber's recognition of the United Rubber Workers at the corporation's central facility in Detroit late in the summer of 1937, the only significant instance of a major industrial employer acceding peacefully to the demands of labor after the onset of the "Roosevelt recession" came in the form of Gerard Swope's long-awaited national agreement with the United Electrical Workers (UE), which took effect officially on 1 April 1938. By that time, however, even though Swope personally might still lay claim to a genuinely pioneering "corporatist" approach to the basic problems of business, the level of dramatic excitement accompanying the compact was greatly diminished because the CIO had already won a series of momentous concessions from other, far less "liberal," industrial employers. And however one may wish to judge that point, it is also worth noting for the sake of perspective

**165**

that the General Electric Company's labor relations policies show nearly as pronounced a pattern of long-term variability, depending upon prevailing competitive and productive conditions, as the labor policies of any other major industrial employer of the modern era. The UE's 1938 master contract with GE was largely procedural in nature, formalizing many of the company's already relatively well-regarded personnel practices but granting no specific wage concessions to the union. Indeed, with the return of more difficult economic circumstances in the industrial sector generally, it seems that even the prince of the corporate liberals, Gerard Swope, was disposed to negotiate a rather hard bargain with his employees. Nor did Swope's legacy of liberalism in the arena of industrial relations survive World War II. By 1946, no matter what it may have been worth to labor during the Depression or earlier, the moderate approach as practiced by Swope had been abandoned by the company's new vice-president, Lemuel Boulware, whose single-minded pursuit of managerial control put GE in the forefront of business' general postwar initiative to contain and undermine much of the strategic impact of organized labor's New Deal gains.[2]

If nothing else, the case of General Electric's personnel policies illustrates that the course of industrial relations generally at the end of the 1930s had not been set unalterably on any one particular path of development. Nor, as yet, was there a truly definitive sense of the federal government's proper role therein. Correlatively, it was not until somewhat later, with the end of World War II and reconversion to a peacetime economy, that labor's place within the confines of the American corporate system was established with any precision. Then, finally, in a clear rebuttal to the excessive generosity of New Deal liberalism, all the most important details of the issue were settled by the Taft-Hartley (Federal Labor Management Relations) Act of 1947. Upon the adoption of this bitterly contested new measure, organized labor henceforth was legally obligated as a party to the basic contractual relations of capitalism to conduct its affairs "responsibly," not only in deference to the "public interest" in an uninterrupted flow of commerce but also in recognition of "management's right to manage."[3]

An abundance of colorfully hysterical conservative rhetoric to the contrary notwithstanding, the forces of American labor were not poised on the brink of expropriating the means of production in a stupendous triumph of revolutionary will when the Eightieth Congress passed the Taft-Hartley law, ultimately over President Harry S. Truman's veto. Certainly the trade unionism of the 1930s, whether represented by the activities of the AFL or the CIO, communists and all, amounted to little more than simply that—trade unionism. Even the newer industrial unions, in the course of their dramatic rise to strength during the latter half of the Depression decade, were fighting for essentially the same representational status, standards of material dignity, job security, and tolerable factory regimen that trade unionists in the United States had always coveted. And with the exception of the odd "renegade" tendency here and there, the younger labor organizations pursued those traditional aims without ever seriously broaching the issue of workers' control or otherwise becoming engaged in the sort of activity that one might reasonably expect to have evolved into a programmatic assault on the capitalist system.[4]

During the war, it is true, certain broadly influential elements within the leadership of the CIO indicated a clear desire to move beyond the well-known limitations of ordinary business unionism by their advocacy of national planning and the prospective creation of "industrial councils," which were conceived as a means of allowing labor the chance to assume a coequal role with management in the running of wartime industry.[5] Walter Reuther, Philip Murray, and other labor chieftains acting as proponents of what Sidney Lens labeled "social unionism" and what David Brody has characterized as "mainstream CIO progressivism" kept this advocacy alive in the aftermath of the war by championing an overtly redistributive wage-price policy as part of the groundwork for an era of industrial democracy and full employment. In addition, both during and after World War II, not a few industrial unions made considerable headway in restricting managerial discretion on a wide range of personnel and production issues: hiring, promotion, job content, rates of operation, and more. When a perceptible erosion of informal authority on the shop floor is added to the equation, these union advances readily explain management's motivation in mounting a vigorously waged post–New Deal counteroffensive in the realm of labor relations that in its common aspects clearly looked to General Electric's "Boulwarism" as a model of accomplishment.[6]

It is equally important, however, that management's principal strategic goal vis-à-vis labor in the early postwar years was not to crush the unions and thus be rid of them altogether. That might have been an easily attainable goal in some industries before 1933, but it was not typically recognized as such by corporation personnel officers in 1946, 1947, or 1948. With the benefit of a generally favorable political climate and the protection of a new federal labor law that severely restricted the freedom of unions to exercise certain forms of coercive leverage in their dealings with management, after the war most industrial employers happily accepted the prospect of a formal, mutually agreed-upon delineation of power and responsibility in the workplace. And clearly the easiest way of achieving this equilibrium without either jeopardizing the fundamental prerogatives of capital or further limiting basic union rights was systematically to filter every "legitimate" issue of controversy between business and labor through the inherently biased contractual net of the collective bargaining process.[7]

The unions ultimately lacked the capacity to resist. The political support of

New Deal liberalism was a thing of the past. And the economics of inflation after 1940 had the effect of elevating the issue of wage security and the promise of material betterment at what seemed to be the dawn of an era of potentially limitless middle-class affluence to a position of overwhelming immediate importance relative to the attainment of this or that transcendent vision of industrial democracy. As to why this actually happened, we have at least three possible scenarios from which to choose. We may fall in behind those who would raise the question inspired originally by the early twentieth-century theorizations of Robert Michels of whether American trade union leaders, in the course of becoming professionally adept at the administration of power, inevitably managed along the way to betray the basic trust of their constituency.[8] Alternatively, we might follow the lead of those analysts who are inclined to stress the broader, sociologically more complex implications of the essentially ambivalent nature of that "trust."[9] Or, indeed, we might adopt certain aspects of the classical Leninist critique of trade unionism, which argues that because trade unions do not in and of themselves represent a force for political change in society, they are incapable of imposing on capitalist exploitation any restriction more burdensome than what the conjuncture of the market at a particular stage of development will bear.[10]

All three of these critical perspectives have some explanatory value with respect to the immediate issue at hand. Each in its own way points to the significance of key societal attributes in the United States that bear more than a tangential relationship to the unremitting confinement of latent proletarian radicalism safely within the operative strictures of narrowly conceived "laborist" reform.[11] The untoward fate of labor's progressive stance at the end of World War II was not a simple accident of history. Organized labor's intrinsic limitations in this country are indisputably a matter of cultural-institutional inheritance, and the capacity of industrial unions under the organizational wing of the CIO to effect social change in America during the 1940s and beyond was unavoidably influenced by certain basic patterns of development set in part during the Great Depression. National politics during the 1930s was fluid with new possibilities. And it is not farfetched to imagine that events then might have taken a truly significant turn in the direction of industrial democracy had that decade witnessed a much more forceful articulation of popularly based yet genuinely radical alternatives to all the trappings of the status quo— but especially to the institutionalized limits of trade unionism and collective bargaining—than the social history of the era managed to produce.[12]

An elaborate explanation of the absence of a strong anticapitalist labor movement in twentieth-century America is beyond the scope of the present study. Any such effort would require a detailed analysis of the impact of a number of highly complex political, social, and economic circumstances more or less peculiar to the American historical experience, beginning perhaps with the comparatively early unrestricted enfranchisement of adult white males. Undergirded by the basic precepts of bourgeois morality evident in the rise of Republican nationalism and the historic alignment of popular sentiment in the North and West antagonistic to the culture of slavery, a widely extended franchise and various collateral benefits of formal democracy effectively undermined every appeal to the logic of sharply delineated class politics during the formative years of the Unitd States's development as an industrial nation in the nineteenth century.[13] Similarly important in this regard from as early as the 1830s forward has been the repeated distortion of popular perceptions and attitudes as a result of exceptionally deep and continually reproduced racial, ethnic, and religious subcultural cleavages in society, compounded by the effect of strongly divergent regional economic peculiarities, a perniciously intricate hierarchical division of labor,[14] and certain "natural" obstacles to ideological and programmatic coalescence in the American two-party, single-member-constituency electoral system. All of these factors, in various combinations and permutations, are given greater force because they have been operative in the most highly diversified, technologically proficient industrial economy in the modern world and, as such, seem to have militated decisively against what otherwise might have emerged historically as a more deeply rooted and generally coherent working-class political opposition. Politically oriented labor radicalism in the United States has appeared only intermittently and even then was prone to any number of parochial and sectarian tendencies that resulted in a marked inability to provide a viable grass-roots alternative to mainstream "bread-and-butter" unionism.[15]

Although partially counteracted by the polarizing effects of a moribund economy, labor's traditional limitations as a force for radical change in the United States were still sufficiently important during the 1930s to command the immediate attention of anyone seeking to explain the relatively narrow boundaries of political struggle within which the various components of New Deal labor policy ultimately took shape.[16] Organized labor was no more inclined to make materially exorbitant or otherwise lavish demands upon the state during the Depression than previously in American history. Labor's strategic position in the American economy, it must be remembered, had already been thoroughly undermined by nearly a decade of involuntary organizational backstepping when the financial collapse of 1929–31 finally traumatized the entire country. Yet there was a certain irony here in relation to the deeper crosscurrents of change in the American political economy, for in hindsight it is clear that the peculiar circumstances of labor's demonstrated inability to hold its own amid the superficial prosperity of the 1920s was a central factor preparatory to massive government intervention in the private sector during the years immediately ahead. Indeed, as this book endeavors to establish, the uniquely pervasive and profound character of the continuing deflationary spiral and the absence of any preexisting means of resistance to it by the early 1930s greatly increased the likelihood that certain appropriately limited "concessions" to labor would not be so universally disturbing to the nation's industrialists as to deprive Roosevelt and the New Dealers of the necessary political latitude within which to pursue moderate, recovery-oriented labor reform. Least disturbed of all were those employers engaged in labor-intensive basic industries such as cotton textiles, garment manufacturing, and bituminous coal mining, many of whom were inclined to regard either the strong union or federally regulated employment standards as perhaps the only available means by which to protect, and possibly advance, their own normally precarious position in the overall competitive structure of the product market.

Although the extent of employer backing for certain labor reforms during the early New Deal may have been somewhat unusual, there was nothing extraordinary about the attitude of the employers per se. No less a legend among American industrialists than Andrew Carnegie, for example, when discussing the limits of his commitment to Spencerian social philosophy with a Scottish journalist in 1891, reasoned that the natural humanitarian proclivities of the "fair" employer would forever be held in check by the determined competition of unscrupulous "hard men" in the absence of uniform labor standards enforced by the state.[17]

A little earlier, Marx confronted a similar phenomenon in his discussion of the English Factory Acts in the first volume of *Capital*.[18] He partially obscured the politics of the issue by implying that the ten-hour law and related measures that served to protect the proletariat against sheer physical exhaustion must somehow be linked historically to the enlightened self-interest of the bourgeoisie.[19] Nevertheless, he acknowledged that the establishment of a "normal working day" was the "result of centuries of struggle between capitalist and labourer" and that the former had been obliged at the end of it all to function under the imposition of an artificial constraint on his ability to exploit the hireling worker. Marx also had interesting evidence in hand in the form of a petition and memorial from "26 firms owning extensive potteries in Staffordshire, amongst others, Josiah Wedgwood & Sons," which indicated how easily the desire of a specific group of employers either to achieve or to preserve a position of viability in "competition with other capitalists" might lead them to favor "some legislative enactment" affecting the basic conditions of labor.[20]

If any general analytic principle can be derived from this observation it is that the struggle for control and domination in the realm of industrial enterprise in nineteenth-century England was waged in a state of complete interpenetration with the larger world of politics and public values that ordinarily produced social reform. Much the same is true of twentieth-century America, particularly with regard to the relationship between labor, capital, and the state during the early New Deal.[21] As in the case of Marx's twenty-six Staffordshire potteries, the immediately practical (if also rather easily circumvented) application of Section 7a and the other regulatory provisions of the National Industrial Recovery Act, not the broader ideological goals of corporatism allegedly manifest in a self-conscious effort on the part of the ruling class to co-opt latent proletarian radicalism, accounts for the acceptance or rejection of such policies by specific constituencies within the business community during the formative stages of the New Deal experience. By this reasoning, moreover, I think it would be a mistake to generalize too freely about whether business clearly won or lost vis-à-vis the material claims of labor during the early New Deal. In a political economy completely overlain with formal democratic rights, power is manifest as an extremely complex relational phenomenon in which basic features of dependence and domination automatically tend to become blurred.[22] And to the extent that the interests of both labor and capital could be accommodated within the framework of the recovery program's commitment to essentially conservative economic objectives, any resulting change in the actual distribution of power in society would appear to have been correspondingly indistinct.

In the case of the Wagner Act, however, the articulated preferences of the industrial employer clearly took a back seat at the policy-making level to the articulated interests of labor. This, in fact, seems to have been one of the few occurrences during the entire New Deal experience when it can be said that the politics of reform were not easily reducible to a simple function of the institutionalized relations of economic power in society—ample testimony, some undoubtedly would be quick to observe, that the rule of law under capitalism may amount to a great deal more than a bourgeois sham.[23]

Insofar as the adoption of the Wagner Act attests to the possibilities of democratic reform within the framework of capitalism, such a perspective may be entirely appropriate.[24] From another analytical viewpoint, however, a somewhat different emphasis would seem most appropriate: that the National Labor Relations Act of 1935 was formulated, by acknowledgment of its chief legislative sponsor, with the primary intention of restoring capitalism in the United States to the status of acceptably good health. Because that was to be accomplished by encouraging a potentially significant adjustment in the differential bargaining capacities of labor and capital in the industrial sector, industry's opposition was unmistakably, and almost uniformly, vehement. There is no question as to whether the Wagner Act threatened the lifeblood of the system: it surely did not. It did signal an unusually direct intrusion by the state into a traditionally autonomous sphere of employer discretion, which certainly was not unimportant. But even in American history there is nothing to indicate that an ideal conception of entrepreneurial freedom has ever been compatible with a more broadly conceived definition of the common good. With respect to the events of 1935, there is little question that the basic thrust and direction of reform were significantly influenced by the loyal perceptions of various parties to the debate over economic recovery whose relatively more expansive social vision and apparent sensitivity to the precarious legitimacy of the established material order ultimately took precedence over the highly particularistic interests of industrial management. One might mention investment bankers, large retail merchants, liberal journalists and academicians, up-and-coming industrial relations experts, or any number of other "public welfare"–oriented elements as being among those groups that seem to have played an especially important role along with labor and its closest allies in constituting the broadly receptive political climate in which the Wagner Act eventually came to pass.[25]

Industry's sufferance of "defeat" in 1935, in any event, represented a setback of objectively tolerable proportions. Within limits dictated by economic good sense, the managers of the nation's leading industrial corporations, almost without exception, resisted both the adoption of the National Labor Relations Act and the rise of the CIO, and in the process these employers' estrangement from the relatively progressive orientation of the New Deal Democrats became steadily more acute. Business attitudes and perceptions are not impervious to reality, however, and soon industry's initially unqualified opposition to the Wagner Act was completely overshadowed by the failure of either the new law or the new unionism to contribute to circumstances in which the essential requisites of profitable enterprise were likely to be subordinated to the boundless aggrandizement of labor's material well-being.[26] Instead, the contemporary world was to witness the disastrous effects of labor's own civil war, a relentless political and legal assault on the administrative integrity of the National Labor Relations Board, and the eventual displacement of New Deal liberalism by the ascendant priorities of military Keynesianism.

In the context of these and related developments in the panoply of public affairs after 1938, it is difficult to imagine how labor's critically diminished strategic position versus that of management in the technological organization of modern industry could have constituted anything but a patent guarantee of the continued preeminence of capital in the American political economy.[27] New Deal labor policy offered the industrial worker not so much a refuge from as a practical incentive to acquiesce in this steadily shifting balance of power in the marketplace of productive talent. Having been so enticed, labor ultimately acceded to a double dependency. First, there was the worker's traditional and obviously unchanged reliance upon the capitalist for the material means of sustenance through employment. And now, suddenly, labor also had become dependent upon the state's capacity to assure that the worker's effective subordination to capital would be rewarded equitably. That expectation meshed perfectly with the New Dealers' own sense that capitalism in the United States could very likely thrive only if a proper balance were struck between the private incentive to produce and the private incentive to consume. Indeed, insofar as it may be possible to perceive a degree of sustained intentionality in the labor reforms of the Depression decade, the proof of consistency is locked somewhere deep within the contemporaneous appeal of the purchasing power thesis. Beyond that, New Deal labor policy was notably devoid of the fore-sighted wisdom and nearly flawless programmatic continuity with which it has mistakenly been credited by some recent analysts. The history of the 1930s may provide a valuable lesson in the conservative functions of liberal reform. But if the evidence presented in this study bears any conclusive weight, it should be clear that the driving force behind the formulation and enactment of federal labor policy during the New Deal era resembled nothing so much as a common variety of political expedience and interest brokering, the only effective boundaries of which were a fundamentally biased configuration of social power and the remarkably resilient institutional structures of American capitalism.

# Notes

## Introduction

1. I use the word "prestige" here in keeping with the meaning of *prestigio* as employed by Antonio Gramsci in his analysis of bourgeois cultural hegemony. The idea is very capably evaluated in context with a number of closely allied concepts in Marxist social theory by Femia, "Hegemony and Consciousness."

2. Williams, *Contours of American History*, pp. 345 ff.; Weinstein, *Corporate Ideal*, for the problem of interclass conflict and its attempted resolution along essentially conservative lines. For the politics and attempted resolution of intraclass conflict during the Progressive era, see Kolko, *Triumph of Conservatism*.

3. For a recent review of the topic see Foner, "Why Is There No Socialism in the United States?"

4. Kolko, "Intelligence and the Myth of Capitalist Rationality."

5. Gilbert, *Designing the Industrial State*.

6. As to the matter of "allied" revisionist currents, perhaps the most notable example of what I have in mind here is Hays, "Politics of Reform."

7. Bernstein, "New Deal"; Conkin, *FDR and the Origins of the Welfare State*; Zinn, *Politics of History*, pp. 118–36.

8. Leuchtenburg, *Franklin D. Roosevelt and the New Deal*, pp. 336, 347.

9. Bernstein, "New Deal," p. 281.

10. A short list of relevant sources in this regard might include Hofstadter, *American Political Tradition*; Holt, "The New Deal and the American Anti-Statist Tradition"; Hawley, *The New Deal and the Problem of Monopoly*; Rosenof, *Dogma, Depression, and the New Deal*; Arnold, *Folklore of Capitalism*; and Lynd and Lynd, *Middletown in Transition*.

11. Auerbach, "New Deal, Old Deal."

12. For example, Radosh, "Myth of the New Deal." See also Domhoff, *Higher Circles*, pp. 218–50; and Hurd, "New Deal Labor Policy." What emerges here is something approximating a slightly sophisticated version of "Labor Frontism," which was first developed by Robert A. Brady as a comparative thesis on the origins of modern industrial totalitarianism: *Business as a System of Power*, pp. 274–87. Cf. Corey, *Decline of American Capitalism*, p. 99 and passim, who, along with Brady,

also anticipated much of the later revisionist argument on the conservative implications of New Deal reform.

13. I have addressed some of the problems connected with this more fully elsewhere: Vittoz, "Economic Foundations of Industrial Politics." See also Skocpol, "Political Response to Capitalist Crisis."

14. As discussed, for example, in Hurst, *Law and Markets*.

# Chapter 1

1. Steindl, *Maturity and Stagnation*, is perhaps the most rigorously conceived theoretical analysis of the long-term sources of capital stagnation in the American economy. See also Baran and Sweezy, *Monopoly Capital*, chap. 8; and Bernstein, "Long-Term Economic Growth." For the 1920s specifically, see, in particular, Moulton, *Formation of Capital*, esp. chap. 10; but also Kolko, *Main Currents*, pp. 101–5. Finally, all of the foregoing should be supplemented with Leven, Moulton, and Warburton, *America's Capacity to Consume*.

2. Habakkuk, *American and British Technology*, for a highly regarded evaluation of the primary forces at work here.

3. Spengler, "Some Economic Aspects of Immigration," for a summary of data that describe the long-term phenomenon in more detail. See also Sumner H. Slichter, "Recent Employment Movements," *Survey*, 1 Apr. 1929, rpt. in U.S. Senate, Committee on Labor and Public Welfare, *History of Employment and Manpower Policy*, 5:1592–93.

4. Kendrick, *Productivity Trends*, p. 118; Creamer, Dobrovolsky, and Borenstein, *Capital in Manufacturing and Mining*, p. 95.

5. Jerome, *Mechanization in Industry*, pp. 218, 224–25; Soule, *Prosperity Decade*, p. 128.

6. Fabricant, *Employment in Manufacturing*, p. 148. Overall manufacturing employment did increase during 1929, ultimately reaching a point just below that of 1920. See Kendrick, *Productivity Trends*, p. 465.

7. Kendrick, *Productivity Trends*, pp. 334, 464–65. For the special significance of the declining capital-output ratio in manufacturing during the post–World War I decade, see ibid., p. 165; and Creamer, Dobrovolsky, and Borenstein, *Capital in Manufacturing and Mining*, p. xxxvii.

8. I have explored the details of this and related issues elsewhere: Vittoz, "World War I and the Political Accommodation of Transitional Market Forces."

9. Easterlin, *Population, Labor Force, and Long Swings*, p. 194; Lebergott, "Labor Force and Employment," p. 119, table 2. The proportion of national income attributable to manufacturing declined from about 25 percent in 1919 to 22–23 percent in 1923 and then remained at that level for the duration of the postwar decade (Fabricant, *Output of Manufacturing Industries*, p. 4). For the key components of domestic labor force growth after 1920, see Lescohier and Brandeis, *History of Labor*, pp. 34–43; and Miller, "Components of Labor Force Growth."

10. Fabricant, *Employment in Manufacturing*, chap. 5; Slichter, "Current Labor Policies of American Industries," pp. 425–26; Weintraub, "Displacement of Workers."

11. Mills, *Economic Tendencies*, p. 312.

12. Taeuber and Taeuber, *Changing Population*, p. 99; Goodrich, *Migration and Economic Opportunity*, pp. 421–59, 475, 675–99.

13. Both the hourly wages and average annual earnings of manufacturing workers nearly doubled between 1914 and 1918 because of uniquely favorable market conditions fostered by the war. Skyrocketing living costs held the corresponding improvement in real earnings to just under 12 percent, but this still represented an annual compound rate of increase substantially greater than prewar averages (Fabricant, *Basic Facts on Productivity Change*, p. 48, table C; Rees, *New Measures*, p. 19, table 8).

14. The greatest regional and subregional out-migration during the 1920s occurred among both blacks and native whites in the rural South. See Eldridge and Thomas, *Population Redistribution and Economic Growth*, 3:90, 118–21, 125. See also Thomas, *Migration and Urban Development*, pp. 140–48. The net transfer of population to industrial or nonfarming regions of the country from 1920 to 1930 amounted to an estimated 5.8 million (U.S. Bureau of the Census, *Historical Statistics*, p. 47, Series C 74-79).

15. Bernstein, *Lean Years*, pp. 47–63, is the only major synthesis that portrays the reality with true success.

16. U.S. Congress, Joint Economic Committee, *Productivity, Prices and Incomes*, p. 157, table 57; Ozanne, "Impact of Unions on Wage Trends and Income Distribution," p. 116, table 6.

17. Keller, "Factor Income Distribution."

18. Troy, *Trade Union Membership*, p. 2, table 2; Levinson, *Unionism, Wage Trends, and Income Distribution*, pp. 32–40, 42, 46–47.

19. Levinson, *Unionism, Wage Trends, and Income Distribution*, pp. 40–44, 90–93.

20. On this point, Harold Levinson's findings in the study cited above are generally supported by the work of other experts in the field. Appropriate reviews of the specialized literature include Hildebrand, "Economic Effects of Unionism"; and Livernash, "Wages and Benefits."

21. Backman and Gainsburgh, *Economics of the Cotton Textile Industry*, pp. 17–19. See also Stelzer, "Cotton Textile Industry," pp. 48–49; U.S. Congress, Temporary National Economic Committee, *Structure of Industry*, pp. 254–56; U.S. National Resources Committee, *Structure of the American Economy*, Part 1, pp. 250–51.

22. Clark, *History of Manufactures*, 3:171–72; Copeland, *Cotton Manufacturing Industry*, pp. 34–35. For a general account of the rise of the industry in the South, see Mitchell, *Rise of Cotton Mills in the South*, along with an important corrective piece on the characteristics of the regional labor supply by Wright, "Cheap Labor and Southern Textiles."

23. Galambos, *Competition and Cooperation*, p. 40; Copeland, *Cotton Manufac-*

*turing Industry*, p. 21; Clark, *History of Manufactures*, 3:179. The domestic market was crucial for American textile producers. In 1914 the United States exported only about 5 percent of its annual cotton textile product, compared to 75 percent for the British. In 1922 exports of U.S. cotton goods reached an all-time high of 7.6 percent of the industry's total product (Clark, *History of Manufactures*, 3:187; Backman and Gainsburgh, *Economics of the Cotton Textile Industry*, p. 181).

24. Copeland, *Cotton Manufacturing Industry*, pp. 86–87.

25. Ibid., pp. 36–39; Clark, *History of Manufactures*, 3:173; Potter, "Historical Development of Eastern-Southern Freight Rate Relationships."

26. Evans, "Southern Labor Supply and Working Conditions," pp. 159–62. See also Smith, *Mill on the Dan*, pp. 9, 48–49, 241–44.

27. Backman and Gainsburgh, *Economics of the Cotton Textile Industry*, p. 89; Berglund, Starnes, and DeVyver, *Labor in the Industrial South*, pp. 16–17, 69–104; Lester, "Trends in Southern Wage Differentials," pp. 319–21, 339; Smith, *Mill on the Dan*, pp. 101–5.

28. U.S. Bureau of Labor, *Report on the Condition of Woman and Child Wage-Earners*, 1:28–36.

29. For the early development of state legislation governing the employment of women and children, see Lescohier and Brandeis, *History of Labor*, pp. 403–500. For the degree of effective enforcement, see U.S. Bureau of Labor, *Report on the Condition of Woman and Child Wage-Earners*, 1:84–86; and Kelley, "Child Labor Legislation." Also of more general interest in this connection are two detailed studies of the child labor reform movement: Felt, *Hostages of Fortune*; and Trattner, *Crusade for the Children*.

30. The standard source here is Davidson, *Child Labor Legislation in the Southern Textile States*.

31. U.S. Bureau of Labor, *Report on the Condition of Woman and Child Wage-Earners*, 1:170ff.; Ogburn, *Progress and Uniformity in Child-Labor Legislation*, pp. 71, 94–96, 108–9, 124, 194–95.

32. Lea, "Cotton Textiles." The same author makes an even more persuasive argument for this in his M.A. thesis: "The Cotton Textile Industry and the Federal Child Labor Act of 1916." See also Graebner, "Federalism in the Progressive Era," pp. 335–37.

33. Clark, *History of Manufactures*, 3:340–42; Murchison, "Requisites of Stabilization," p. 72.

34. Backman and Gainsburgh, *Economics of the Cotton Textile Industry*, p. 89; U.S. Bureau of Labor Statistics, "Wages and Hours of Labor in Cotton-Goods Manufacturing," p. 24; Tolles, "Regional Differences in Cotton-Textile Wages," pp. 37–38.

35. *Textile World*, 4 Feb. 1928, p. 128.

36. Backman and Gainsburgh, *Economics of the Cotton Textile Industry*, p. 173; Murchison, "Requisites of Stabilization," p. 72; Nourse, *America's Capacity to Produce*, pp. 196–200; U.S. Bureau of Labor Statistics, "Wages and Hours of Labor in Cotton-Goods Manufacturing," pp. 24–25.

37. Murchison, *King Cotton Is Sick*, pp. 148–49, for the economics of night work.

38. Backman and Gainsburgh, *Economics of the Cotton Textile Industry*, pp. 138–39, 189, 212.

39. Galambos, *Competition and Cooperation*, pp. 92, 136, 167.

40. Ibid., pp. 11–85, for the early development of cotton textile trade associations.

41. Ibid., pp. 77–81; Kolko, *Triumph of Conservatism*, p. 268.

42. Galambos, *Competition and Cooperation*, pp. 82–83.

43. Ibid., pp. 89–112, for the events leading to the creation of the Cotton Textile Institute.

44. Ibid., pp. 103–7, 116; Murchison, "Requisites of Stabilization," p. 72.

45. See Bernstein, *Lean Years*, pp. 1–43, for the labor insurgency during the late 1920s in the textile districts of the Southeast.

46. Ibid., p. 11.

47. This was one of the principal topics of discussion at a conference in New Bedford, Massachusetts, in mid-November 1928 between a state congressional delegation and representatives of both manufacturer and union interests in the northeastern branch of the textile industry (*Textile World*, 24 Nov. 1928, p. 39).

48. In 1931 the combined value of cotton textiles produced in the Carolinas, Georgia, and Alabama was more than twice the value attributable to the top four producing states in the Northeast (U.S. Bureau of the Census, *Census of Manufactures: 1931*, p. 225).

49. See, for example, Murchison, "Southern Textile Manufacturing."

50. Lester, "Trends in Southern Wage Differentials," pp. 323–25, 341; U.S. Bureau of Labor Statistics, "Wages and Hours of Labor in Cotton-Goods Manufacturing," p. 24; Otey, "Women and Children in Southern Industry," pp. 166–68; Galambos, *Competition and Cooperation*, pp. 116–17.

51. Galambos, *Competition and Cooperation*, pp. 117–38.

52. Galambos, *Competition and Cooperation*, pp. 141–49; Berglund, Starnes, and DeVyver, *Labor in the Industrial South*, p. 100; *Textile World*, 14 Dec. 1929, pp. 38–39; ibid., 1 Mar. 1930, p. 56.

53. Galambos, *Competition and Cooperation*, p. 149; *Textile World*, 3 May 1930, pp. 82–82d. Also ibid., 28 June 1930, p. 47; 6 Sept. 1930, p. 43; and 7 Feb. 1931, pp. 90–91.

54. *Textile World*, 20 Sept. 1930, p. 22; ibid., 11 Oct. 1930, p. 29, and 18 Oct. 1930, p. 76.

55. Ibid., 20 June 1931, p. 23.

56. Galambos, *Competition and Cooperation*, pp. 150–57.

57. Ibid., pp. 157–61, 165, 173.

58. *Textile World*, 27 Feb. 1932, p. 20.

59. Galambos, *Competition and Cooperation*, pp. 174–75; B. B. Gossett, president, American Cotton Manufacturers Association, to the membership, 8 July 1932, Subject-Case File 165-913, Box 26, Records of the Federal Mediation and Conciliation Service, National Archives, Washington, D.C.; *Business Week*, 3 Nov. 1932, p. 8.

60. C. K. Moser to R. P. Lamont, 16 Nov. 1932, Robert P. Lamont Correspondence, Box 23, General Records of the U.S. Department of Commerce, National Archives; *Business Week*, 3 Nov. 1932, p. 8.

61. Galambos, *Competition and Cooperation*, pp. 176–78.

## Chapter 2

1. U.S. Bureau of the Census, *Census of Manufactures: 1931*, pp. 325–26; U.S. National Resources Committee, *Structure of the American Economy*, Part 1, p. 251; Pope, *Clothing Industry in New York*, pp. 64–65; Levine, *Women's Garment Workers*, pp. 14–17, 384–89, 394, 397–402; Seidman, *Needle Trades*, pp. 9, 11, 21–22; National Recovery Administration, Division of Review, "The Men's Clothing Industry," Work Materials No. 58, Mar. 1936, p. 55, Box 7057, Records of the National Recovery Administration, National Archives.

2. See, in particular, Carpenter, *Competition and Collective Bargaining*. See also Cohen, *Law and Order in Industry*; Budish and Soule, *New Unionism*; Robinson, *Collective Bargaining and Market Control*; Wolfson, "Role of the ILGWU"; and Braun, *Union-Management Co-operation*.

3. Levine, *Women's Garment Workers*, chaps. 6–14.

4. Perlman and Taft, *History of Labor*, p. 290.

5. Ibid. More detailed accounts of the early phases of trade unionism in the garment industry include Levine, *Women's Garment Workers*, chaps. 6–21; Seidman, *Needle Trades*, chap. 4; and Stolberg, *Tailor's Progress*, chaps. 2–3. For the unique role of Jewish culture and tradition in the early formation of the garment unions, see, in particular, Tcherikower, *Early Jewish Labor Movement*, chap. 10. See also Dubofsky, "Organized Labor and the Immigrant"; Epstein, *Jewish Labor in the USA*; and Laslett, *Labor and the Left*, chap. 4.

6. Levine, *Women's Garment Workers*, chap. 15.

7. Ibid., chaps. 16–20.

8. For a complete account of the 1909 shirtwaist strike, see Levine, *Women's Garment Workers*, chap. 21. See also Dubofsky, *When Workers Organize*, pp. 49–58; and Tax, *Rising of the Women*, chap. 8.

9. Levine, *Women's Garment Workers*, pp. 169–70.

10. Ibid., pp. 170–71.

11. Ibid., pp. 172–74.

12. Ibid., p. 175.

13. Ibid., p. 176.

14. Quoted in Carpenter, *Competition and Collective Bargaining*, p. 40.

15. Ibid., pp. 40, 43.

16. Chapter 2 of Carpenter's book is the best source for the details of the protocol arrangement. See also ibid., p. 503; and Robinson, *Collective Bargaining and Market Control*, p. 41. For a detailed account of the 1910 cloak and suitmakers' strike, as well as the negotiations that eventually led to the signing of the protocol, see Levine, *Women's Garment Workers*, pp. 178–95; and Dubofsky, *When Workers Organize*, pp. 58–66.

17. U.S. Commission on Industrial Relations, *Final Report and Testimony*, 2:1025–1161. See also Carpenter, *Competition and Collective Bargaining*, pp. 43–54, 229–51, 492–94, 577–84; Levine, *Women's Garment Workers*, chaps. 23–29; and Dubofsky, *When Workers Organize*, chap. 4.

18. Carpenter, *Competition and Collective Bargaining*, pp. 418–20.

19. For an evaluation of the Amalgamated Clothing Workers' rapid rise to power in the men's industry and the apparently advantageous "corporate syndicalist" orientation of the union in that connection and more generally as well, see Fraser, "Dress Rehearsal for the New Deal." See also Cobrin, *Men's Clothing Industry*, chaps. 7–9; and Myers and Bloch, "Men's Clothing."

20. Between 1914 and 1919, the total number of establishments in the women's wear industry increased by more than one-third; the men's by about one-fourth (Seidman, *Needle Trades*, pp. 335, 340).

21. Baum, "Fifty Years in America," p. 180.

22. The combined total of both types of shops declined between 1929 and 1933 by approximately 34 percent, with the annual mortality rate in some branches of the industry running as high as 25 percent (U.S. Bureau of the Census, *Census of Manufactures: 1933*, pp. 192, 194–95. See also Carpenter, *Competition and Collective Bargaining*, p. 33).

23. There was one marked exception to the general trend for the period 1919–29. During the economywide slump of 1920–21, the proportion of contract shops that were forced out of the market in the women's wear industry far exceeded the number of regular shops unfortunate enough to suffer the same fate: 27.6 and 0.8 percent, respectively. This pattern reversed itself, however, with a gradual recovery of demand in 1922–23, when subcontracting once again began to flourish (U.S. Bureau of the Census, *Census of Manufactures: 1931*, pp. 324–26).

24. Ibid., pp. 309–11.

25. International Ladies' Garment Workers' Union, *Report of the General Executive Board*, pp. 24–32.

26. Carpenter, *Competition and Collective Bargaining*, pp. 30–31, 522; Robinson, *Collective Bargaining and Market Control*, p. 44. See also Levine, *Women's Garment Workers*, pp. 402–6.

27. Rayack, "Impact of Unionism on Wages," p. 682; U.S. Bureau of the Census, *Census of Manufactures: 1931*, p. 309; U.S. Bureau of Labor Statistics, "Wages and Hours of Labor in the Men's Clothing Industry: 1932," p. 2; Levinson, *Unionism, Wage Trends, and Income Distribution*, p. 45; Slichter, *Union Policies and Industrial Management*, pp. 505–6, 526–27.

28. Carpenter, *Competition and Collective Bargaining*, p. 505; Slichter, *Union Policies and Industrial Management*, pp. 431–32.

29. Presumably the pressure for wage reductions was even greater in the men's wear industry. Thus one finds that whereas wages as a proportion of value added declined more or less equally during the 1920s in both the women's wear industry and in manufacturing generally (by about 14–15 percent), in the men's wear industry the proportion increased by an average of 5 percent. These figures are based on data compiled by the U.S. Bureau of the Census, *Census of Manufactures: 1931*, p. 324; and Levinson, *Unionism, Wage Trends, and Income Distribution*, p. 89.

30. Carpenter, *Competition and Collective Bargaining*, pp. 502ff.

31. Quoted in ibid., p. 477.

32. Ibid., pp. 492–94.

33. *Business Week*, 17 Aug. 1932, p. 6, 11 Jan. 1933, pp. 20, 22; and Seidman, *Needle Trades*, pp. 66–67.

34. Julius H. Cohen, chief counsel to several manufacturers' associations in the women's trade, anticipated the ultimate utility of "political regulation" in the garment industry nearly two decades before the implementation of federally sanctioned controls as provided in the National Industrial Recovery Act of June 1933. Inspired by the example of the British Trade Disputes Act, in January 1914 Cohen submitted a brief to the U.S. Commission on Industrial Relations that argued for the adoption of legislation creating a "National Industrial Board" empowered to enforce, on a marketwide basis, the terms of any agreement reached between a "substantial proportion" of the workers and employers in any of the various branches of the clothing industry, after "proper hearings" (Cohen, *Law and Order in Industry*, pp. 225–28, 291–92). Cohen later extended his advocacy to the adoption of a national labor policy, based on the same governing principle as his plan for the garment trades but applied to industry in general: *An American Labor Policy*, esp. pp. 103–10. See also Carpenter, *Competition and Collective Bargaining*, pp. 586–89.

# Chapter 3

1. See Parker, *Coal Industry*, for the best general study of the economics of bituminous mining in the United States during the interwar period. Although a less well-ordered presentation than the Parker study, a wealth of information on the bituminous industry during the 1920s and the first half of the 1930s, otherwise unavailable, can be found in Berquist, *Economic Survey*. See also National Bureau of Economic Research, Conference on Price Research, *Report of the Committee on Prices*, pp. 10–27; Hendry, "Bituminous Coal Industry." For a useful compilation of secondary sources on the American coal mining industry, see Munn, *Coal Industry*.

2. Parker, *Coal Industry*, pp. 9, 12.

3. Nourse, *America's Capacity to Produce*, pp. 48–55.

4. See, generally, Wiebe, "Anthracite Coal Strike of 1902"; but also Nash, *Conflict and Accommodation*, pp. 73–74, 91. For the contrasting market structures of bituminous and anthracite coal mining as they affected the industrial relations of each branch of the industry during the Progressive era, see Ramirez, *When Workers Fight*, chaps. 1–2.

5. Goodrich, *Migration and Economic Opportunity*, pp. 94–95.

6. Warne, *Coal-Mine Workers*; U.S. Industrial Commission, *Reports*, 12:xxiv, xxx–xxxi, cx, cxxxiv–cxxxvii, cxlii, and passim; *Coal Age*, 1 Oct. 1925, pp. 459–62; Gowaskie, "From Conflict to Cooperation"; Kerr, "Labor-Management Cooperation"; Nash, *Conflict and Accommodation*, pp. 26–28, 154; Lubin, *Miners' Wages*, pp. 51–55; Fisher, "Bituminous Coal," pp. 233–35, 238–40, 280; Ethelbert Stewart, "Equalizing Competitive Conditions," *Eleventh Special Report of the U.S. Commissioner of Labor, 1904*, rpt. in Commons, *Trade Unionism and Labor Problems*, pp. 521–33; Berquist, *Economic Survey*, 1:155–56; Tryon, "Effect of Competitive Condi-

tions," pp. 84–85, 87; Ulman, *Rise of the National Trade Union*, pp. 28–32, 513, 522. For the effect of "spatial limitations" on the competitive structure of the product market and its special relationship to the early and relatively successful unionization of both the anthracite and bituminous coal mining industries, see Levinson, *Determining Forces*, pp. 266–67; and Wolman, *Ebb and Flow*, p. 87.

7. Hinrichs, *United Mine Workers*, pp. 112–25; Baratz, *The Union and the Coal Industry*, p. 46; Fisher, "Bituminous Coal," pp. 253–54, 262–64. William Graebner has produced several exceptionally fine works on the political economy of the bituminous mining industry during the Progressive era: "The Coal Mine Operator and Safety"; "Great Expectations"; and *Coal Mining Safety in the Progressive Period*.

8. Lubin, *Miners' Wages*, p. 5; Tryon, "Effect of Competitive Conditions," p. 89. Unless otherwise indicated, all information on levels of production and fluctuating market shares among mining interests in different geographic regions of the country is either taken or computed from data compiled in various reports and publications of the U.S. Geological Survey and the U.S. Bureau of Mines, 1922–48, and reproduced in U.S. National Labor Relations Board, "Effect of Labor Relations," Appendix A, pp. 49, 57–58; and U.S. Senate, Committee on Banking and Currency, *Hearings: Economic Power of Labor Organizations*, Part 1, p. 266.

9. U.S. Bureau of Mines, *Minerals Yearbook, 1957*, 2:49; U.S. National Labor Relations Board, "Effect of Labor Relations," pp. 20–23, 25, 59; U.S. Federal Trade Commission, *Preliminary Report*, pp. 6, 59; National Industrial Conference Board, *Competitive Position of Coal*, p. 279; Nourse, *America's Capacity to Produce*, pp. 48–49; Parker, *Coal Industry*, p. 36; Fisher, "Bituminous Coal," p. 264; Kiessling, "Coal Mining in the South," pp. 88–90. All figures on changing mine capacity are computed from Bureau of Mines data and, unless otherwise indicated, are calculated on the basis of an annual 280-day period of operation. For an explanation of the formula used, see Hendry, "Bituminous Coal Industry," pp. 82–83.

10. U.S. Bureau of Mines, *Minerals Yearbook, 1957*, 2:10–11, 49; Kendrick, *Productivity Trends*, p. 400; "Employment in Relation to Mechanization in the Bituminous Coal Industry," *Monthly Labor Review* 36 (Feb. 1933): 256–78; Berquist, *Economic Survey*, 1:19–21; 2:291, 294; Parker, *Coal Industry*, pp. 38, 56–57; Baratz, *The Union and the Coal Industry*, p. 42.

11. The contemporary economics and sociology of mechanization are elaborated in Goodrich, *Miner's Freedom*.

12. U.S. Coal Commission, *Report*, Part 3, pp. 1317, 1330–31; Hunt, Tryon, and Willits, *What the Coal Commission Found*, pp. 230–33, 243, 247; Barger and Schurr, *Mining Industries*, pp. 178–79; Fisher, *Collective Bargaining*, p. 26; Fisher, "Bituminous Coal," pp. 258–59; Parker, *Coal Industry*, pp. 64–65.

13. *Coal Age*, 21 Jan. 1926, p. 105. Cf. Hendry, "Bituminous Coal Industry," p. 89; and Fisher, "Bituminous Coal," p. 264. The weakening of the UMW in bituminous mining during the post–World War I decade held certain measurable consequences for the material position of the coal miners. The hourly earnings of unionized bituminous miners increased between 1919 and 1923 by approximately 30 percent, finally reaching the equivalent of 12 percent above the average wage level of union workers in other industries and 24 percent above that of comparable nonunion groups.

By 1929, however, bituminous wages in Ohio, Indiana, and Illinois had fallen to a point about 28 percent below average union rates and 9 percent below average nonunion rates. Indeed, during a period when the hourly earnings of the industrial labor force as a whole generally had risen, the average hourly earnings of bituminous coal miners declined by about 22 percent. By contrast, the average hourly earnings of anthracite miners, whose industrywide organizational capacity remained fairly stable throughout the decade, increased by about 5 percent during the lean years from 1923 to 1929. See Levinson, *Unionism, Wage Trends, and Income Distribution*, pp. 43, 90–91. Cf. Douglas, *Real Wages*, pp. 144, 154.

14. "Earnings of Union and Non-Union Miners as Affected by Changes in Wage Rates in 1921," n.d., Commerce Files, Box 101, Hoover Papers, Herbert Hoover Presidential Library, West Branch, Iowa. See also Lubin, *Miners' Wages*, pp. 210–12.

15. R. A. Good to Herbert Hoover, 6 Feb. 1922 (with enclosures), Commerce Files, Box 98, Hoover Papers.

16. Lubin, *Miners' Wages*, p. 215; U.S. House of Representatives, Committee on Labor, *Hearings: Investigation of Wages and Working Conditions*, p. 140. See also Johnson, *Politics of Soft Coal*, pp. 113–14; and Dubofsky and Van Tine, *John L. Lewis*, p. 80.

17. The reluctance of a numerically significant element among the coal operators in this respect continued to be a source of frustration to three successive Republican administrations. See Hawley, "Secretary Hoover and the Bituminous Coal Problem."

18. U.S. Bureau of Mines, *Minerals Yearbook, 1957*, 2:49; U.S. National Labor Relations Board, "Effect of Labor Relations," pp. 18–24, 58; Fisher, "Bituminous Coal," p. 259; Tryon, "Effect of Competitive Conditions," p. 92; Parker, *Coal Industry*, p. 70; Zieger, *Republicans and Labor*, pp. 110–17; Dubofsky and Van Tine, *John L. Lewis*, p. 87.

19. U.S. National Labor Relations Board, "Effect of Labor Relations," pp. 25, 58; Beame, "Jacksonville Agreement"; Dubofsky and Van Tine, *John L. Lewis*, pp. 106–7. There can be little question that a relatively high current level of demand and the fear of market losses to nonunion competition during another prospective industrywide strike were jointly responsible in 1924 for a predominantly favorable opinion among major producers in the Central Competitive Field as to the advisability of extending the provisions of the Cleveland agreement. For the view that pressure brought to bear by both the Harding and Coolidge administrations via the direct intervention of Herbert Hoover may have been the critical factor ultimately accounting for the decision of the coal producers, see Hawley, "Secretary Hoover and the Bituminous Coal Problem," p. 264; and Zieger, *Republicans and Labor*, pp. 227–32, 238–39. Hawley and Zieger both stress the probable significance of a link between Hoover, Treasury Secretary Andrew Mellon, and the belated cooperation of the Pittsburgh Coal Company, which had recently come under the control of the Mellon banking interests. Yet in testimony before Congress, Hoover later flatly denied any significant government responsibility for the Jacksonville agreement. Rather, in the course of explaining the tenor of his personal communications with various mine owners before the settlement, Hoover claimed merely to have affirmed the acceptability of a solution to the

problem with which most producers in the Central Competitive Field were already in complete agreement—expressing himself, as he put it, in the capacity of a knowledgeable public official "upon the necessity of continuous production as vital to the elimination of speculative mining" (U.S. House of Representatives, Committee on Interstate and Foreign Commerce, *Hearings: Coal Legislation*, Part 3, p. 529. See also Herbert Hoover to C. J. Goodyear, 26 Jan. 1924; Hoover to Julius H. Barnes, 28 Jan. 1924, Commerce Files, Box 98, Hoover Papers; and Eugene McCauliffe to Hoover, 11 Jan. 1924; F. R. Wadleigh to Hoover, 5 Feb. 1924; F. R. Wadleigh, "Jacksonville Meeting," 12 Feb. 1924, Commerce Files, Box 101, ibid.).

20. Tryon and Mann, *Coal in 1923*, Part 2, p. 506.

21. Kiessling, "Coal Mining in the South," p. 90.

22. F. M. Shore to Richard Emmett, 7 Apr. 1924 (and enclosures); Shore to Emmett, 28 Apr. 1924; Shore to Emmett, 1 May 1924, Commerce Files, Box 98, Hoover Papers.

23. For example, A. R. Hamilton to Herbert Hoover, 9 Feb. 1925, ibid.

24. John L. Lewis's address to a meeting of bituminous coal miners at Fairmont, West Virginia, 26 Sept. 1925, ibid., Box 104. For further details, see Bernstein, *Lean Years*, pp. 127–36; Perlman and Taft, *History of Labor*, pp. 562–71; and U.S. Senate, Committee on Interstate Commerce, *Hearings: Conditions in the Coal Fields*.

25. W. K. Kavanaugh to Herbert Hoover, 22 Sept. 1924, Commerce Files, Box 98, Hoover Papers. See also *Twelfth Annual Report of the Secretary of Commerce* (Washington, 1924), pp. 13–14.

26. C. P. White to Herbert Hoover, 29 Dec. 1924, Commerce Files, Box 109, Hoover Papers.

27. Richard Campbell to Herbert Hoover, 23 Jan. 1925, ibid., Box 98.

28. C. P. White to Herbert Hoover, 26 Feb. 1925, ibid., Box 104.

29. Typescript report by Paul Wooton, Washington correspondent for *Coal Age*, 6 Mar. 1925, ibid., Box 98.

30. Wooton, 20 Mar. 1925. Also C. P. White to Herbert Hoover, 3 Apr. 1925, both in ibid.

31. Wooton, 20 Mar. 1925. Also C. P. White to Herbert Hoover, 9 Apr. 1925, ibid., Box 101.

32. *Coal Age*, 2 July 1925, p. 8. See also ibid., 26 Mar. 1925, p. 479; 8 Oct. 1925, pp. 491–95; Philip Murray to James J. Davis, 10 Dec. 1927, Case File 170/3918-5, Box 180, Records of the Federal Mediation and Conciliation Service (hereafter FMCS Records), National Archives; Berquist, *Economic Survey*, 1:174–77; U.S. National Labor Relations Board, "Effect of Labor Relations," pp. 27–28; Beame, "Jacksonville Agreement," pp. 198–201; Parker, *Coal Industry*, pp. 70–71; and Zieger, *Republicans and Labor*, pp. 234–35.

33. *Coal Age*, 1 Oct. 1925, pp. 461–62; U.S. Bureau of Mines, *Minerals Yearbook, 1957*, 2:49; U.S. National Labor Relations Board, "Effect of Labor Relations," pp. 26, 49, 58; U.S. Senate, Committee on Banking and Currency, *Hearings: Economic Power of Labor Organizations*, Part 1, p. 266; Baratz, *The Union and the Coal Industry*, pp. 23–33; Kiessling, "Coal Mining in the South," p. 90.

34. *Employes' Magazine*, Apr. 1927, pp. 113–14.

35. C. P. White to Herbert Hoover, 9 Feb. 1927, Commerce Files, Box 99, Hoover Papers.

36. U.S. National Labor Relations Board, "Effect of Labor Relations," pp. 28, 29, 59; Berquist, *Economic Survey*, 1:178; Beame, "Jacksonville Agreement," p. 202; Hawley, "Secretary Hoover and the Bituminous Coal Problem," p. 267; Fisher, "Bituminous Coal," pp. 261–62; Dubofsky and Van Tine, *John L. Lewis*, pp. 144–45.

37. U.S. Bureau of Mines, *Minerals Yearbook, 1957*, 2:49; U.S. House of Representatives, Committee on Interstate and Foreign Commerce, *Hearings: Coal Legislation*, Part 2, pp. 185–86; Frank E. Taplin, North American Coal Corporation, to James J. Davis, 22 Dec. 1927, Case File 170/3918-B, Box 179, FMCS Records.

38. U.S. Department of Labor, press release, 14 Dec. 1927, Box 43, Davis Papers, Library of Congress, Washington, D.C. See also Zieger, *Republicans and Labor*, p. 253; Dubofsky and Van Tine, *John L. Lewis*, p. 146; Johnson, *Politics of Soft Coal*, p. 121; and the *Washington Post*, 11 Dec. 1927, pp. 1, 16.

39. U.S. House of Representatives, Committee on Interstate and Foreign Commerce, *Hearings: Coal Legislation*, Part 3, p. 352. See also Hoover, *Memoirs: The Cabinet and the Presidency*, p. 71; and Zieger, *Republicans and Labor*, pp. 243, 245.

40. Secretary Davis's memorandum to joint committee of operators and miners, 14 Dec. 1927; Davis memo to operators and union representatives not in attendance, 17 Dec. 1927, Box 43, Davis Papers. See also Dubofsky and Van Tine, *John L. Lewis*, pp. 146–47. Related correspondence, memorandums, press releases, and lists of those in attendance at the December meeting in Washington can be found in the case files (170/3918-4) of the FMCS, Box 179.

41. Coal Operators Association of Illinois to Robert F. Wagner, 11 Feb. 1928, Wagner Papers, Georgetown University, Washington, D.C. See also Parker, *Coal Industry*, p. 72; and Fisher, "Bituminous Coal," p. 265.

42. *Coal Age*, Aug. 1928, p. 507; U.S. National Labor Relations Board, "Effect of Labor Relations," p. 39; Parker, *Coal Industry*, p. 72; Perlman and Taft, *History of Labor*, p. 567; Dubofsky and Van Tine, *John L. Lewis*, pp. 147–48.

43. *Coal Age*, Jan. 1929, pp. 56–59; U.S. National Labor Relations Board, "Effect of Labor Relations," p. 58.

44. The industry as a whole suffered a progressively greater net loss every year between 1928 and 1933 (U.S. Senate, Committee on Banking and Currency, *Hearings: Economic Power of Labor Organizations*, Part 1, p. 260).

45. *Coal Age*, May 1929, p. 314.

46. *Coal Age*, Feb. 1933, p. 35; *Business Week*, 1 July 1931, pp. 15–16; Bernstein, *Lean Years*, pp. 132–36; Perlman and Taft, *History of Labor*, pp. 567–71; Parker, *Coal Industry*, pp. 77–78; Dubofsky and Van Tine, *John L. Lewis*, pp. 155–72.

47. Taplin's open letter to coal operators, 27 June 1931 (portions of which are reprinted in Berquist, *Economic Survey*, 1:184–85; and also U.S. National Labor Relations Board, "Effect of Labor Relations," p. 40); Taplin to Hoover, 29 June 1931, Robert P. Lamont Correspondence, Box 4, General Records of the U.S. Department of Commerce (hereafter Commerce Records), National Archives. See also Parker, *Coal Industry*, p. 78; Dubofsky and Van Tine, *John L. Lewis*, pp. 173–74.

48. Howard W. Showalter, president, Continental Coal Company, to Robert P. Lamont, 22 July 1931, Lamont Correspondence, Box 3, Commerce Records. See also Ross, *Machine Age in the Hills*, p. 108, who quotes one unnamed southern operator as finally having concluded that "any employee has a right to a voice in an organization to protect himself. And if we give them that right they can do for us what we can't do for ourselves—stabilize coal prices. It can't be done from the top. Operators don't trust each other. We need the unions as a police agency to see that we operators act square with each other. We've got to give the miners a voice to stop this damnable cut-throat competition and the taking out of our stupidities on the miners. Blood is paying today for what brains should have done."

49. *Coal Age*, Aug. 1931, p. 345; Oct. 1931, p. 538; Sept. 1931, pp. 470–71.

50. Much of the relevant correspondence between union officials and members of the Hoover cabinet is reprinted in the *Proceedings of the Thirty-Second Consecutive Constitutional Convention of the United Mine Workers of America*, Indianapolis, Indiana, 26 Jan.–5 Feb. 1932, 2 vols. (Indianapolis, 1932), 1:51–65.

51. The primary documentation is available in Subject-Case File 165-944, Box 27, FMCS Records; and the Presidential File, Box 104, Hoover Papers. See also Dubofsky and Van Tine, *John L. Lewis*, pp. 174–75.

52. *Coal Age*, Aug. 1931, pp. 453–54; *Business Week*, 15 July 1931, p. 7, 22 July 1931, pp. 9–10; Lewis to Hoover, 29 June 1931; William H. Coolidge to Lamont and Doak, 6 July 1931; Lamont to William H. Coolidge, 8 July 1931; Frank E. Taplin to Lamont, 13 July 1931; J. D. A. Marrow to Lamont, 17 July 1931, all in Lamont Correspondence, Box 4, Commerce Records. See also Matthew Woll to Lamont, 8 July 1931; J. A. Paisley to Lamont, 1 Aug. 1931; Doak to Lewis, 29 Aug. 1931, ibid., Box 3; and Lamont to Matthew Woll, 9 July 1931, ibid., Box 25.

53. Doak to Lamont, 18 July 1931; Lamont to Doak, 13 July 1931 (and enclosure), Subject-Case File 165-944, Box 27, FMCS Records. This sentiment was in keeping with the opinion expressed by one operator more than three and a half years earlier that "the coal industry must be regulated" by an agency with the indisputable powers of a "Czar" (W. A. Brewerton, Brewerton Coal Company, to James J. Davis, 19 Dec. 1927, Case File 170/3918-A, Box 179, ibid.).

54. Robert P. Lamont to Frank E. Taplin, 1 Dec. 1931, Lamont Correspondence, Box 3, Commerce Records.

55. As quoted in *Business Week*, 16 Dec. 1931, p. 18.

56. Fisher and James, *Minimum Price Fixing*, p. 21.

57. *Coal Age*, Feb. 1932, pp. 65–67.

58. U.S. Senate, Committee on Interstate Commerce, *Hearings: Bituminous Coal Commission*, Part 2, passim. See also *Coal Age*, Feb. 1929, pp. 123–24; Parker, *Coal Industry*, p. 100; Hawley, "Secretary Hoover and the Bituminous Coal Problem," p. 267; Zieger, *Republicans and Labor*, p. 258; and Johnson, *Politics of Soft Coal*, pp. 123–24.

59. John L. Lewis to W. Jett Lauck, 27 Feb. 1932; Lauck to Lewis, 29 Feb. 1932, Box 39, Lauck Papers, Alderman Library, University of Virginia, Charlottesville; Van A. Bittner to Lauck, 2 Mar. 1932, ibid., Box 33; *Coal Age*, Apr. 1932, p. 168; Godfrey Tait to Daniel Roper, 25 May 1933, File 94694, Box 775, Commerce Records.

See also U.S. Senate, Committee on Mines and Mining, *Hearings: To Create a Bituminous Coal Commission*. A useful digest of testimony on the Davis-Kelly bill taken by a subcommittee of the Senate Committee on Mines and Mining is contained in Box 232, Lauck Papers.

60. James J. Davis to W. Jett Lauck, 12 Apr. 1932, Box 50, Davis Papers.

61. *Coal Age*, July 1932, p. 258; *Business Week*, 17 Feb. 1932, p. 11, 8 Oct. 1932, p. 5; Dubofsky and Van Tine, *John L. Lewis*, pp. 176–77; Johnson, *Politics of Soft Coal*, pp. 130–32. The attitude of the operators was no doubt affected in part by President Hoover's failure to support the Davis-Kelly bill, even in the face of his labor secretary's conviction that it might have presented "a way of solving many of the ills which are afflicting the [bituminous mining] industry" (William N. Doak, "Memorandum for the President," 17 Feb. 1932, Presidential File, Box 104, Hoover Papers). For Hoover's unsympathetic response, see W. Jett Lauck to John L. Lewis, 21 Nov. 1932, Box 39, Lauck Papers.

62. "Confidential: Coal," 14 Mar. 1932, Box 231, Lauck Papers.

63. *Business Week*, 18 Jan. 1933, p. 9.

64. W. H. Haskins to William N. Doak, 16 Apr. 1932, Subject-Case File 165-944, Box 27, FMCS Records. See also W. Jett Lauck to John L. Lewis, 24 Mar. 1933, Box 39, Lauck Papers.

65. Ickes, *Secret Diary*, pp. 24, 30. See also "Docket—Coal & Stabilization," 4 May 1933, Box 165, Lauck Papers; Harry S. Gay to Frances Perkins, 30 Mar. 1933; George A. Blackford to Perkins, 30 Mar. 1933, Subject-Case File 165-1082, Box 30, FMCS Records; Perkins, *The Roosevelt I Knew*, pp. 228–30; Farr, *Origins of Recent Labor Policy*, pp. 31–32; Himmelberg, *Origins of the National Recovery Administration*, p. 188; Johnson, "Drafting the NRA Code," p. 523; and Johnson, *Politics of Soft Coal*, p. 140.

# Chapter 4

1. Huthmacher and Susman, *Herbert Hoover and the Crisis of American Capitalism*, pp. 3–33; Hawley, "Herbert Hoover."

2. See, for instance, Schwarz, *Interregnum of Despair*, which is the best political history of the period.

3. Historians and political scientists have analyzed in great detail what generally is understood to have been a decisive shift between 1928 and 1940 in the voting pattern of the urban lower and middle classes toward concentration of electoral support for the Democratic party. The key to this shift for most analysts has appeared to lie with a sharply higher voter participation rate among these groups during a sustained period of economic adversity. Of particular importance, as one recent study has demonstrated, was the electoral mobilization of previous nonvoters, including a disproportionate number of women, but also the pre–World War I generation of European immigrants who, on the eve of the Great Depression, were just beginning to take part in American electoral politics and whose children were reaching voting age. See Ander-

sen, *Creation of a Democratic Majority*. Various other lines of analysis as they have appeared in the specialized literature are reviewed by Sternsher, "Emergence of the New Deal Party System"; and Lichtman, "Critical Election Theory."

4. Hoover, *Memoirs: The Great Depression*, pp. 85–86; Myers and Newton, *Hoover Administration*, p. 118.

5. Nash, "Herbert Hoover and the Origins of the Reconstruction Finance Corporation"; Olson, *Herbert Hoover and the Reconstruction Finance Corporation*, chap. 3.

6. Hoover explained the situation in reference to the many difficulties posed by an uncooperative and politically self-seeking Congress, especially citing the motives of the Democratic majority (Hoover, *Memoirs: The Great Depression*, pp. 100–103, 105–6, 159–60).

7. *Commercial and Financial Chronicle*, 23 Apr. 1932, p. 2973. See also *Business Week*, 11 Apr. 1931, p. 5; Bernstein, *Lean Years*, pp. 259, 313–14; Perlman and Taft, *History of Labor*, pp. 615–17.

8. Quoted in Romasco, *Poverty of Abundance*, p. 63.

9. *Business Week*, 14 May 1932, pp. 5–6.

10. Bernstein, *Lean Years*, pp. 393–415; Seidman, "Yellow Dog Contract"; Zieger, *Republicans and Labor*, pp. 258–70.

11. Norris, *Fighting Liberal*, p. 309.

12. Robert W. Hansen to George W. Norris, 14 Mar. 1932, Tray 79, Box 7; and Norris press release, 24 Mar. 1932, Tray 42, Box 8, Norris Papers, Library of Congress. See also Bernstein, *Lean Years*, p. 414; and Lowitt, *George W. Norris*, pp. 525–26.

13. Donald R. Richberg to George W. Norris, 11 Feb. 1930, Tray 79, Box 7, Norris Papers; Bernstein, *Lean Years*, pp. 395–403, 410–12.

14. *Congressional Record*, 26 Feb. 1932, pp. 4754–55, 8 Mar. 1932, p. 5465. Felix Frankfurter advised Norris to pursue his advocacy of the anti-injunction bill by stressing some of its more politically neutral benefits, such as "a needed reduction in the litigation that goes to the federal courts instead of an increase in the number of federal judges"—in line with an "impetus of the economy plea" (Frankfurter to Norris, 5 Jan. 1932, Box 87, Frankfurter Papers, Library of Congress).

15. Selznick, *Law, Society, and Industrial Justice*, pp. 135, 212.

16. U.S. House of Representatives, Committee on the Judiciary, *Hearings: Defining and Limiting the Jurisdiction of Courts Sitting in Equity*, pp. 50, 61, 67. For a legal history of the labor provisions of the Clayton Act, see Kutler, "Labor, the Clayton Act, and the Supreme Court."

17. See, in particular, Nash, "Franklin D. Roosevelt and Labor." See also Bernstein, *New Deal Collective Bargaining Policy*, pp. 19–20; Leuchtenburg, "The New Deal and the Analogue of War," pp. 86–88, 118–19; and Saposs, "The American Labor Movement since the War," pp. 238–39.

18. Conner, *National War Labor Board*.

19. It is not at all clear, however, that the president was very impressed with these possible similarities. According to Hugh Johnson (soon to be appointed chief administrator of the National Recovery Administration), in the early spring of 1933 FDR was silently unreceptive to the suggestion that a federal "Labor Policies Board"

might, as part of a general recovery program, serve essentially the same laudable political and administrative purposes as the government's wartime agencies (Johnson, *Blue Eagle*, p. 209).

20. Burns, *Roosevelt*, p. 42.

21. Ibid., pp. 43, 105, 116, 124, 215, 218; Rollins, "Franklin Roosevelt's Introduction to Labor"; Schlesinger, *Coming of the New Deal*, p. 402; Freidel, *The Apprenticeship*, pp. 120–21, 192–206, 330–31; Freidel, *The Ordeal*, pp. 23–25, 263; Freidel, *The Triumph*, pp. 24, 54, 160, 358; Bellush, *Franklin D. Roosevelt as Governor of New York*, pp. 21–22, 207; Fusfeld, *Economic Thought*, pp. 46–47, 50–51, 66–70, 74, 93, 155, 164–65; Tugwell, *In Search of Roosevelt*, p. 242.

22. Rollins, "Franklin Roosevelt's Introduction to Labor," p. 18.

23. Schlesinger, *Crisis of the Old Order*, p. 455.

24. Ibid., pp. 420, 424; Tugwell, "The Protagonists"; Tugwell, *Brains Trust*, pp. 75, 153–54, 170, 172, 174, 270–71, 273, 305, 312, 379, 495–96; Tugwell, *In Search of Roosevelt*, pp. 230, 286–89; Tugwell, *Democratic Roosevelt*, pp. 220–21, 239–42; Moley, *First New Deal*, pp. 6–7, 223–25, 228; Perkins, *The Roosevelt I Knew*, pp. 136–37, 163–64, 166–67; Peel and Donnelly, *1932 Campaign*, chaps. 6–7; Leuchtenburg, *Franklin D. Roosevelt and the New Deal*, p. 33; Freidel, *The Triumph*, pp. 247–49, 331, 342, 356–57; Freidel, *Launching the New Deal*, pp. 60–82, 409; Fusfeld, *Economic Thought*, pp. 202–3, 226, 246–48; Conkin, *FDR and the Origins of the Welfare State*, pp. 10–19; Hofstadter, *American Political Tradition*, chap. 12. Cf. Rosen, *Hoover, Roosevelt, and the Brains Trust*, for a positive assessment of Roosevelt's political flexibility and moderation in the prevailing transitional context of 1932.

25. Moley, *First New Deal*, p. 223. The immediate political consequences of this void in planning were clearly anticipated by John Dickinson in a letter to Felix Frankfurter, 10 Nov. 1932, Box 52, Frankfurter Papers.

26. What I have to say on the "five main currents of thought" is adapted largely from Himmelberg, *Origins of the National Recovery Administration*, chap. 10; and Hawley, *The New Deal and the Problem of Monopoly*, chaps. 1–2.

27. Tugwell, *Brains Trust*, pp. 34–36, 43–44, 57–60, 97–100, 104–5, 129, 132–35, 158, 168–69, 174–75, 277–78, 303–5, 307, 380, 385, 401–11, 416–18, 462, 471–72, 494, 520–21. See also Tugwell, *Democratic Roosevelt*, p. 246; Berle and Jacobs, eds., *Navigating the Rapids*, pp. 56–59; Moley, *After Seven Years*, pp. 23–24; Sternsher, *Rexford Tugwell and the New Deal*, pp. 39–50, 109–21; Hawley, *The New Deal and the Problem of Monopoly*, pp. 13, 44–46; Himmelberg, *Origins of the National Recovery Administration*, pp. 182–83; Leuchtenburg, *Franklin D. Roosevelt and the New Deal*, p. 35; Schlesinger, *Coming of the New Deal*, pp. 179–84; and Rosen, *Hoover, Roosevelt, and the Brains Trust*, pp. 154–56, 318–23. Even Tugwell's "collectivist" tendencies were somewhat ambivalent, as is best indicated in his well-known contemporary study *The Industrial Discipline and the Governmental Arts*.

28. Robert Wagner was one of the first to offer a clear position on this issue: "Will Congress Choose a Way Out of Unemployment?" *American Labor Legislation Review* 20 (Sept. 1930): 293–96. See also Huthmacher, *Senator Robert F. Wagner*, p. 71.

29. Moley went so far as to say that Roosevelt "distrusted public works pro-

foundly" (*After Seven Years*, p. 174). See also Moley, *First New Deal*, pp. 267–71, 273–75; Sargent, *Roosevelt and the Hundred Days*, pp. 254–55, 265–66; Leuchtenburg, *Franklin D. Roosevelt and the New Deal*, p. 52; Schlesinger, *Coming of the New Deal*, p. 95; Huthmacher, *Senator Robert F. Wagner*, pp. 138–39, 142–43; Perkins, *The Roosevelt I Knew*, pp. 268–70; and Himmelberg, *Origins of the National Recovery Administration*, pp. 189–90.

30. Frederick, *Swope Plan*; Harriman, "Stabilization of Business and Employment." For a digest of these and other plans offered as the prospective means of business stabilization, see U.S. Senate, Committee on Finance, *Hearings: Investigation of Economic Problems*, pp. 933–1008.

31. Berle and Jacobs, eds., *Navigating the Rapids*, pp. 62–70, 77.

32. Moley, *First New Deal*, pp. 230–32.

33. Himmelberg, *Origins of the National Recovery Administration*, pp. 185–89; Galambos, *Competition and Cooperation*, pp. 186–94.

34. Himmelberg, *Origins of the National Recovery Administration*, pp. 192–96.

35. Moley, *After Seven Years*, pp. 185–86. See also Moley, *First New Deal*, pp. 285–87.

36. It has been written of Senator David I. Walsh (Democratic governor of Massachusetts during the final years of the Progressive era and later a committed New Dealer more or less representative of those who supported the work-sharing approach), for example, that his deepest political concerns were "directed toward [purely] functional objectives, not structural change. . . . His policies were aimed at the improvement of conditions for the working class. He believed that legislation for their benefit was an economically sound approach. Consumption was the factor which underlay successful production; and wages measured its extent. The market thus defined determined the functioning of the factory system. A general rise in income, therefore, would stimulate industrial expansion. The remedy for inadequate recompense lay in government regulation of hours, wages, and the conditions of labor, and the extension of social benefits for the working class. Their welfare was that of society at large, in which the business community would eventually share" (Grattan, "David I. Walsh and His Associates," pp. 251, 253–54). Hugo Black generally shared Senator Walsh's interpretation of the current economic situation, and he was also deeply concerned about its implications for the basic legitimacy of public authority, warning on one occasion that "the very safety and perpetuity of any government demands that its citizens may by honest work earn their living" (*Congressional Record*, 10 Jan. 1933, p. 1443). George W. Norris, another outstanding supporter of the work-sharing approach in the Senate, cast his warning in the same dire imagery when he admonished the forces of immovable conservatism to take heed of the obvious: "We must readjust our civilization or we are going to sink" (*Congressional Record*, 6 Apr. 1933, p. 1339). See also Lowitt, *George W. Norris*, p. 10.

37. Steve Fraser has developed a highly original perspective on the historical sources of what he identifies as the "anticipatory Keynesianism" of the early New Deal in "From the 'New Unionism' to the New Deal."

38. Rosenof, *Dogma, Depression, and the New Deal*, p. 39. See also Lyon, *National Recovery Administration*, p. 25.

39. Among reform-minded analysts of the Depression, the political debate over re-

covery centered squarely on the concept of "economic maturity." In vogue since the beginning of the downward plunge, this ultimately lamentable achievement was promptly identified as the systemic companion of a marked increase during the previous decade in the level of technological unemployment and generally a condition, as Hugo Black saw it, in which "the possibilities of production have far outdistanced the realities of production." Reminiscent in some respects of Thorstein Veblen's more penetrating assessment of the problem in his 1921 classic *The Engineers and the Price System*, Senator Black's acquaintance with technocratic theory and the notion of economic maturity led him directly to the purchasing power thesis, a doctrine that enabled him and other New Dealers to pursue essentially conservative ends through a professed commitment to universally acknowledged progressive means. As Black put it: "Men without jobs cannot buy. [And] I am not willing to sit silent and permit the capitalistic system to destroy itself by reason of blind adherence to old forms" (quoted in Hamilton, *Hugo Black*, p. 216). Black's remarks on "the realities of production" were delivered in a radio broadcast on 26 May 1937, the text of which can be found in Box 478, Black Papers, Library of Congress. For the concept of economic maturity in the context of the political debate over recovery policy, see Rosenof, *Dogma, Depression, and the New Deal*, chap. 2. Contending viewpoints on this and related issues among professional economists are expertly evaluated by Stoneman, *History of the Economic Analysis*. For a critical discussion of the purchasing power thesis in relation to the actual functioning of the NRA, see Lyon, *National Recovery Administration*, pp. 756–75.

40. Most of the official correspondence pertaining to the minimum wage issue and related topics to be discussed at the 6 March Conference of Governors is contained in the Franklin D. Roosevelt File, Box 1, Moley Papers, Hoover Institution, Palo Alto, Calif. See also Box 150, Frankfurter Papers; Perkins, *The Roosevelt I Knew*, pp. 151–52; Freedman, *Roosevelt and Frankfurter*, pp. 125–26; Bellush, *Franklin D. Roosevelt as Governor of New York*, pp. 194, 200; Fusfeld, *Economic Thought*, pp. 205–6, 245–46, 254; Himmelberg, *Origins of the National Recovery Administration*, pp. 190–92; Leuchtenburg, *Franklin D. Roosevelt and the New Deal*, p. 36; Schlesinger, *Coming of the New Deal*, p. 91; and Rosen, *Hoover, Roosevelt, and the Brains Trust*, who has written (on p. 324) that "if Roosevelt had little contact or sympathy with organized labor in the early years of the New Deal, the labor movement's concrete goals harmonized [nonetheless] with the Brains Trust's aspirations and his own for a better economic balance and attainment of certain economic minima."

41. *Business Week*, 18 Jan. 1933, p. 9.

42. The best account of the genesis of the Black bill is in Farr, *Origins of Recent Labor Policy*, pp. 46–69.

43. Several months earlier, the AFL had asked President Hoover to support the thirty-hour workweek as the single most viable road to recovery, stating: "We challenge industrial management to offer a better plan. We insist that the exigencies and the gravity of the situation demand action. We cannot delay longer. . . . The executive council of the American Federation of Labor now demands and shall continue to demand that industrial management be compelled to act through the pressure of public opinion expressed, as we hope it will be, through the Chief Executive of the nation" (*New York Times*, 21 July 1932, p. 9).

44. U.S. Senate, Committee on the Judiciary, *Hearings: Thirty-Hour Work Week*, Part 2, pp. 330–42, 483–87. See also *Textile World* (1933 Annual), pp. 60–61; and Brandeis, "Organized Labor and Protective Labor Legislation," p. 202.

45. Edwin S. Smith to Frances Perkins, 28 Mar. 1933, Correspondence of Secretary Perkins, Subject File, Box 76, General Records of the U.S. Department of Labor (hereafter Department of Labor Records), National Archives. See also Henry P. Kendall, "The Effect of Uniform Labor Standards on Interstate Competition," typescript, n.d., Box 129, Frankfurter Papers; Frankfurter to Kendall, 18 Nov. 1932; Kendall to Frankfurter, 21 Nov. 1932, ibid., Box 71; *Textile World*, Dec. 1932, p. 65; *Business Week*, 7 Dec. 1932, p. 6, 15 Mar. 1933, p. 18; and Wolfbein, *Decline of a Cotton Textile City*, pp. 126–27.

46. U.S. Senate, Committee on the Judiciary, *Hearings: Thirty-Hour Work Week*, pp. 585–89.

47. *Business Week*, 15 Feb. 1933, p. 3. Other passages from the same dispatch are worth quoting in their entirety: "Businessmen are talking it [the proposed legislative trade-off] over. They want anti-trust law modification badly, worse now than ever before. The proposal is decidedly attractive. The price, at first inspection, does not seem excessive. It is thoroughly appreciated also that if this is a chance for modification, it is the only one. Any casual canvass of Senators yields convincing proof that if a revision of anti-trust laws were to be put through the next session, the result would be stricter laws, not more lenient. . . .

"Meanwhile, sentiment in favor of the shorter week has been growing. Progressives who have been advocating something of the kind have discovered they can get support from conservatives. A considerable number of staunch conservatives are coming rapidly to the belief that shorter hours and wage increases are the only road to solid prosperity. In fact, their chief concern is that they have been unable to suggest any practical means of bringing this about.

"If that were the whole picture the Progressives might start a fight right away to enforce shorter hours and a 5-day week by law. But staring them in the face is the decision of the Supreme Court on the child labor law. No one of them has evolved any way of surmounting that constitutional hurdle.

"That is why the idea of permitting the big interests to 'conspire in restraint of trade' if they will only agree to conspire at the same time to reduce hours and working days per week may be very appealing. So Roosevelt thinks, and so do a few of the business men with whom he has discussed his idea."

48. Bernstein, *New Deal Collective Bargaining Policy*, p. 30.

49. Moley, *First New Deal*, p. 287. The legislative record of the Black bill in the early spring of 1933 notwithstanding, there was still a deep undercurrent of uncertainty about the economic feasibility of such a measure, which ran back to the first serious discussion of a legislated reduction in the length of the workweek during the Hoover administration. See, for instance, a brief but revealing memorandum from Edward E. Hunt to Dr. Julius Klein (both of the Commerce Department), 16 Oct. 1930, Files of E. E. Hunt, Series 1, Tray 419, Records of the President's Organization on Unemployment Relief, National Archives. See also Donald R. Richberg, "The Spread-Work Folly," typescript, 17 Aug. 1932, Subject File, Box 44, Richberg Papers, Library of Congress. For industry's objections to the initial thirty-hour-week

proposal, see, in particular, the testimony of Paul W. Litchfield, chairman of the U.S. Chamber of Commerce Special Committee on Work Periods in Industry, in U.S. Senate, Committee on Finance, *Hearings: Investigation of Economic Problems*, p. 498; U.S. Chamber of Commerce, *Report: Working Periods in Industry*, passim; and Roos, *NRA Economic Planning*, pp. 18–20. See also James A. Emery, general counsel, National Association of Manufacturers, to Daniel C. Roper, 10 Apr. 1933, Box 775, Commerce Records; Donald Comer to Hugo Black, 15 Apr. 1933, Official File 372, Box 1, Roosevelt Papers, Franklin D. Roosevelt Library, Hyde Park, N.Y.; *Business Week*, 19 Apr. 1933, pp. 4–5; T. H. Gerken, "Thirty-Hour Week Would Not Work in the Steel Industry," *Iron Age*, 20 Apr. 1933, pp. 613ff.; *Iron Age*, 13 Apr. 1933, pp. 596–97; and Loth, *Swope of G.E.*, p. 222.

50. U.S. House of Representatives, Committee on Labor, *Hearings: Thirty-Hour Week Bill*, pp. 1–24. See also Perkins, *The Roosevelt I Knew*, pp. 192–96; Martin, *Madam Secretary*, pp. 260–63; and Farr, *Origins of Recent Labor Policy*, pp. 63–64.

51. Hillman, a relentless advocate of the purchasing power thesis, was also an early supporter of federal minimum-wage controls. See, in particular, his "Memorandum—December 1932," which was sent to Frances Perkins for Roosevelt's consideration, Hillman Papers, New York State School of Industrial and Labor Relations, Cornell University, Ithaca, N.Y. See also Soule, *Sidney Hillman*, pp. 165–66; and Fraser, "From the 'New Unionism' to the New Deal."

52. U.S. House of Representatives, Committee on Labor, *Hearings: Thirty-Hour Week Bill*, p. 66, for the Green amendment.

53. U.S. House of Representatives, Committee on Labor, House Report No. 124 to accompany S. 158, 73d Cong., 1st sess., 10 May 1933 (Washington, 1933).

54. National Association of Manufacturers, "Government Control of Industry—and Industry's Alternative," policy declarations adopted at NAM National Emergency Industrial Conference, Washington, D.C., 28 Apr. 1933, Box 775, Commerce Records. See also U.S. House of Representatives, Committee on Labor, *Hearings: Thirty-Hour Week Bill*, particularly the testimony of Alfred P. Sloan, Jr., Thomas W. Lamont, Gerard Swope, Walter C. Teagle, and Henry I. Harriman for the U.S. Chamber of Commerce, as well as James A. Emery of the NAM. For a supplement to Lamont's testimony on behalf of the steel industry, see *Iron Age*, 27 Apr. 1933, p. 677, 4 May 1933, p. 717, and 11 May 1933, p. 746. Excellent detailed accounts of the controversy can be found in Farr, *Origins of Recent Labor Policy*, pp. 64–66; and Himmelberg, *Origins of the National Recovery Administration*, pp. 203–4.

55. *Business Week*, 3 May 1933, p. 9.

56. Ibid., 10 May 1933, p. 3; *Textile World*, May 1933, p. 47, thus satisfying the author's (and presumably much of the textile industry's) only serious objection to the basic thrust of the Perkins amendments, with respect to which he stated: "If we were asked to write a prescription for the textile industry, we could not improve upon the one contained in that bill. In a masterly way, the Secretary summarized all the aspirations of industry itself, or rather of the enlightened majority in industry. The only difference is that we insist the job must be done by industry, and not by government." See also *Textile World*, May 1933, pp. 50–51; U.S. House of Representatives, Committee on Labor, *Hearings: Thirty-Hour Week Bill*, testimony of Henry P. Kendall; and A. C. Stapter to Robert F. Wagner, 9 May 1933, Wagner Papers.

57. U.S. House of Representatives, Committee on Labor, *Hearings: Thirty-Hour Week Bill*, p. 18. See also Perkins, *The Roosevelt I Knew*, p. 196.

58. Huthmacher, *Senator Robert F. Wagner*, pp. 143–46. See also Himmelberg, *Origins of the National Recovery Administration*, pp. 195, 199–200.

59. See Lauck, *New Industrial Revolution*, for an excellent example of the labor economist's critique.

60. Lauck to Lewis, 20 Nov. 1929, 13 May 1930, 8 July 1930, 26 Aug. 1931; Lewis to Lauck, 31 Aug. 1931; Lauck to Lewis, 4 Sept. 1931, all in Box 39, Lauck Papers.

61. W. Jett Lauck to Philip Murray, 12 Aug. 1932, Box 41, Lauck Papers. See also Lauck to FDR, 11 Oct. 1932, ibid., Box 44, in which Lauck attempts to persuade the Democratic presidential candidate "to make a statement" in support of stabilization legislation.

62. "Docket—Coal & Stabilization," 25–27 Apr. 1933, Box 172, Lauck Papers. See also W. Jett Lauck to John L. Lewis, 27 Apr. 1933, ibid., Box 39, in which Lauck reports that his "effort has been to secure the adoption of a plan which would provide for a general recovery and stabilization board under which there would be similar boards for each major industry which would proceed in accordance with the provisions of the coal bill. If I am successful in this, we would then have a coal stabilization board proceeding in general along the lines of the Davis-Kelly Bill, and our purposes in this direction would be accomplished." Cf. Lewis, "Labor and the National Recovery Administration," p. 58; McFarland, *Roosevelt, Lewis, and the New Deal*, pp. 17–18; Dubofsky and Van Tine, *John L. Lewis*, pp. 182–83; and Huthmacher, *Senator Robert F. Wagner*, pp. 146–47. Three separate drafts of the legislative proposal prepared by the Moulton-Lauck subcommittee (dated 28 April, 29 April, and 1 May 1933), all titled, "A bill to create employment and purchasing power through the revival of industry," are in Box 285, Lauck Papers.

63. Himmelberg, *Origins of the National Recovery Administration*, p. 201.

64. Ibid., pp. 201–2.

65. John Dickinson to Raymond Moley, 26 Apr. 1933 (and enclosed memorandums), Indexed Correspondence, Box 67, Moley Papers.

66. Moley, *First New Deal*, p. 288. See also Himmelberg, *Origins of the National Recovery Administration*, p. 203.

67. Huthmacher, *Senator Robert F. Wagner*, p. 147. See also "Docket—Coal & Stabilization," 2–3 May 1933, Boxes 165 and 172, Lauck Papers.

68. W. Jett Lauck to John L. Lewis, 5 May 1933, Box 39, Lauck Papers. In the same letter, Lauck, brimming with optimism, also wrote that he did "not see any reason why the coal bill as drafted should not be passed at this session [of Congress along with the recovery bill], and I hope that some way may be found for bringing it out. If it does not, however, and everything goes well with the other bill, it will suit our purposes almost as well. Fundamentally, it will be all right as a basis for organizing the industry."

69. Himmelberg, *Origins of the National Recovery Administration*, pp. 204–5.

70. Rosenman, ed., *Public Papers and Addresses*, 2:155–58.

71. John H. Fahey to Daniel C. Roper, 16 May 1933, Box 4, Commerce Records. See also Henry I. Harriman to Roosevelt, 11 May 1933, Official File 466, Box 1,

Roosevelt Papers; Moley, *First New Deal*, p. 290; Schlesinger, *Coming of the New Deal*, p. 97; and Himmelberg, *Origins of the National Recovery Administration*, pp. 205–6.

72. For the complete text of the National Industrial Recovery Act, see Lyon, *National Recovery Administration*, Appendix A. Title II of the NIRA authorized the president to create an emergency Public Works Administration with the initial authority to expend up to $3.3 billion on highways, dams, federal buildings, and various other public construction projects.

73. See, for instance, "Docket—Coal & Stabilization," 3 May 1933, Box 165, Lauck Papers, in which Lauck writes of his arrival in Washington only to "read in the New York Times that a conference of the Manufacturers Association and the Chamber of Commerce representatives had been arranged with Senator Wagner. I called up Assistant Counsel Gall of the Association who informed me that this was a movement on their part growing out of their general determination to play ball with the Act, or, in other words, not to needlessly oppose it or its labor provisions. I advised Mr. Warrum [Henry Warrum, general counsel for the UMW] over the telephone about the conference, and he said he would look out for it but had no fear on account of Senator Wagner's attitude."

74. U.S. House of Representatives, Committee on Ways and Means, *Hearings: National Industrial Recovery*, pp. 117–18.

75. Robert L. Lund to Daniel C. Roper, 27 May 1933, Box 774, Commerce Records. Farr, *Origins of Recent Labor Policy*, is an excellent guide to the congressional debate on Section 7a, especially pp. 72–76, 78–94, 101–2, 105. See also Bernstein, *New Deal Collective Bargaining Policy*, pp. 33–39; and *Iron Age*, 8 June 1933, pp. 917-A-C; as well as the relevant public documents: U.S. House of Representatives, Committee on Ways and Means, *Hearings: National Industrial Recovery*; and U.S. Senate, Committee on Finance, *Hearings: National Industrial Recovery*.

76. Himmelberg, *Origins of the National Recovery Administration*, p. 207.

77. Robert L. Lund to Hugh S. Johnson, 3 July 1933, Box 774, Commerce Records. See also Lund to Daniel C. Roper, 3 July 1933, ibid.; Bureau of Foreign and Domestic Commerce, "Bulletin No. 8," 17 June 1933 (mimeo), Box 8447, Records of the National Recovery Administration (hereafter NRA Records), National Archives; *Commercial and Financial Chronicle*, 17 June 1933, p. 4199; and *Steel*, 19 June 1933, p. 20.

78. The President's Reemployment Agreement could best be described as a voluntary precode contract. Its adherents were authorized to display the insignia of the Navajo thunderbird, or Blue Eagle, which was later used to signal compliance with the NRA industrial codes. In the PRA pledge, under the terms of a so-called "blanket code," a compliant firm promised to end child labor, to pay a minimum wage to all employees (from thirty to forty cents an hour), and to limit the number of working hours for certain specified groups of employees to a total of either forty or thirty-five per week. Officially instituted on 1 August 1933, the PRA campaign had its origins in Hugh Johnson's desire to stimulate greater haste on the part of industry generally in the final code formulation process. See Himmelberg, *Origins of the National Recovery Administration*, p. 210, who is of the opinion that other motives may have been involved as well.

79. "Joint Statement Concerning Section 7(a) of the National Industrial Recovery Act," 24 Aug. 1933, Subject File, Box 45, Richberg Papers. See also "Employee Representation: Chronological History of Interpretations," n.d., General Correspondence of the Industrial Advisory Board, 1933–35; Raymond S. Rubinow, "Section 7(a): Its History, Interpretation and Administration," Work Materials No. 45, a section of Part E, *The Labor Program under the NRA*, Mar. 1936, pp. 50–57, Division of Review, Labor Studies Section, Box 7055; Minutes of the Special Industrial Recovery Board, 18 July 1933, p. 23, Boxes 8462–63; Minutes of the Industrial Advisory Board, 3 Aug. 1933, p. 5, 24 Aug. 1933, pp. 1–2, Boxes 8415–16, all in NRA Records; Fred I. Kent to H. H. Heimann, 27 July 1933, Box 784, Commerce Records; and *Business Week*, 15 July 1933, pp. 7–8, 9 Sept. 1933, pp. 4–5. For a general account of the many political uncertainties facing business during the first few weeks after the adoption of the recovery act, see Himmelberg, *Origins of the National Recovery Administration*, pp. 207–9.

80. Minutes of the Industrial Advisory Board, 30 Aug. 1933, pp. 1–4, 1 Sept. 1933, p. 2, 7 Sept. 1933, pp. 1–3, 3 Oct. 1933, pp. 4–6, 5 Oct. 1933, p. 2; and Minutes of the Joint Meeting of the Labor and Industrial Advisory Boards, 7 Sept. 1933, pp. 1–4, 12 Sept. 1933, pp. 1–5, Boxes 8415–16, NRA Records. See also Minutes of the Special Industrial Recovery Board, 11 Sept. 1933, pp. 22–24, ibid., Boxes 8462–63; as well as a perceptive appraisal of the situation by Saposs, "American Labor Movement since the War," pp. 249–50. The open-shop controversy was a particularly contentious issue in the steel industry. See, for instance, *Iron Age*, 3 Aug. 1933, pp. 41–46, 10 Aug. 1933, pp. 40–41, and 17 Aug. 1933, pp. 36–37.

81. "Protection for Wages above the Minimum," n.d., NRA Staff Studies, Division of Industrial Economics, pt. 3, chap. 12, p. 25, Box 8127, NRA Records. See also Farr, *Origins of Recent Labor Policy*, p. 98.

82. Felix Frankfurter to Donald Richberg, 7 July 1933, Box 159, Frankfurter Papers.

83. Johnson, *Blue Eagle*, p. 201; "Argument on S. 3055 (Walsh-Healy Bill)," n.d., Wagner Papers. See also Alexander Sachs, "National Recovery Administration Policies and the Problem of Economic Planning," Swarthmore College Lectures on America's Recovery Program, Oxford University Press (typescript summary, n.d.), p. 2, Box 779, Commerce Records. The underconsumption/purchasing power interpretation of the Depression and its relationship to the "underlying purposes" of Title I of the recovery act are analyzed in what one might call "world-historical perspective" in a five-page communication from Felix Frankfurter to Robert Wagner, 30 May 1933, Wagner Papers; also Box 159, Frankfurter Papers.

84. U.S. House of Representatives, Committee on Ways and Means, *Hearings: National Industrial Recovery*, especially the testimony of Richberg and Harriman, pp. 67, 91, 134. See also "Legislative History of NIRA," n.d., NRA Staff Studies, Division of Industrial Economics, pt. 1, chap. 4, pp. 123–25, Box 8126, NRA Records. Roosevelt represented the issue in very much the same manner. In a 7 May "fireside chat," for instance, he remarked that "the so-called anti-trust laws were intended to prevent the creation of monopolies and to forbid unreasonable profits to those monopolies. That purpose of the anti-trust laws must be continued," he agreed, "but these laws were never intended to encourage the kind of unfair competition that results in

long hours, starvation wages and overproduction" (quoted in Galambos, *Competition and Cooperation*, p. 198).

85. The political background of this debate is developed in the context of a more general analysis of the Depression experience by Mulder, "Insurgent Progressives."

86. *Congressional Record*, debates of 9 and 13 June 1933, passim; "Legislative History of NIRA," n.d., NRA Staff Studies, Division of Industrial Economics, pt. 1, chap. 4, pp. 135–37, Box 8126, NRA Records; Hawley, *The New Deal and the Problem of Monopoly*, pp. 29–31; Schlesinger, *Coming of the New Deal*, pp. 100–101; Freidel, *Launching the New Deal*, pp. 450–52; Leuchtenburg, *Franklin D. Roosevelt and the New Deal*, p. 58; Roos, *NRA Economic Planning*, pp. 45–46, 50–51; Huthmacher, *Senator Robert F. Wagner*, pp. 148–51.

# Chapter 5

1. For the concept of "political capitalism" in its original historiographical context, see Kolko, *Triumph of Conservatism*, p. 3. For the underlying fragility of the New Deal consensus, see Hawley, *The New Deal and the Problem of Monopoly*, pp. 52–90.

2. Minutes of the Special Industrial Recovery Board, 14 Aug. 1933, pp. 9–10, 18 Sept. 1933, pp. 5–7, Boxes 8462–63, Records of the National Recovery Administration (hereafter NRA Records), National Archives; "The NRA Compliance Problem," n.d., pt. 1, chap. 3, pp. 57–65; "Labor's Role in the Administration of the Act," n.d., pt. 3, chap. 2, pp. 11, 38–44; and "The Experience with the Labor Program under the NIRA," n.d., pt. 3, chap. 21, pp. 2, 8, 10, NRA Staff Studies, Division of Industrial Economics, Boxes 8126–27, ibid.; National Recovery Administration, Division of Review, "Code Compliance Activities of the National Recovery Administration," Work Materials No. 61, Mar. 1936, pp. 15–16, Box 7057, ibid. See also National Recovery Administration, *Report of the President's Committee of Industrial Analysis*, pp. 107, 157–59; and Elinore M. Herrick (New York Regional Labor Board), "Enforcement of Codes through Organized Labor," n.d., Wagner Papers.

3. Reprinted in Stein, *Out of the Sweatshop*, pp. 229–30.

4. *Business Week*, 22 July 1933, p. 7.

5. Carpenter, *Competition and Collective Bargaining*, p. 593.

6. Quoted in Robinson, *Collective Bargaining and Market Control*, p. 103.

7. Carpenter, *Competition and Collective Bargaining*, p. 625.

8. Quoted in ibid., p. 595. See also Robinson, *Collective Bargaining and Market Control*, pp. 104ff.

9. National Recovery Administration, Division of Industrial Economics, "History of the Code of Fair Competition for the Coat and Suit Industry," p. 84, Box 7573, NRA Records.

10. National Recovery Administration, Division of Review, "The Men's Clothing Industry," Work Materials No. 58, Mar. 1936, p. 8, Box 7057, NRA Records; Connery, *Administration of an NRA Code*, pp. 8–21.

11. Quoted in Carpenter, *Competition and Collective Bargaining*, p. 607.

12. Ibid., pp. 622–29.

13. ILGWU, *Financial and Statistical Report*, 6 May 1971, pp. 44–45, rpt. in Brandes, "From Sweatshop to Stability," p. 132, table 1.

14. The forty-hour limitation in the cotton garment code (among a number of other provisions) was intended to correspond to the strictures of the NRA code for the cotton textile industry. All of the other garment codes prescribed a maximum thirty-five-hour week.

15. M. Harris (Levin & Harris Shirt Co., New York) to the Industrial Advisory Board, 3 Oct. 1933; and M. Harris to Thomas R. Taylor, 16 Oct. 1933, both in General Correspondence of the Industrial Advisory Board, 1933–35, NRA Records.

16. U.S. Bureau of the Census, *Census of Manufactures: 1933*, pp. 184, 193–94; *Census of Manufactures: 1935*, pp. 363, 365, 395, 398.

17. National Recovery Administration, Division of Review, "Report of the Commission for the Coat and Suit Industry," Work Materials No. 10, Mar. 1936, pp. 65, 67–68, 72, Box 7050, NRA Records.

18. Stein, *Out of the Sweatshop*, p. 241. See also Robinson, *Collective Bargaining and Market Control*, p. 119.

19. J. R. McMullen to Robert F. Wagner, 5 Apr. 1935, Wagner Papers. See also Samuel Klein, executive director, Industrial Council of Cloak, Suit, and Skirt Manufacturers, to Robert F. Wagner, ibid.; U.S. House of Representatives, Committee on Ways and Means, *Hearings: Extension of NIRA*, p. 514 and passim. Testimony of a similar nature was presented earlier before the U.S. Senate, Committee on Finance, *Hearings: Investigation of the National Recovery Administration*, a useful summary of which appears in a "Memorandum Supporting Extension of the NIRA Based upon the Testimony Presented to the Senate Committee on Finance," n.d., Box 8296, NRA Records.

20. Marx Lewis, executive secretary, United Hatters, Cap and Millinery Workers International Union, to R. M. Wilmotte, 2 July 1935, General Correspondence of the Labor Advisory Board, Subject File, Boxes 8180–90, NRA Records. See also Marx Lewis to R. M. Wilmotte, 29 June 1935, ibid.; and *Business Week*, 1 June 1935, p. 8.

21. *Monthly Labor Review* 42 (Apr. 1936): 934–38.

22. Carpenter, *Competition and Collective Bargaining*, p. 815.

23. Ibid. See also Robinson, *Collective Bargaining and Market Control*, chap. 5.

24. Untitled report of the Millinery Stabilization Commission, New York, 1937, p. 11, Box 8481, NRA Records.

25. See, primarily, Johnson, "Drafting the NRA Code"; and Johnson, *Politics of Soft Coal*, pp. 150–63, 165–71. See also Parker, *Coal Industry*, pp. 107–10; and Berquist, *Economic Survey*, 1:188–90; 2:302–3. For the catalyzing organizational accomplishments of the UMW during the code negotiations, see "Docket—Coal & Stabilization," 19 June 1933, Box 165, Lauck Papers; "Appalachian Agreements, 1934" (typescript), pp. 1–5, Box 12, Edward A. Wieck Papers, Archives of Urban and Labor Affairs, Wayne State University, Detroit, Mich.; Dubofsky and Van Tine, *John L. Lewis*, pp. 185–90; and Bernstein, *Turbulent Years*, pp. 40–61. For a behind-the-scenes glimpse of the code negotiations, see Felix Frankfurter's memorandum of 6 Sept. 1933, rpt. in Freedman, *Roosevelt and Frankfurter*, pp. 150–55.

26. Parker, *Coal Industry*, pp. 110–13; Berquist, *Economic Survey*, 2:303–8.

27. *Coal Age*, Oct. 1933, pp. 325–26.

28. Berquist, *Economic Survey*, 2:308–11.

29. Ibid., pp. 311–13. See also Johnson, *Politics of Soft Coal*, pp. 185–87.

30. Berquist, *Economic Survey*, 2:315. See also *Business Week*, 21 Apr. 1934, p. 14.

31. Berquist, *Economic Survey*, 2:316–22. See also "Appalachian Agreements, 1934," pp. 10–13, Wieck Papers; and Johnson, *Politics of Soft Coal*, pp. 187–88.

32. Johnson, *Politics of Soft Coal*, chap. 7, discusses the issue of bituminous pricing under the NRA in much more elaborate detail than I am able to provide here.

33. *Coal Age*, Oct. 1934, p. 380.

34. Parker, *Coal Industry*, pp. 125–26. See also U.S. Congress, Temporary National Economic Committee, *Economic Standards of Government Price Control*, p. 257.

35. *Coal Age*, Feb. 1935, p. 54.

36. J. P. Williams, Jr., president, National Coal Association, to Clay Williams, chairman, National Industrial Recovery Board, 1 Feb. 1935, Subject File, Box 45, Richberg Papers. See also *Coal Age*, Feb. 1935, p. 51.

37. Johnson, *Politics of Soft Coal*, pp. 217–19. See also *Proceedings of the Thirty-Fourth Constitutional Convention of the United Mine Workers of America*, Washington, D.C., 28 Jan.–7 Feb. 1936, 4 vols. (Washington, 1936), 1:26–27.

38. John L. Lewis to Robert F. Wagner, 11 Apr. 1935, Wagner Papers.

39. W. Jett Lauck's optimistic (but by all other indications inaccurate) assessment of the situation was that "operators and districts representing more than 50 percent of the tonnage of the industry are supporting the Guffey Bill." See his "Memorandum for Mr. Lewis," 2 Mar. 1935, Box 278, Lauck Papers. Cf. Johnson, *Politics of Soft Coal*, p. 220.

40. U.S. Senate, Subcommittee of the Committee on Interstate Commerce, *Hearings: Stabilization of the Bituminous Coal Mining Industry*, p. 233; *Coal Age*, Apr. 1935, p. 168.

41. Charles O'Neill (National Conference of Bituminous Coal Operators) to the members of Congress, 17 Aug. 1935, Wagner Papers; *Coal Age*, Aug. 1935, pp. 354ff., Feb. 1936, p. 44. See also U.S. House of Representatives, Subcommittee of the Committee on Ways and Means, *Hearings: Stabilization of the Bituminous Coal Mining Industry*, passim; *Business Week*, 8 June 1935, pp. 16–17; U.S. Congress, Temporary National Economic Committee, *Economic Standards of Government Price Control*, p. 258.

42. Mr. Dewey to Mr. Kerwin (confidential memorandum), 25 May 1935, Case File 182/471, Records of the Federal Mediation and Conciliation Service (hereafter FMCS Records).

43. Oddly, even J. D. A. Morrow and several other former supporters of the Guffey-Snyder bill among the operators now also rejected it on constitutional grounds. See Morrow's testimony, House Committee on Ways and Means, *Hearings: Stabilization of the Bituminous Coal Mining Industry*, pp. 268–69.

44. W. P. Tams, Jr., president, Gulf Smokeless Coal Co., to the Secretary of Labor, 29 July 1935, Correspondence of Secretary Perkins, Subject File, Box 11, Gen-

eral Records of the U.S. Department of Labor; Committee Against Guffey Coal Bill, memorandum to members of Congress re H.R. 9100, 19 Aug. 1935, Wagner Papers; "Views of Various Coal Fields re Guffey Coal Bill," n.d., General Correspondence of the Industrial Advisory Board, NRA Records; Andrew Pangrace, "Preliminary Abstract of Work on Labor Compliance Activities of the Bituminous Coal Labor Boards," 15 Nov. 1935, p. 58, Records of the Organization Studies Section, Preliminary Drafts of Reports, ibid., Box 7739; Berquist, *Economic Survey*, 2:323–28; *Coal Age*, Aug. 1935, pp. 353–54; Hawley, *The New Deal and the Problem of Monopoly*, pp. 207–8; Johnson, *Politics of Soft Coal*, pp. 221–23.

45. For the details, see James F. Dewey to H. L. Kerwin, "Re Bituminous Coal Strike," 8 Oct. 1935, Case File 182/471, FMCS Records. See also Dubofsky and Van Tine, *John L. Lewis*, p. 374.

46. Berquist, *Economic Survey*, 2:329; U.S. National Labor Relations Board, "Effect of Labor Relations," p. 42.

47. *Coal Age*, Sept. 1935, p. 360.

48. The best source for the extent of operator resistance to the code, both in and out of the courts, is the files of the short-lived NBCC: General Correspondence, Box 9, Records of the National Bituminous Coal Commission, 1935–36, National Archives. See also *Business Week*, 2 Nov. 1935, p. 14.

49. Parker, *Coal Industry*, p. 141. See also *Business Week*, 4 Jan. 1936, p. 16.

50. *Carter* v. *Carter Coal Co.*, 298 U.S. 238 (1936), decided on the precedent of the *Schechter* case and the opinion that the labor provisions of the Guffey Act (which were virtually inseparable from the price provisions of the measure) sought to regulate an aspect of production having only an indirect effect upon interstate commerce. See U.S. Congress, Senate, Senate Report No. 2370 to accompany S. 4668, 74th Cong., 2d sess., 15 June 1936 (Washington, 1936), pp. 7ff. See also Kelly and Harbison, *American Constitution*, pp. 747–49; and Johnson, *Politics of Soft Coal*, pp. 224–28.

51. Johnson, *Politics of Soft Coal*, pp. 228–31.

52. U.S. Senate, Committee on Interstate Commerce, *Hearings: To Regulate Interstate Commerce in Bituminous Coal*, pp. 46–65, 70–77, 125–31, 157–71, 195–213; *Coal Age*, June 1936, p. 260, July 1936, p. 301, Feb. 1937, pp. 95–96; *Proceedings of the Thirty-Fifth Constitutional Convention of the United Mine Workers of America*, Washington, D.C., 25 Jan.–3 Feb. 1938, 2 vols. (Washington, 1938), 2:54–55. See also U.S. National Labor Relations Board, "Effect of Labor Relations," pp. 45–47.

53. *Coal Age*, June 1936, p. 261.

54. Donald Richberg to James Roosevelt, 17 Feb. 1938, General Correspondence, Box 2, Richberg Papers. See also *Business Week*, 28 Aug. 1937, pp. 18, 20, 22; Parker, *Coal Industry*, pp. 144–48; Hawley, *The New Deal and the Problem of Monopoly*, pp. 210–11; and Johnson, *Politics of Soft Coal*, pp. 231–35.

55. *Coal Age*, June 1936, p. 261. The best consecutive twelve-month period for the industry in at least a decade occurred in 1936. Bituminous coal, however, was still commonly being marketed below cost, which resulted in an aggregate industrywide loss for the year of about $6.5 million (U.S. Congress, Temporary National Economic Committee, *Economic Standards of Government Price Control*, p. 266).

56. *Coal Age*, July 1937, p. 303. See also Baratz, *The Union and the Coal Indus-*

*try*, chaps. 7–8; Glasser, "Union Wage Policy"; and Johnson, *Politics of Soft Coal*, pp. 236–38.

57. The rate of employee compensation per unit of labor time worked in bituminous mining increased between 1939 and 1953 by more than 350 percent. As a result, the "employment cost" per ton of coal mined increased during the same period by more than a factor of two, whereas the overall productivity of the industry improved by only about one-fourth (U.S. Bureau of Labor Statistics, "Technological Change," p. 120; Kendrick, *Productivity Trends*, p. 400).

# Chapter 6

1. George A. Sloan to Roosevelt, 10 May 1933, Official File 372, Box 1, Roosevelt Papers. See also Galambos, *Competition and Cooperation*, pp. 178–203; and Hodges, "New Deal Labor Policy and the Southern Cotton Textile Industry," p. 165.

2. Galambos, *Competition and Cooperation*, pp. 204–5.

3. Ibid., pp. 208–12.

4. Ibid., pp. 213–14; National Recovery Administration, Division of Industrial Economics, "History of the Code of Fair Competition for the Cotton Textile Industry," Exhibit 3, p. 4, Box 7571, NRA Records.

5. *Textile World*, July 1933, p. 50.

6. Transcript of Code Hearing No. 1, 27–29 June 1933, Box 7152, NRA Records. See also Galambos, *Competition and Cooperation*, pp. 216–25; Hodges, "New Deal Labor Policy and the Southern Cotton Textile Industry," pp. 176–88; and *Textile World*, July 1933, pp. 50–53.

7. George A. Sloan, "How the Oldest Code Is Working," *Nation's Business*, Feb. 1934, pp. 17–18, 65. See also Oscar W. Gridley to Robert F. Wagner, 29 Aug. 1933, Wagner Papers; *Business Week*, 2 Sept. 1933, pp. 9–10; *Textile World*, Dec. 1933, p. 85, Feb. 1934, p. 61, Apr. 1934, p. 104; Backman and Gainsburgh, *Economics of the Cotton Textile Industry*, p. 212, table 47; Hodges, "New Deal Labor Policy and the Southern Cotton Textile Industry," pp. 194–98.

8. Comments by Donald Comer (president, Avondale Mills, Birmingham, Alabama) before the NRA Committee of Code Authorities, Washington, D.C., 6 Mar. 1934, General Correspondence of the Industrial Advisory Board, 1933–35, NRA Records; "Wages and Hours of Labor in Cotton-Goods Manufacturing," *Monthly Labor Review* 35 (July 1932): 150–56; Tolles, "Regional Differences in Cotton-Textile Wages," pp. 37–38. See also Hodges, "New Deal Labor Policy and the Southern Cotton Textile Industry," pp. 199–200.

9. Hodges, "New Deal Labor Policy and the Southern Cotton Textile Industry," pp. 201–6. See also *Business Week*, 11 Aug. 1934, pp. 15–16. Galambos, on the other hand, tends to stress the industry's relative contentment with the code: *Competition and Cooperation*, esp. pp. 255–56.

10. Galambos, *Competition and Cooperation*, pp. 230–33. See also Hodges, "New Deal Labor Policy and the Southern Cotton Textile Industry," pp. 219–24.

11. See, for instance, "Confidential Memorandum," H. Weiss to L. C. Marshall, 27 Aug. 1934, Hillman Papers.

12. U.S. Bureau of Labor Statistics, "Textile Report, Part I: Wage Rates and Weekly Earnings in the Cotton Goods Industry from July 1933 to August 1934," 4 Feb. 1935 (mimeo), Box 8467, NRA Records; "Cotton Textile Industry: Examples of Benefits under the Code," n.d., ibid., Box 8376; Hinrichs, "Wage Rates and Weekly Earnings in the Cotton-Textile Industry," pp. 623–25. See also *Textile World*, Mar. 1934, pp. 62–63; Galambos, *Competition and Cooperation*, pp. 243–46, 257; and Hodges, "New Deal Labor Policy and the Southern Cotton Textile Industry," pp. 225–27, 258–60.

13. Galambos, *Competition and Cooperation*, pp. 257–60; Hodges, "New Deal Labor Policy and the Southern Cotton Textile Industry," pp. 240–41.

14. Galambos, *Competition and Cooperation*, p. 260.

15. Memorandum, V. S. Von Szeliski to Prentiss L. Coonley, 22 Aug. 1934, Personal Files of Victor S. Von Szeliski, Research and Planning Division, Box 7414, NRA Records.

16. Bernstein, *Turbulent Years*, pp. 298–315, is the best general account of the 1934 textile workers' strike.

17. "Report of the Board of Inquiry for the Cotton Textile Industry to the President," 20 Sept. 1934, Hillman Papers.

18. Backman and Gainsburgh, *Economics of the Cotton Textile Industry*, p. 212, table 47. See also Galambos, *Competition and Cooperation*, pp. 264, 269; Hodges, "New Deal Labor Policy and the Southern Cotton Textile Industry," pp. 231–34, 260, 329–30; and Wolfbein, *Decline of a Cotton Textile City*, p. 128.

19. Robert M. Harris to Raymond V. Ingersoll, 11 Sept. 1934, Correspondence of the President's Board of Inquiry for the Cotton Textile Industry, Box 4476, NRA Records; Memorandum, Leon Henderson to Donald Richberg, 12 Jan. 1935, Office Files of Leon Henderson, ibid., Box 7402. See also Hodges, "New Deal Labor Policy and the Southern Cotton Textile Industry," pp. 330–31.

20. Memorandum, Charles E. Wyzanski to Secretary of Labor Perkins, 27 Dec. 1934, Correspondence of Secretary Perkins, Subject File, Box 75, Department of Labor Records. See also Galambos, *Competition and Cooperation*, pp. 269–70; and Hodges, "New Deal Labor Policy and the Southern Cotton Textile Industry," p. 332.

21. Donald Comer to Harry Hopkins, 5 Oct. 1934, Subject File of Leon Henderson, Box 7399, NRA Records; Turner W. Battle to Frances Perkins, 18 Sept. 1934, Correspondence of Secretary Perkins, Subject File, Box 33, Department of Labor Records.

22. Backman and Gainsburgh, *Economics of the Cotton Textile Industry*, p. 212, table 47; Galambos, *Competition and Cooperation*, p. 286, table 12; *Business Week*, 12 Jan. 1935, pp. 20–21; Memorandum, "Difficulties Faced by the Cotton Textile Industry," A. F. Hinrichs to the secretary, 19 Apr. 1935, Correspondence of Secretary Perkins, Subject File, Box 75, Department of Labor Records; Daniel C. Roper to Franklin D. Roosevelt, 19 Apr. 1935; Roper to Roosevelt, 14 Aug. 1935, Correspondence of Secretary Roper, Box 2, General Records of the U.S. Department of Commerce; "Cabinet Committee's Recommendations for Cotton-Textile Industry," *Monthly Labor Review* 41 (Oct. 1935): 944–46.

23. U.S. House of Representatives, Subcommittee of the Committee on Labor, *Hearings: To Rehabilitate and Stabilize Labor Conditions in the Textile Industry*, passim. See also F. B. Williams to Hugo Black, 4 Feb. 1936; Black to John J. Sparkman, 15 Feb. 1936; and Black to Leslie Thornthwaite, 29 Apr. 1936, Box 170, Black Papers.

24. U.S. House of Representatives, Subcommittee of the Committee on Labor, *Hearings: To Regulate the Textile Industry*.

25. George A. Sloan to Kenneth P. Budd, 21 July 1937, Box 579, Edward R. Stettinius, Jr., Papers, Alderman Library, University of Virginia, Charlottesville.

26. *Textile World*, June 1936, p. 76, Dec. 1936, p. 64, Apr. 1937, p. 107, 1937 Annual, p. 113; Hodges, "New Deal Labor Policy and the Southern Cotton Textile Industry," pp. 354–55; Backman and Gainsburgh, *Economics of the Cotton Textile Industry*, p. 173, table 12; Galambos, *Competition and Cooperation*, pp. 288–89; Tolles, "Regional Differences in Cotton-Textile Wages," p. 38, table 1; U.S. Bureau of Labor Statistics, "Wages in Cotton-Goods Manufacturing," p. 71; U.S. Congress, Temporary National Economic Committee, *Industrial Wage Rates, Labor Costs and Price Policies*, pp. 43–59.

27. U.S. Bureau of Labor Statistics, "Wages in Cotton-Goods Manufacturing," p. 72; Wolfbein, *Decline of a Cotton-Textile City*, p. 134; Bernstein, *Turbulent Years*, pp. 620–21; *Textile World*, Aug. 1937, p. 70; *Congressional Record*, 23 May 1938, p. 7304.

28. U.S. Department of Labor, *Proceedings of the National Conference for Labor Legislation*; Rosenman, ed., *Public Papers and Addresses*, 3:259–60; Leon Henderson, "N.R.A." (typescript report), 27 June 1934, p. 6, President's Secretary's File, Box 115, Roosevelt Papers.

29. According to Frances Perkins, FDR's interest in bringing wage-and-hour legislation out at this time was inspired at least in part by the desire to find an issue that might serve to reunite the Democratic majority in Congress in the wake of the recent uproar over the famous "court packing" episode. See *The Roosevelt I Knew*, pp. 256–57; Rosenman, ed., *Public Papers and Addresses*, 4:209–14; Felt, "Child Labor Provisions."

30. *Business Week*, 10 Sept. 1938, p. 14.

31. Ibid.

32. *Textile World*, July 1937, p. 63.

33. There was the usual "ritualistic" opposition from the National Association of Manufacturers and the U.S. Chamber of Commerce, but *Business Week* captured the essence of the issue months before the bill was finally enacted: "The wage-hour bill has its roots in the textile industry, and, as circumstances have shaped up, it will be strange if the pattern for all industry is not cut by Congress with that in mind" (3 July 1937, p. 24).

34. In Alabama, business opposition to the wage-and-hour bill seems to have been centered in both the lumber and textile industries: Box 159, Black Papers.

35. Daugherty, "Economic Coverage." In July 1937 the average hourly hiring rate for unskilled labor in twenty selected industries, not including textiles, was 49.5 cents in six New England states compared to 40.8 cents in nine South Atlantic states, in-

cluding the District of Columbia (*Business Week*, 18 Dec. 1937, p. 26). See also ibid., 29 May 1937, p. 14, 26 June 1937, pp. 17–18, 18 June 1938, pp. 13–14; *Congressional Record*, 24 May 1938, p. 7415.

36. A comment such as that made by Walter Lippmann in the pages of the *New York Herald Tribune* on 21 May 1938 that the FLSA was "in truth a sectional bill disguised as humanitarian reform" was a partially misleading, if essentially accurate, characterization of a complex political-economic reality. See *Congressional Record*, 23 May 1938, p. 7305; also Hyman L. Battle to Hugo L. Black, 2 Aug. 1937, Box 164, Black Papers; *Textile World*, Nov. 1937, pp. 106–9; *Business Week*, 21 May 1938, p. 14; and Hodges, "New Deal Labor Policy and the Southern Cotton Textile Industry," pp. 416–19, 425–26. The best step-by-step legislative history of the Black-Connery bill is Douglas and Hackman, "The Fair Labor Standards Act of 1938." See also Forsythe, "Legislative History"; and Patterson, *Congressional Conservatism and the New Deal*, pp. 149–54.

37. *Congressional Record*, 14 Dec. 1937, Appendix, pp. 517–18.

38. U.S. Senate, Committee on Education and Labor, and U.S. House of Representatives, Committee on Labor, *Fair Labor Standards Act of 1937*, p. 814.

# Chapter 7

1. Brody, "Labor and the Great Depression," p. 235.

2. Perhaps the most direct clarification of the administration's position on the question came early in December 1933, when chief NRA administrator Hugh Johnson assured the National Association of Manufacturers that, although the government had a mandate under the recovery act "to foster the organization of industry for cooperative action among the trade groups," he was quite sure it had "no such mandate as to labor" (*NRA Notes*, Jan. 1934, p. 2, quoted in Foner, "Some Reflections on Ideology and American Labor History," p. 471). Cf. Johnson, *Blue Eagle*, p. 345: "It is not the function of government to organize labor. The whole intent of the Act was to leave organization and representation to the men themselves, unhampered and uninfluenced by any outside source. Repeatedly the President made this clear and (following his lead) also so did every spokesman for NRA." See also, in addition to the detail provided below, Bellush, *Failure of the NRA*, chaps. 4–5.

3. U.S. Bureau of Labor Statistics, "Strikes in the United States," p. 46, table 21; U.S. Bureau of the Census, *Historical Statistics*, p. 99, series D 764-778.

4. The business press was full of such warnings. See, in particular, *Iron Age*, 14 Sept. 1933, p. 37.

5. The best contemporary source for information on the origins and history of the National Labor Board is Lorwin and Wubnig, *Labor Relations Boards*, chaps. 4–10. A number of more recent secondary works also report the facts in reliable detail. See, in particular, Gross, *Making of the National Labor Relations Board*, chaps. 1–2.

6. Rosenman, ed., *Public Papers and Addresses*, 2:524–25.

7. Lorwin and Wubnig, *Labor Relations Boards*, p. 108, n. 41.

8. "Personal Notes, CIO Period," n.d., Box 29, Lauck Papers.

9. Lorwin and Wubnig, *Labor Relations Boards*, p. 270. See also *Iron Age*, 8 Feb. 1934, pp. 41B–D; and, for a summary and verification of contemporary interpretations, "Employee Representation: Chronological History of Interpretations," n.d., General Correspondence of the Industrial Advisory Board, 1933–35, NRA Records.

10. One student of Roosevelt's apparent inconsistency on this score (albeit in connection with a slightly later phase of developments) attributes the president's waffling to his "short-term view and empirical approach to economic recovery," and especially to his extreme sensitivity to the "incidence of power," which made him "ready to compromise" and to be "flexible about majority rule" (Gross, *Making of the National Labor Relations Board*, p. 103). The chief source of Gross's impressions is a memoir by Biddle, *In Brief Authority*, pp. 36–40. Cf. Irons, *New Deal Lawyers*, pp. 211–12.

11. In reference to this settlement Roosevelt declared happily a short time later: "I [finally] defined 7-a when I settled the automobile strike" (Confidential summary of president's conference with members of the Senate, 14 Apr. 1934, p. 2, President's Secretary's File, Box 129, Roosevelt Papers). Roosevelt's apparent satisfaction that he had at last settled all that needed to be settled in this respect may have been encouraged in part by praise from Walter Teagle and Louis Kirstein for the way he and Johnson had handled the recent auto industry dispute. Of this, FDR and Johnson would likely have taken particular note, because both Teagle and Kirstein, as employer representatives on the NLB, regularly concurred with the board's "majority rule" decisions—most notably in the Denver Tramway case, which was decided on 1 March 1934. On Denver Tramway, see Teagle to Jesse I. Miller, 1 Mar. 1934; Teagle to Kirstein, 1 Mar. 1934; and Kirstein to Teagle, 2 Mar. 1934, File A-19, Case 7, Louis E. Kirstein Papers, Baker Library, Harvard University Graduate School of Business Administration, Cambridge, Mass. For Teagle and Kirstein on the automobile settlement, see Kirstein to Johnson, 26 Mar. 1934; Kirstein to Teagle, 26 Mar. 1934; and Teagle to Kirstein, 27 Mar. 1934, in ibid. Teagle's position here (in his personal dedication to one or the other currently competing principles of industrial democracy) may not have been as inconsistent as it would appear at first glance. Thus, though I do not have the evidence with which to argue the point in connection with Kirstein, it seems that Teagle tended to equate the principle of majority rule with the ideal defense of company unions where they already existed as the predominant mode of employee representation. See C. W. Bergquist to William P. Witherow, 24 Aug. 1934, General Correspondence of the Industrial Advisory Board, NRA Records. See also n. 54, below.

12. Lorwin and Wubnig, *Labor Relations Boards*, pp. 332–81, 415–27.

13. "Labor Organization and Collective Bargaining," n.d., NRA Staff Studies, Division of Industrial Economics, pt. 3, chap. 20, pp. 30–31, Box 8127, NRA Records.

14. See Bernstein, *Turbulent Years*, chap. 6, for the best general account of the 1934 strike wave; and *Business Week*, 28 July 1934, p. 7, for an indication of the growing fear in Washington that the recent strike activity signaled a possible "turn to the left" in the labor movement, beginning with the eclipse of the predictably conservative, old-line AFL leadership by "young and inexperienced radicals."

15. This impression was conveyed by Edward A. Filene in his "Report of a Study Tour of Business Conditions in Fourteen Large Cities in the United States as Affected by the President's Recovery Program," 1 Mar. 1934, President's Personal File 2116, Roosevelt Papers.

16. *Business Week*, 24 Mar. 1934, p. 9. This "deepening conviction" was attributed by the magazine to various industry representatives in attendance at a recent Code Authority Conference whose main concern apparently was to convince the administration that henceforth economic recovery "must be based on [the] revival of capital goods."

17. Johnson, *Blue Eagle*, pp. 342–43, 348.

18. Somewhat later, this general economic pattern was partially documented by Kreps, "Dividends, Interest, Profits, and Wages."

19. Huthmacher, *Senator Robert F. Wagner*, pp. 158–59, 163–71, 193–95. See also Tomlins, "The State and the Unions," pp. 117–20, 137–38, 148. Many other individuals, of course, shared these and related concerns with Senator Wagner, even though they may not all have had a direct role in shaping the labor legislation with which Wagner himself is most closely associated. There were also a number of recent studies on the subject of labor and income distribution sponsored by the Brookings Institution and the Twentieth Century Fund of which Wagner was undoubtedly aware. But the underconsumption/purchasing power interpretation of the Depression (and the implied need for policy action like that being pursued by Wagner) was pervasive in the minds of New Deal liberals as well—and certainly among those individuals who had been active in the debate on recovery legislation in 1932 and 1933. Hugo Black, for example, was still warning early in 1935 that federal policy makers had not yet taken seriously enough the fact that the consumer had become the most important component of the American economic system. And indeed (although he uttered the following words at a somewhat later time), the senator felt that "the only chance for labor [as consumer] to receive enough of the income from our national business system to buy the products of that system is through [as Robert Wagner would have heartily agreed] its own bargaining power or through [the] operation of law." For Senator Black's thoughts on the "consumer as producer," see "My Views on the Short Work Week," *Common Sense*, Feb. 1935, pp. 22–23; and on the importance of labor's bargaining power in that connection, "The Shorter Work Week and Work Day," Jan. 1936, pp. 6–7, Speech File, Box 477, Black Papers. These and related issues were pursued in elaborate detail throughout 1935 and 1936. Among Black's most valuable allies in the campaign were Sidney Hillman and other members of the Committee on National Industrial Policy of the Council for Industrial Progress. See, in particular, a lengthy statement before the committee by Edward A. Filene, 9 Dec. 1935; along with an address by Filene, "What Price Prosperity?" Annual Convention of the Wholesale Dry Goods Institute, New York, 16 Jan. 1936, Hillman Papers. Also, "Business and the Wage Problem," an address before the Commonwealth Club, San Francisco, 6 Feb. 1935; and "Why We Must Make Higher Wages Compulsory," a statement issued during the 1936 campaign to reelect President Roosevelt, both in Filene, *Speaking of Change*, pp. 100–109, 275–80.

20. *Business Week*, 10 Mar. 1934, p. 12.

21. U.S. Senate, Committee on Education and Labor, *Hearings: To Create a National Labor Board*, pp. 502, 618, 638, 643, 648, 651, 731.

22. Schlesinger, *Coming of the New Deal*, p. 402.

23. Rosenman, ed., *Public Papers and Addresses*, 3:322–27.

24. C. W. Bergquist to Thomas R. Taylor, 19 July 1934, General Correspondence of the Industrial Advisory Board, NRA Records.

25. The facts of the matter, in much greater detail than I have been able to provide here, are readily available elsewhere. See, in particular, Lorwin and Wubnig, *Labor Relations Boards*, chaps. 9–11; but also Gross, *Making of the National Labor Relations Board*, pp. 64–74.

26. Lloyd G. Garrison, "7(a) and the Future," *Survey Graphic*, Feb. 1935, p. 53, as quoted in Cortner, *Wagner Act Cases*, p. 65. Garrison was succeeded as NLRB chairman in November 1934 by Francis Biddle, a Philadelphia lawyer and former counsel for the Pennsylvania Railroad.

27. F. J. Dufficy to Linton M. Collins, 6 Sept. 1934, Office Files of Leon C. Marshall, Box 7551, NRA Records; Gross, *Making of the National Labor Relations Board*, pp. 89–97; Vadney, *Wayward Liberal*, p. 150.

28. *Business Week*, 2 Mar. 1935, pp. 9–10.

29. H. I. Harriman to Donald Richberg, 6 Oct. 1934, General Correspondence, Box 2, Richberg Papers. See also *Business Week*, 15 Sept. 1934, p. 7, 13 Oct. 1934, p. 9, and 1 Dec. 1934, p. 5.

30. Biddle, *In Brief Authority*, p. 41.

31. Bernstein, *New Deal Collective Bargaining Policy*, pp. 114–15. See also Keyserling, "Wagner Act," p. 202; and Gross, *Making of the National Labor Relations Board*, pp. 140–41.

32. In a referendum conducted during the winter of 1934, even the membership of the U.S. Chamber of Commerce, one of the NIRA's original supporters, voted for drastic revision of the recovery act—or, failing that, discontinuance altogether (Wilson, "How the Chamber of Commerce Viewed the NRA," pp. 105–6).

33. George A. Sloan, chairman, NRA Consumers Goods Committee, to the president, 5 May 1935, Official File 466, Box 4, Roosevelt Papers. See also "Information Memorandum: Code of Fair Competition for the Iron and Steel Industry," Apr. 1935, NRA Iron and Steel Code Section, Box 8478, NRA Records. Appended to this document are several dozen letters from "Little Steel" interests supportive of the NRA code system and recommending extension of the law for at least an additional two-year period. There is also some indication, however, that NRA renewal may have been desired by many of these interests as a means of diverting Congress's attention from other, much less agreeable, pending legislation. At this point, the Wagner Labor Relations bill was probably of less immediate concern than a new, even more burdensome, version of the Black thirty-hour week proposal. See U.S. Senate, Committee on Finance, *Hearings: Investigation of the National Recovery Administration*, pp. 2816, 2821, 2828–29.

34. See, for instance, Donald Richberg's confidential memorandum to the president, dated 13 Apr. 1935, in which Richberg calls Roosevelt's attention to the growing influence of the "anti-monopoly" lobby and its Senate allies, who "fail to compre-

hend the minimum necessities of any legislation which is worth passing—or which can be legally upheld and enforced" (Official File 466, Box 4, Roosevelt Papers). See also *Business Week*, 16 Mar. 1935, pp. 18, 20, 25 May 1935, pp. 16, 18.

35. FDR created the National Industrial Recovery Board on 27 September 1934 to take over the duties of Hugh Johnson just a few days after Johnson resigned his post as head of the NRA. S. Clay Williams, a southern conservative and former president of the R. J. Reynolds Tobacco Company, was appointed chairman of the NIRB. The other board members were Arthur D. Whiteside, a former NRA division administrator and, before that, president of Dun and Bradstreet, to represent business; Sidney Hillman of the Amalgamated Clothing Workers to represent labor; and two university professors, Leon C. Marshall and Walton H. Hamilton, to represent the interests of consumers and the public. Richberg succeeded Williams as NIRB chairman on 21 March 1935. See Richberg to Roosevelt, 26 Apr. 1935, Official File 466, Box 4, Roosevelt Papers; Richberg to Roosevelt, 1 May 1935, Subject File, Box 45, Richberg Papers.

36. Murphy, *Brandeis/Frankfurter Connection*, pp. 153–55.

37. See Brinkley, *Voices of Protest*, esp. pp. 79–81, 207–15.

38. What this meant, of course, as Arthur Schlesinger, Jr., has described FDR's not entirely unfamiliar predicament in the spring of 1935, was that, once again, "events were imposing policy on him" (*Politics of Upheaval*, p. 264). Roosevelt's contemporaries were similarly impressed by his subservience to Wagner's initiative on labor policy in 1935. For example, Frances Perkins wrote: "It ought to be on record that the President did not take part in developing the National Labor Relations Act and, in fact, was hardly consulted about it. It was not a part of the President's program. It did not particularly appeal to him when it was [first] described to him. All the credit for it belongs to Wagner" (*The Roosevelt I Knew*, p. 239). See also Moley, *After Seven Years*, p. 304, who invokes FDR's need for support from Wagner on other legislation, as well as the invalidation of the NIRA, as the principal reasons for the president's willingness, ultimately, to support the senator and his Labor Relations bill.

39. Keyserling, "Wagner Act," pp. 203, 208.

40. Frances Perkins, memorandum to the president, 18 May 1935, "Selected Correspondence from the Papers of FDR Concerning Robert F. Wagner [FDR Library]," J. Joseph Huthmacher Notes (microfilm), Wagner Papers; Huthmacher, *Senator Robert F. Wagner*, p. 198; Felix Frankfurter to Roosevelt, 29 May 1935; Frankfurter to Roosevelt, 30 May 1935, Box 98, Frankfurter Papers.

41. National Labor Relations Act, Secs. 1, 8(2), and 9(b), rpt. in Bernstein, *New Deal Collective Bargaining Policy*, pp. 153–60.

42. Tomlins, "The State and the Unions," pp. 152–62, 173ff.; Sipe, "A Moment of the State," pp. 171–75; Gross, *Making of the National Labor Relations Board*, pp. 98, 138, 146; Bernstein, *New Deal Collective Bargaining Policy*, p. 89.

43. The definitive source is the U.S. National Labor Relations Board, *Legislative History*, which includes the complete texts of both the House and Senate labor committees' hearings on the Wagner bill. The most comprehensive secondary treatment is provided by Bernstein, *New Deal Collective Bargaining Policy*, pp. 88–128.

44. Frey to Sumner H. Slichter, 21 Dec. 1934, Box 15, Frey Papers, Library of

Congress; also Slichter to Frey, 13 Feb. 1935, ibid.; Radosh, "Myth of the New Deal," p. 180; and Sipe, "A Moment of the State," chap. 6, esp. pp. 176–90.

45. The usual portrayal by historians is of an organization that generally espoused the interests of small to medium-sized manufacturing firms, which is a fairly apt characterization for the period before 1933. From 1933 until the late 1940s, however, the representatives of "big" business seem to have played a distinctly important role in all NAM affairs. See, in particular, Burch, "The NAM," pp. 97–130. See also U.S. Congress, Temporary National Economic Committee, *Economic Power and Political Pressures*, chap. 6, esp. pp. 95, 106–7. The NAM, or even the ideologically more extreme American Liberty League, offered some of the larger corporate interests in the United States during the New Deal era the symbolic value of the small business, rags-to-riches entrepreneurial ideal, which, as one student of the phenomenon has noted, became "a particularly useful buffer for big business in the struggle against [unwanted] government controls and the rising power of labor unions" (Zeigler, *Politics of Small Business*, p. 69). See also Rudolph, "American Liberty League," p. 31; Mills, *White Collar*, chap. 3; and Burch, "The NAM," pp. 110–14.

46. Business Advisory Council, "Report of the Committee on the Wagner National Labor Relations Bill," 10 Apr. 1935, Official File 3Q, Box 22, Roosevelt Papers. In all of the testimony on the Wagner bill taken by the Senate Labor Committee, only two employers (both of whom happened to be tobacco processors) offered what might legitimately be interpreted as a "corporatist" defense of the measure (U.S. National Labor Relations Board, *Legislative History*, 1:1592–98).

47. Memorandum, Mr. Lubin to the secretary, 7 June 1934, Correspondence of Secretary Perkins, Subject File, Box 81, General Records of the U.S. Department of Labor; Schlesinger, *Coming of the New Deal*, p. 405.

48. McQuaid, "Frustration of Corporate Revival," p. 693.

49. The most commonly noted example is Gerard Swope's unsuccessful attempt in 1926 to persuade AFL president William Green to form a nationwide union of electrical manufacturing workers organized specifically along industrial, as opposed to craft, lines.

50. Chapin Hoskins, "The Labor Background of Business Administration," *Personnel*, Aug. 1934, p. 11, cited in Scheinberg, "Development of Corporation Labor Policy," p. 179.

51. Fine, *The Automobile under the Blue Eagle*, p. 56.

52. Memorandum of a conversation with Arthur H. Young, 3 Apr. 1934, Office Files of Leon C. Marshall, Box 7549, NRA Records.

53. *Fortune*, July 1935, p. 140, as quoted in Leuchtenburg, *Franklin D. Roosevelt and the New Deal*, p. 177. See also *Iron Age*, 3 Oct. 1935, pp. 39, 74, for Young's continuing defense of the company union approach to employee representation in an address before a gathering of the Association of Iron and Steel Electrical Engineers in Pittsburgh, 24–26 Sept. 1935. Young, incidentally, resigned from U.S. Steel shortly after Myron Taylor reached an agreement with the Steel Workers Organizing Committee in February 1937 and upon that occasion was distinguished by the *New York World Telegram* as the "Daddy" of the company union idea (J. Carlisle MacDonald to E. R. Stettinius, Jr., 12 Aug. 1937, Box 65, Stettinius Papers).

54. Walter C. Teagle, "Employee Representation and Collective Bargaining," Report of the Chairman of the Industrial Relations Committee, Business Advisory and Planning Council of the Department of Commerce, ca. 1934, cited in Radosh, "Myth of the New Deal," p. 179. Along with Swope, Teagle also had been a member of the first National Labor Board.

55. Stolberg, "Government in Search of a Labor Movement." See also Stolberg, *Story of the CIO*, chap. 1; *Business Week*, 9 Sept. 1933, p. 5; and Adamic, "Collapse of Organized Labor."

56. Johnson, *Blue Eagle*, pp. 338–42, 349. See also Perkins, *The Roosevelt I Knew*, pp. 308–9.

57. The price for this institutional security, of course, was a not altogether appealing dependence upon the friendly assertion of public authority. See, generally, Tomlins, "The State and the Unions," esp. chaps. 5–6.

# Chapter 8

1. The definitive source for industry's continued resistance to union labor subsequent to the adoption of the Wagner Act is the voluminous published hearings and reports of the famous La Follette Committee, a subcommittee of the Senate Committee on Education and Labor, which conducted an exceptionally thorough four-year investigation of the entire phenomenon: *Violations of Free Speech and Rights of Labor*. The best scholarly treatment of the committee's investigations is Auerbach, *Labor and Liberty*.

2. Harris, *Right to Manage*, p. 32.

3. Rae, *American Automobile Manufacturers*, pp. 191–98.

4. Chandler, *Giant Enterprise*, p. 3, table 1.

5. Fine, *Sit-Down*, p. 20.

6. Ibid., p. 21.

7. Ibid.

8. *Business Week*, 20 Apr. 1935, p. 10, 8 June 1935, p. 18.

9. *Automotive Industries*, 4 Apr. 1936, p. 487.

10. *Business Week*, 11 Apr. 1936, p. 28, 18 Apr. 1936, p. 11.

11. The details of the 1936–37 strikes at GM have been recounted too frequently to warrant yet another narrative description here. The definitive study is Fine, *Sit-Down*. See also Bernstein, *Turbulent Years*, chap. 11. The distinctly less impressive accomplishments of the UAW during the formative, and particularly fractious, stages of the union's history before the victory over GM are analyzed in Fine, *The Automobile under the Blue Eagle*, chap. 12; Skeels, "Background of UAW Factionalism"; and Boryczka, "Seasons of Discontent." Various aspects of the rise and eventual triumph of the auto workers' union at the level of the union local have been examined in considerable detail by Kruchko, *Birth of a Union Local*.

12. *Business Week*, 23 Jan. 1937, p. 15.

13. H. B. Personal Note: "Settlement of General Motors Strike, February 10," 25 Feb. 1937, Box 1, Folder 37, Blankenhorn Papers, Archives of Urban and Labor Affairs, Wayne State University, Detroit, Mich. (rpt. in Fine, "John L. Lewis"). Heber Blankenhorn, at one point, had been on the staffs of both the NRA and the National Labor Board, but in February 1937 he was serving as an investigator for the NLRB as well as the unofficial liaison between the board and the La Follette Civil Liberties Committee. Prepared by Blankenhorn on the basis of a conversation with John L. Lewis two weeks after the conclusion of the strike, the document, according to Fine, "is the best available contemporaneous source for Lewis' views concerning the settlement of the strike and the factors that contributed to the victory of the United Automobile Workers." See also Fine, *Frank Murphy*, chap. 8. For the general background of the Democrats', and especially Roosevelt's, political indebtedness to Lewis, see McFarland, "Coalition of Convenience"; and Dubofsky and Van Tine, *John L. Lewis*, pp. 248–54, 268–70.

14. Fine, "John L. Lewis," p. 566. The Fisher Body No. 1 plant in Flint was the corporation's installation for the production of Buick bodies as well as certain parts for Pontiacs and Oldsmobiles. The Chevrolet No. 4 plant, also in Flint, was the only producer of Chevrolet engines. The Cleveland Fisher Body plant produced the body stampings for two-door Chevrolet models as well as some parts for all Chevrolet bodies—and these were the GM factories in which the sit-down strikes took place (ibid., nn. 6 and 7).

15. Fine, *Sit-Down*, chap. 10, esp. p. 303. The complete text of the 11 February 1937 settlement can be found in Chandler, *Giant Enterprise*, pp. 221–22.

16. U.S. Congress, Temporary National Economic Committee, *Structure of Industry*, pp. 24–26.

17. Adams, "Steel Industry," pp. 150–51.

18. Ibid., pp. 151–52, 173, table 2; Daugherty, de Chazeau, and Stratton, *Economics of the Iron and Steel Industry*, 1:412; U.S. Congress, Temporary National Economic Committee, *Hearings: Investigation of Concentration of Economic Power*, pp. 13948–52.

19. Memorandum, J. H. Osmers to E. R. Stettinius, Jr. (with enclosures), 16 Dec. 1936; A. W. Vogt to Myron C. Taylor, 11 Feb. 1937, Boxes 64 and 65, Stettinius Papers. Production capacity in operation increased steadily throughout the winter, reaching about 90 percent in March–April 1937 (United States Steel Corporation, *TNEC Papers*, 1:23, table 1).

20. *Business Week*, 27 Feb. 1937, p. 13.

21. The standard account is Brooks, *As Steel Goes*, chap. 4. See also Bernstein, *Turbulent Years*, pp. 459–65; and Galenson, *CIO Challenge to the AFL*, pp. 84–91.

22. J. R. Steelman to Frances Perkins, 19 Oct. 1936, Correspondence of Secretary Perkins, Subject File, Box 32, Department of Labor Records.

23. The NLRB conducted a series of highly publicized hearings from December 1936 to February 1937 on the question of Carnegie-Illinois's alleged domination of its ERPs. The hearings, according to Irving Bernstein, "seriously damaged both the corporation and the company unions. The testimony established the weakness of the ERPs as bargaining agents and exposed their dependence upon the corporation for fi-

nancing, a condition that often deteriorated into graft" (*Turbulent Years*, p. 465). See also Brooks, *As Steel Goes*, pp. 104–5, 107; and *Business Week*, 26 Dec. 1936, pp. 17–18.

24. "It Happened in Steel," *Fortune*, May 1937, p. 179.

25. Ibid. According to another contemporary account, Governor Earle had pledged that "if a strike came, the steel workers would enjoy complete freedom of picketing and assemblage, and, while striking, might expect aid from governmental relief funds" as well (Levinson, *Labor on the March*, p. 199).

26. *Business Week*, 6 Mar. 1937, p. 13. The Walsh-Healey Public Contracts Act of 1936 stipulated that U.S. government contracts in excess of $10,000 require observance of certain specified minimum labor standards, including overtime pay for hours worked over eight per day and forty per week. In this instance, therefore, U.S. Steel "conceded" to SWOC precisely what it would have had to offer its employees anyway to be in a position to bid on government contracts.

27. "It Happened in Steel," p. 179.

28. In January and February 1937 domestic bookings of steel fell below the level for December 1936 by approximately 35 percent. A large backlog of orders placed in the last quarter of 1936, however, had the countervailing effect of pushing the volume of steel production and shipments during the first two months of the new year over and above the corresponding rate for the previous December. Roughly the same profit-sustaining pattern of market behavior occurred again between March and September 1937, subsequent to which the entire industrial economy, including steel, collapsed into recession (U.S. Congress, Temporary National Economic Committee, *Hearings: Investigation of Concentration of Economic Power*, pp. 13953–56).

29. "It Happened in Steel," p. 92. See also Stolberg, "Big Steel, Little Steel," p. 119.

30. Taylor, *Ten Years of Steel*, p. 40; Stolberg, *Story of the CIO*, pp. 74–78; and Stolberg, "Big Steel, Little Steel," p. 120, for a contemporary account of the details. See also Wechsler, *Labor Baron*, p. 68. Thomas W. Lamont feared that a strike in 1937 might cost the corporation as much as $100 million ("Memorandum for Mr. Ingersoll," 29 Mar. 1937, File 227-3, Lamont Papers, Baker Library, Harvard University Graduate School of Business Administration, Cambridge, Mass.

31. "It Happened in Steel," p. 176; Stolberg, "Big Steel, Little Steel," p. 119.

32. "Memorandum for the President: The Lewis Diatribe against J. P. M. and M. C. T.," 3 Nov. 1941, President's Personal File 70, Roosevelt Papers; File 127-7, Lamont Papers. When this explanation was voiced (largely as speculation) by Philadelphia radio broadcaster Boake Carter, it provoked a defensive and seemingly anxious response from the officers of the corporation: Thomas W. Lamont to Boake Carter, 30 June 1937; E. R. Stettinius, Jr., to Edward T. Sanders, 1 July 1937, File 227-4, Lamont Papers. Cf. Parry, "Steel Management and the Acceptance of Unionism," who essentially agrees with my reasoning but emphasizes the possible importance of Taylor's widely noted ideological detachment with respect to the issue of union recognition in general, relative to the distinctly belligerent attitude of the "Little Steelers." Tom Girdler, for example, chairman of the board at Republic Steel, whose reaction to the prospect of labor organization in the industry seemed to epitomize the thinking of

the smaller steel barons, found the "psychic costs" of unionism too great to bear; see Girdler, *Boot Straps*.

33. Wages throughout the industry increased by an average of 18 percent during March 1937 (*Iron Age*, 27 Oct. 1937, p. 73).

34. Lauderbaugh, "Business, Labor, and Foreign Policy."

35. Isador Lubin to Frances Perkins, 10 Mar. 1937, Correspondence of Secretary Perkins, Box 32, Department of Labor Records.

36. The sizable increase in U.S. Steel's profits was second only to that of Bethlehem, which easily topped the list of steel companies with higher profits in 1937 by posting a gain of 128.9 percent over the previous year (*Wall Street Journal*, 14 Apr. 1938, p. 5).

37. Isador Lubin to Frances Perkins, 6 Aug. 1937, Correspondence of Secretary Perkins, Box 32, Department of Labor Records.

# Conclusion

1. Brody, "Emergence of Mass-Production Unionism."

2. Meyerowitz, "Development of General Electric's Labor Policies"; Schatz, "End of Corporate Liberalism"; Galenson, *CIO Challenge to the AFL*, p. 251; Bernstein, *Turbulent Years*, pp. 589–613; Matles and Higgins, *Them and Us*, chap. 6; Harris, *Right to Manage*, pp. 34, 157–58; Northrup, *Boulwarism*.

3. Harris, *Right to Manage*, pp. 125–27, for a concise but well-balanced assessment of the Taft-Hartley Act's historical significance. For the story in greater detail, with special emphasis on the administrative practices of the NLRB, see Gross, *Reshaping of the National Labor Relations Board*.

4. Krueger, "Another Reflection."

5. Lichtenstein, *Labor's War at Home*, pp. 41, 85–86.

6. Lens, *Crisis of American Labor*, p. 20 and passim; Brody, *Workers in Industrial America*, pp. 177–82, 186.

7. Brody, *Workers in Industrial America*, pp. 182–211. See also Montgomery, *Workers' Control in America*, pp. 161ff.

8. Michels, *Political Parties*. See also Rogin, "Voluntarism"; and Radosh, "Corporate Ideology."

9. Perhaps the classic appraisal in this vein was provided by Perlman, *Theory of the Labor Movement*, esp. chap. 5.

10. The point, as formulated here, is adapted from Rosa Luxemburg's famous 1899 polemic against Edward Bernstein and his Social Democrat revisionist cohorts: "Social Reform or Revolution," rpt. in Howard, ed., *Selected Political Writings*, pp. 52–134.

11. I borrow the term "laborist" from Joseph Schumpeter's usage in application of the concept "laborist capitalism"—that particular order of capitalism that promises "indefinitely higher mass standards of life, supplemented by gratis services *without* complete 'expropriation of the expropriators.' " (*Capitalism, Socialism, and Democracy*, p. 419).

12. Dubofsky, "Not So 'Turbulent Years.' "

13. See, for example, Dawley and Faler, "Working Class Culture and Politics."

14. One important study on this subject is Burawoy, *Manufacturing Consent*.

15. For a highly capable discussion of the primary interpretive issues here, see Davis, "Why the U.S. Working Class Is Different." See also Katznelson, *City Trenches*, esp. pp. 1–72.

16. Davis, "Barren Marriage."

17. Wall, *Andrew Carnegie*, p. 392.

18. Marx, *Capital*, 1:chap. 10, secs. 2, 5–7; chap. 15, sec. 9.

19. Kolko, *Triumph of Conservatism*, pp. 290–94. See also the discussion in Steinberg, *Wages and Hours*, pp. 212–16.

20. Marx, *Capital*, 1:297.

21. See, for example, Graebner, "Federalism in the Progressive Era," which is highly suggestive in this context even though the author is not concerned with the issue of New Deal reform specifically.

22. Lukes, *Power*, for a discussion of some of the conceptual problems involved in the study and meaning of power in liberal democratic societies.

23. For a particularly forceful statement in this vein, see Thompson, *Whigs and Hunters*, pp. 258ff. Cf. Neumann, "Change in the Function of Law."

24. Klare, "Judicial Deradicalization."

25. Ferguson, "From Normalcy to New Deal," provides an engaging new perspective.

26. For the post–World War II legal framework of labor's rights and obligations under American capitalism see Atleson, *Values and Assumptions*; and Stone, "Post-War Paradigm."

27. See, for example, Aglietta, *Theory of Capitalist Regulation*, chap. 3; who depicts "the transformation of the wage earners' conditions of life" via the "legal codification" of collective bargaining during the 1930s as a prime catalyst in the realization of capitalism's greatest exploitive potential under what the author calls the regime of "intensive accumulation" and its contemporary variant, "Fordism." See also the discussion provided by Davis, " 'Fordism' in Crisis."

# Bibliography

## Manuscript Collections

Cambridge, Massachusetts
  Baker Library, Harvard University Graduate School of Business Administration
    Louis E. Kirstein Papers
    Thomas W. Lamont Papers
Charlottesville, Virginia
  Alderman Library, University of Virginia
    W. Jett Lauck Papers
    Edward R. Stettinius, Jr., Papers
Detroit, Michigan
  Archives of Urban and Labor Affairs, Wayne State University
    Heber Blankenhorn Papers
    Edward A. Wieck Papers
Hyde Park, New York
  Franklin D. Roosevelt Library
    Franklin D. Roosevelt Papers
Ithaca, New York
  New York State School of Industrial and Labor Relations, Cornell University
    Sidney Hillman Papers
Palo Alto, California
  Hoover Institution on War, Revolution, and Peace
    Raymond Moley Papers
Washington, D.C.
  Georgetown University
    Robert F. Wagner Papers
  Library of Congress
    Hugo L. Black Papers
    James J. Davis Papers
    Felix Frankfurter Papers
    John P. Frey Papers

George W. Norris Papers
Donald R. Richberg Papers
National Archives
   General Records of the U.S. Department of Commerce
   General Records of the U.S. Department of Labor
   Records of the Federal Mediation and Conciliation Service
   Records of the National Bituminous Coal Commission, 1935–36
   Records of the National Recovery Administration
   Records of the President's Organization on Unemployment Relief
West Branch, Iowa
  Herbert Hoover Presidential Library
   Herbert Hoover Papers

## Other Unpublished Sources

Bernstein, Michael A. "Long-Term Economic Growth and the Great Depression in America: Some Notes on Recent Research." Princeton University, 1982.

Grattan, William Joseph. "David I. Walsh and His Associates: A Study in Political Theory." Ph.D. dissertation, Harvard University, 1957.

Hodges, James Andrew. "New Deal Labor Policy and the Southern Cotton Textile Industry, 1933–1941." Ph.D. dissertation, Vanderbilt University, 1963.

Lea, Arden J. "The Cotton Textile Industry and the Federal Child Labor Act of 1916." M.A. thesis, Stetson University, 1972.

Meyerowitz, Ruth Susan. "The Development of General Electric's Labor Policies, 1922–1950." M.A. thesis, Columbia University, 1969.

Mulder, Ronald A. "The Insurgent Progressives and the New Deal, 1933–1939." Ph.D. dissertation, University of Michigan, 1970.

Parry, Byron Lee. "Steel Management and the Acceptance of Unionism, 1937–1942." M.A. thesis, University of Illinois, 1957.

Scheinberg, Stephen J. "The Development of Corporation Labor Policy, 1900–1940." Ph.D. dissertation, University of Wisconsin, 1966.

Sipe, Daniel A. "A Moment of the State: The Enactment of the National Labor Relations Act, 1935." Ph.D. dissertation, University of Pennsylvania, 1981.

Tomlins, Christopher L. "The State and the Unions: Federal Labor Relations Policy and the Organized Labor Movement in America, 1935–1955." Ph.D. dissertation, Johns Hopkins University, 1980.

## Published Sources

Adamic, Louis. "The Collapse of Organized Labor." *Harper's*, Jan. 1932, pp. 167–78.

Adams, Walter. "The Steel Industry." In *The Structure of American Industry: Some Case Studies*, edited by Walter Adams, pp. 144–84. New York: Macmillan, 1961.

Aglietta, Michel. *A Theory of Capitalist Regulation: The U.S. Experience*. Translated by David Fernbach. London: New Left Books, 1979.

Andersen, Kristi. *The Creation of a Democratic Majority, 1928–1936*. Chicago: University of Chicago Press, 1979.

Arnold, Thurman W. *The Folklore of Capitalism*. New Haven: Yale University Press, 1937.

Atleson, James B. *Values and Assumptions in American Labor Law*. Amherst: University of Massachusetts Press, 1983.

Auerbach, Jerold S. *Labor and Liberty: The La Follette Committee and the New Deal*. Indianapolis: Bobbs-Merrill, 1966.

————. "New Deal, Old Deal, or Raw Deal: Some Thoughts on New Left Historiography." *Journal of Southern History* 35 (Feb. 1969): 18–30.

Backman, Jules, and Gainsburgh, M. R. *Economics of the Cotton Textile Industry*. New York: National Industrial Conference Board, 1946.

Baran, Paul A., and Sweezy, Paul M. *Monopoly Capital: An Essay on the American Economic and Social Order*. New York: Monthly Review Press, 1966.

Baratz, Morton S. *The Union and the Coal Industry*. New Haven: Yale University Press, 1955.

Barger, Harold, and Schurr, Sam H. *The Mining Industries, 1899–1939: A Study of Output, Employment, and Productivity*. New York: National Bureau of Economic Research, 1944.

Baum, Bernard. "Fifty Years in America." *American Jewish Archives* 23 (Nov. 1971): 160–97.

Beame, Edmond M. "The Jacksonville Agreement: Quest for Stability in Coal." *Industrial and Labor Relations Review* 8 (Jan. 1955): 195–203.

Bellush, Bernard. *The Failure of the NRA*. New York: Norton, 1975.

————. *Franklin D. Roosevelt as Governor of New York*. New York: Columbia University Press, 1955.

Berglund, Abraham; Starnes, George T.; and De Vyver, Frank T. *Labor in the Industrial South*. Charlottesville: University of Virginia, Institute for Research in the Social Sciences, 1930.

Berle, Beatrice Bishop, and Jacobs, Travis Beal, eds. *Navigating the Rapids, 1918–1971: From the Papers of Adolf A. Berle*. New York: Harcourt Brace Jovanovich, 1973.

Bernstein, Barton J. "The New Deal: The Conservative Achievements of Liberal Reform." In *Towards a New Past: Dissenting Essays in American History*, edited by Barton J. Bernstein, pp. 263–88. New York: Pantheon, 1968.

Bernstein, Irving. *The Lean Years: A History of the American Worker, 1920–1933*. Boston: Houghton Mifflin, 1960.

————. *The New Deal Collective Bargaining Policy*. Berkeley and Los Angeles: University of California Press, 1950.

————. *Turbulent Years: A History of the American Worker, 1933–1941*. Boston: Houghton Mifflin, 1969.

Berquist, Fred E. *Economic Survey of the Bituminous Coal Mining Industry under Free Competition and Code Regulation.* 2 vols. Washington, D.C.: Office of the National Recovery Administration, 1936.

Biddle, Francis. *In Brief Authority.* Garden City: Doubleday, 1962.

Boryczka, Ray. "Seasons of Discontent: Auto Union Factionalism and the Motor Products Strike of 1935–1936." *Michigan History* 61 (1977): 3–32.

Brady, Robert A. *Business as a System of Power.* New York: Columbia University Press, 1943.

Brandeis, Elizabeth. "Organized Labor and Protective Labor Legislation." In *Labor and the New Deal,* edited by Milton Derber and Edwin Young, pp. 195–237. Madison: University of Wisconsin Press, 1957.

Brandes, Joseph. "From Sweatshop to Stability: Jewish Labor between Two World Wars." *YIVO Annual of Jewish Social Science* 16 (1976): 1–149.

Braun, Kurt. *Union-Management Co-operation: Experience in the Clothing Industry.* Washington, D.C.: Brookings Institution, 1947.

Brinkley, Alan. *Voices of Protest: Huey Long, Father Coughlin, and the Great Depression.* New York: Knopf, 1982.

Brody, David. "The Emergence of Mass-Production Unionism." In *Change and Continuity in Twentieth Century America,* edited by John Braeman, Robert H. Bremner, and Everett Walters, pp. 221–62. Columbus: Ohio State University Press, 1964.

———. "Labor and the Great Depression: The Interpretive Prospects." *Labor History* 13 (Spring 1972): 231–44.

———. *Workers in Industrial America: Essays on the Twentieth Century Struggle.* New York: Oxford University Press, 1980.

Brooks, Robert R. R. *As Steel Goes: Unionism in a Basic Industry.* New Haven: Yale University Press, 1940.

Budish, Jacob M., and Soule, George. *The New Unionism in the Clothing Industry.* New York: Harcourt Brace & Howe, 1920.

Burawoy, Michael. *Manufacturing Consent: Changes in the Labor Process under Monopoly Capitalism.* Chicago: University of Chicago Press, 1979.

Burch, Philip H. "The NAM as an Interest Group." *Politics and Society* 4 (Fall 1973): 97–130.

Burns, James MacGregor. *Roosevelt: The Lion and the Fox.* New York: Harcourt Brace, 1956.

Carpenter, Jesse T. *Competition and Collective Bargaining in the Needle Trades, 1910–1967.* Ithaca: New York State School of Industrial and Labor Relations, 1972.

Chandler, Alfred D., Jr., ed. *Giant Enterprise: Ford, General Motors, and the Automobile Industry, Sources and Readings.* New York: Harcourt Brace and World, 1964.

Clark, Victor S. *History of Manufactures in the United States.* 3 vols. New York: McGraw-Hill, 1929.

Cobrin, Harry A. *The Men's Clothing Industry: Colonial through Modern Times.* New York: Fairchild Publications, 1970.

Cohen, Julius Henry. *An American Labor Policy.* New York: Macmillan, 1919.

_____. *Law and Order in Industry: Five Years' Experience*. New York: Macmillan, 1916.

Commons, John R., ed. *Trade Unionism and Labor Problems*. 1905. Reprint. New York: A. M. Kelley, 1967.

Conkin, Paul K. *FDR and the Origins of the Welfare State*. New York: Crowell, 1967.

Conner, Valerie Jean. *The National War Labor Board: Stability, Social Justice, and the Voluntary State in World War I*. Chapel Hill: University of North Carolina Press, 1983.

Connery, Robert H. *The Administration of an NRA Code: A Case Study of the Men's Clothing Industry*. Chicago: Public Administration Service, 1938.

Copeland, Melvin T. *The Cotton Manufacturing Industry of the United States*. 1912. Reprint. New York: A. M. Kelley, 1966.

Corey, Lewis. *The Decline of American Capitalism*. New York: Covici Friede, 1934.

Cortner, Richard C. *The Wagner Act Cases*. Knoxville: University of Tennessee Press, 1964.

Creamer, Daniel; Dobrovolsky, Sergei P.; and Borenstein, Israel. *Capital in Manufacturing and Mining: Its Formation and Financing*. Princeton: Princeton University Press, 1960.

Daugherty, Carroll R. "The Economic Coverage of the Fair Labor Standards Act: A Statistical Study." *Law and Contemporary Problems* 6 (Summer 1939): 406–15.

Daugherty, Carroll R.; de Chazeau, Melvin D.; and Stratton, Samuel S. *The Economics of the Iron and Steel Industry*. 2 vols. New York: McGraw-Hill, 1937.

Davidson, Elizabeth H. *Child Labor Legislation in the Southern Textile States*. Chapel Hill: University of North Carolina Press, 1939.

Davis, Mike. "The Barren Marriage of American Labour and the Democratic Party." *New Left Review*, no. 124 (Nov.–Dec. 1980): 43–84.

_____. " 'Fordism' in Crisis: A Review of Michel Aglietta's *Régulation et crisis: L'expérience des Etats-Unis*." *Review* 2 (Fall 1978): 207–69.

_____. "Why the U.S. Working Class Is Different." *New Left Review*, no. 123 (Sept.–Oct. 1980): 3–44.

Dawley, Alan, and Faler, Paul. "Working Class Culture and Politics in the Industrial Revolution: Sources of Loyalism and Rebellion." *Journal of Social History* 9 (June 1976): 466–80.

Domhoff, G. William. *The Higher Circles: The Governing Class in America*. New York: Random House, 1970.

Douglas, Paul H. *Real Wages in the United States, 1890–1926*. Boston: Houghton Mifflin, 1930.

Douglas, Paul H., and Hackman, Joseph. "The Fair Labor Standards Act of 1938, I." *Political Science Quarterly* 53 (1938): 491–515.

Dubofsky, Melvyn. "Not So 'Turbulent Years': Another Look at the American 1930s." *Amerikastudien* 24 (1979): 5–20.

_____. "Organized Labor and the Immigrant in New York City, 1900–1918." *Labor History* 2 (Spring 1961): 182–201.

_____. *When Workers Organize: New York City in the Progressive Era*. Amherst: University of Massachusetts Press, 1968.

Dubofsky, Melvyn, and Van Tine, Warren. *John L. Lewis: A Biography*. New York: Quadrangle, 1977.

Easterlin, Richard A. *Population, Labor Force, and Long Swings in Economic Growth: The American Experience*. New York: National Bureau of Economic Research, 1968.

Eldridge, Hope T., and Thomas, Dorothy S. *Population Redistribution and Economic Growth, United States, 1870–1950*. Vol. 3, *Demographic Analyses and Interrelations*. Philadelphia: American Philosophical Society, 1964.

Epstein, Melech. *Jewish Labor in the USA: An Industrial, Political and Cultural History of the Jewish Labor Movement, 1882–1914*. New York: Trade Union Sponsoring Committee, 1950.

Evans, Mercer G. "Southern Labor Supply and Working Conditions in Industry." *Annals of the American Academy of Political and Social Science* 153 (Jan. 1931): 156–62.

Fabricant, Solomon. *Basic Facts on Productivity Change*. National Bureau of Economic Research, Occasional Paper no. 63. New York, 1959.

————. *Employment in Manufacturing, 1899–1939*. New York: National Bureau of Economic Research, 1942.

————. *The Output of Manufacturing Industries, 1899–1937*. New York: National Bureau of Economic Research, 1940.

Farr, Grant N. *The Origins of Recent Labor Policy*. University of Colorado Studies, Series in Economics no. 3. Boulder: University of Colorado Press, 1959.

Felt, Jeremy P. "The Child Labor Provisions of the Fair Labor Standards Act." *Labor History* 11 (Fall 1970): 467–81.

————. *Hostages of Fortune: Child Labor Reform in New York State*. Syracuse: Syracuse University Press, 1965.

Femia, Joseph. "Hegemony and Consciousness in the Thought of Antonio Gramsci." *Political Studies* 23 (1975): 29–48.

Ferguson, Thomas. "From Normalcy to New Deal: Industrial Structure, Party Competition, and American Public Policy in the Great Depression." *International Organization* 38 (Winter 1984): 41–94.

Filene, Edward A. *Speaking of Change: A Selection of Speeches and Articles*. New York: Published by former associates of Edward A. Filene, 1939.

Fine, Sidney. *The Automobile under the Blue Eagle: Labor, Management, and the Automobile Manufacturing Code*. Ann Arbor: University of Michigan Press, 1963.

————. *Frank Murphy: The New Deal Years*. Chicago: University of Chicago Press, 1979.

————. *Sit Down: The General Motors Strike of 1936–1937*. Ann Arbor: University of Michigan Press, 1969.

————, ed. "John L. Lewis Discusses the General Motors Sit-Down Strike: A Document." *Labor History* 15 (Fall 1974): 563–70.

Fisher, Waldo E. "Bituminous Coal." In *How Collective Bargaining Works*, edited by the Twentieth Century Fund, pp. 229–79. New York, 1942.

————. *Collective Bargaining in the Bituminous Coal Industry: An Appraisal*. Philadelphia: University of Pennsylvania Press, 1948.

Fisher, Waldo E., and James, Charles M. *Minimum Price Fixing in the Bituminous Coal Industry*. Princeton: Princeton University Press, 1955.

Foner, Eric. "Why Is There No Socialism in the United States?" *History Workshop*, no. 17 (Spring 1984): 57–80.

Foner, Philip S. "Some Reflections on Ideology and American Labor History." *Science and Society* 34 (Winter 1970): 467–78.

Forsythe, John S. "Legislative History of the Fair Labor Standards Act." *Law and Contemporary Problems* 6 (Summer 1939): 464–90.

Fraser, Steve. "Dress Rehearsal for the New Deal: Shop-Floor Insurgents, Political Elites, and Industrial Democracy in the Amalgamated Clothing Workers." In *Working-Class America: Essays on Labor, Community, and American Society*, edited by Michael H. Frisch and Daniel J. Walkowitz, pp. 212–55. Urbana: University of Illinois Press, 1983.

——. "From the 'New Unionism' to the New Deal." *Labor History* 25 (Summer 1984): 405–30.

Frederick, J. George, ed. *The Swope Plan: Details, Criticisms, and Analysis*. New York: Business Bourse, 1931.

Freedman, Max, ed. *Roosevelt and Frankfurter: Their Correspondence, 1928–1945*. Boston: Little, Brown, 1967.

Freidel, Frank. *Franklin D. Roosevelt*. 4 vols. Vol. 1, *The Apprenticeship*. Vol. 2, *The Ordeal*. Vol. 3, *The Triumph*. Vol. 4, *Launching the New Deal*. Boston: Little, Brown, 1952–73.

Fusfeld, Daniel R. *The Economic Thought of Franklin D. Roosevelt and the Origins of the New Deal*. New York: Columbia University Press, 1956.

Galambos, Louis. *Competition and Cooperation: The Emergence of a National Trade Association*. Baltimore: Johns Hopkins University Press, 1966.

Galenson, Walter. *The CIO Challenge to the AFL: A History of the American Labor Movement, 1935–1941*. Cambridge, Mass.: Harvard University Press, 1960.

Gilbert, James. *Designing the Industrial State: The Intellectual Pursuit of Collectivism in America, 1880–1940*. Chicago: Quadrangle, 1972.

Girdler, Tom. *Boot Straps: The Autobiography of Tom M. Girdler*. Written in collaboration with Boyden Sparkes. New York: Scribner, 1943.

Glasser, Carrie. "Union Wage Policy in Bituminous Coal." *Industrial and Labor Relations Review* 1 (July 1948): 609–23.

Goodrich, Carter. *Migration and Economic Opportunity*. Philadelphia: University of Pennsylvania Press, 1936.

——. *The Miner's Freedom: A Study of the Working Life in a Changing Industry*. Boston: Marshall Jones, 1925.

Gowaskie, Joseph M. "From Conflict to Cooperation: John Mitchell and Bituminous Coal Operators, 1898–1908." *Historian* 38 (Aug. 1976): 669–88.

Graebner, William. "The Coal Mine Operator and Safety: A Study of Business Reform in the Progressive Period." *Labor History* 14 (Fall 1973): 483–505.

——. *Coal Mining Safety in the Progressive Period: The Political Economy of Reform*. Lexington: University of Kentucky Press, 1976.

——. "Federalism in the Progressive Era: A Structural Interpretation of Reform."

*Journal of American History* 64 (Sept. 1977): 331–57.

————. "Great Expectations: The Search for Order in Bituminous Coal, 1890–1917." *Business History Review* 38 (Spring 1974): 49–72.

Gross, James A. *The Making of the National Labor Relations Board.* Albany: State University of New York Press, 1974.

————. *The Reshaping of the National Labor Relations Board: National Labor Policy in Transition, 1937–1947.* Albany: State University of New York Press, 1981.

Habakkuk, H. J. *American and British Technology in the Nineteenth Century: The Search for Labour-Saving Inventions.* Cambridge: At the University Press, 1962.

Hamilton, Virginia Van der Veer. *Hugo Black: The Alabama Years.* Baton Rouge: Louisiana State University Press, 1972.

Harriman, Henry I. "The Stabilization of Business and Employment." *American Economic Review* 22 (Mar. 1932): 63–79.

Harris, Howell John. *The Right to Manage: Industrial Relations Policies of American Business in the 1940s.* Madison: University of Wisconsin Press, 1982.

Hawley, Ellis W. "Herbert Hoover, the Commerce Secretariat, and the Vision of an 'Associative State,' 1921–1928." *Journal of American History* 61 (June 1974): 116–40.

————. *The New Deal and the Problem of Monopoly: A Study in Economic Ambivalence.* Princeton: Princeton University Press, 1966.

————. "Secretary Hoover and the Bituminous Coal Problem, 1921–1928." *Business History Review* 42 (1968): 247–70.

Hays, Samuel P. "The Politics of Reform in Municipal Government in the Progressive Era." *Pacific Northwest Quarterly* 55 (Oct. 1964): 157–69.

Hendry, James B. "The Bituminous Coal Industry." In *The Structure of American Industry*, edited by Walter Adams, pp. 74–112. New York: Macmillan, 1961.

Hildebrand, George H. "The Economic Effects of Unionism." In *A Decade of Industrial Relations Research, 1946–1956*, edited by Neil W. Chamberlain, Frank C. Pierson, and Theresa Wolfson, pp. 98–145. New York: Harper, 1958.

Himmelberg, Robert F. *The Origins of the National Recovery Administration: Business, Government, and the Trade Association Issue, 1921–1933.* New York: Fordham University Press, 1976.

Hinrichs, A. F. *The United Mine Workers of America and the Non-Union Coal Fields.* New York: Columbia University Press, 1923.

————. "Wage Rates and Weekly Earnings in the Cotton Textile Industry." *Monthly Labor Review* 40 (Mar. 1935): 612–25.

Hofstadter, Richard. *The American Political Tradition and the Men Who Made It.* New York: Knopf, 1948.

Holt, James. "The New Deal and the American Anti-Statist Tradition." In *The New Deal: The National Level*, edited by John Braeman, Robert H. Bremner, and David Brody, pp. 27–49. Columbus: Ohio State University Press, 1975.

Hoover, Herbert. *Memoirs: The Cabinet and the Presidency, 1920–1933.* New York: Macmillan, 1951.

————. *Memoirs: The Great Depression, 1929–1941.* New York: Macmillan, 1952.

Howard, Dick, ed. *Selected Political Writings of Rosa Luxemburg*. New York: Monthly Review Press, 1971.

Hunt, Edward Eyre; Tryon, F. G.; and Willits, Joseph H., eds. *What the Coal Commission Found*. Baltimore: Williams & Wilkins, 1925.

Hurd, Rick. "New Deal Labor Policy and the Containment of Radical Union Activity." *Review of Radical Political Economics* 8 (Fall 1976): 32–43.

Hurst, James Willard. *Law and Markets in United States History: Different Modes of Bargaining among Interests*. Madison: University of Wisconsin Press, 1982.

Huthmacher, J. Joseph. *Senator Robert F. Wagner and the Rise of Urban Liberalism*. New York: Atheneum, 1968.

Huthmacher, J. Joseph, and Susman, Warren I., eds. *Herbert Hoover and the Crisis of American Capitalism*. Cambridge, Mass.: Schenkman, 1973.

Ickes, Harold L. *The Secret Diary of Harold L. Ickes, 1933–1936*. New York: Simon & Schuster, 1953.

International Ladies' Garment Workers' Union. *Report of the General Executive Board to the Eighteenth Convention*, 30 Nov. 1925. Philadelphia, 1925.

Irons, Peter H. *The New Deal Lawyers*. Princeton: Princeton University Press, 1982.

Jerome, Harry. *Mechanization in Industry*. New York: National Bureau of Economic Research, 1934.

Johnson, Hugh S. *The Blue Eagle from Egg to Earth*. Garden City: Doubleday, 1935.

Johnson, James P. "Drafting the NRA Code of Fair Competition for the Bituminous Coal Industry." *Journal of American History* 53 (1966–67): 521–41.

_____. *The Politics of Soft Coal: The Bituminous Industry from World War I through the New Deal*. Urbana: University of Illinois Press, 1979.

Katznelson, Ira. *City Trenches: Urban Politics and the Patterning of Class in the United States*. New York: Pantheon, 1981.

Keller, Robert R. "Factor Income Distribution in the United States during the 1920s: A Reexamination of Fact and Theory." *Journal of Economic History* 33 (Mar. 1973): 252–73.

Kelley, Florence. "Child Labor Legislation and Enforcement in New England and the Middle States." *Annals of the American Academy of Political and Social Science* 25 (1905): 480–90.

Kelly, Alfred H., and Harbison, Winfred A. *The American Constitution: Its Origins and Development*. New York: Norton, 1963.

Kendrick, John W. "Employment in Relation to Mechanization in the Bituminous Coal Industry." *Monthly Labor Review* 36 (Feb. 1933): 256–78.

_____. *Productivity Trends in the United States*. Princeton: Princeton University Press, 1961.

Kerr, K. Austin. "Labor-Management Cooperation: An 1897 Case." *Pennsylvania Magazine of History and Biography* 99 (Jan. 1975): 45–71.

Keyserling, Leon H. "The Wagner Act: Its Origins and Current Significance." *George Washington Law Review* (Dec. 1960): 199–233.

Kiessling, O. E. "Coal Mining in the South." *Annals of the American Academy of Political and Social Science* 153 (Jan. 1931): 84–93.

Klare, Karl E. "Judicial Deradicalization of the Wagner Act and the Origins of Modern Legal Consciousness, 1937–1941." *Minnesota Law Review* 62 (1978): 265–339.

Kolko, Gabriel. "Intelligence and the Myth of Capitalist Rationality in the United States." *Science and Society* 14 (Summer 1980): 130–54.

———. *Main Currents in Modern American History.* New York: Harper & Row, 1976.

———. *The Triumph of Conservatism: A Reinterpretation of American History, 1900–1916.* New York: Free Press, 1963.

Kreps, T. J. "Dividends, Interest, Profits, and Wages, 1923–35." *Quarterly Journal of Economics* 49 (Aug. 1935): 561–99.

Kruchko, John G. *The Birth of a Union Local: The History of UAW Local 674, Norwood, Ohio, 1933–1940.* Ithaca: New York State School of Industrial and Labor Relations, 1972.

Krueger, Thomas A. "Another Reflection on the Failure of Socialism in America: The Case of the CIO." A review of *Industriegewerkschaften im Organisierten Kapitalismus; Der CIO in der Roosevelt-Ära*, by Peter Lösche. Opladen, 1975. *Reviews in American History* 5 (June 1977): 269–74.

Kutler, Stanley I. "Labor, the Clayton Act, and the Supreme Court." *Labor History* 3 (Winter 1962): 19–38.

Laslett, John H. M. *Labor and the Left: A Study of Socialist and Radical Influences in the American Labor Movement, 1881–1924.* New York: Basic Books, 1970.

Lauck, W. Jett. *The New Industrial Revolution and Wages.* New York: Funk & Wagnalls, 1929.

Lauderbaugh, Richard A. "Business, Labor, and Foreign Policy: U.S. Steel, the International Steel Cartel, and Recognition of the Steel Workers Organizing Committee." *Politics and Society* 6 (1976): 433–57.

Lea, Arden J. "Cotton Textiles and the Federal Child Labor Act of 1916." *Labor History* 16 (Fall 1975): 485–94.

Lebergott, Stanley. "Labor Force and Employment, 1800–1960." In *Output, Employment and Productivity in the United States after 1800.* National Bureau of Economic Research, Studies in Income and Wealth, vol. 30, pp. 117–204. New York, 1966.

Lens, Sidney. *The Crisis of American Labor.* New York: Sagamore Press, 1959.

Lescohier, Don D., and Brandeis, Elizabeth. *History of Labor in the United States, 1896–1932.* New York: Macmillan, 1935.

Lester, Richard A. "Trends in Southern Wage Differentials since 1890." *Southern Economic Journal* 11 (Apr. 1945): 317–44.

Leuchtenburg, William E. *Franklin D. Roosevelt and the New Deal.* New York: Harper & Row, 1963.

———. "The New Deal and the Analogue of War." In *Change and Continuity in Twentieth Century America*, edited by John Braeman, Robert H. Bremner, and Everett Walters, pp. 81–143. Columbus: Ohio State University Press, 1964.

Leven, Maurice; Moulton, Harold G.; and Warburton, Clark. *America's Capacity to Consume.* Washington, D.C.: Brookings Institution, 1934.

Levine, Louis (pseudonym for Lewis L. Lorwin). *The Women's Garment Workers: A*

*History of the International Ladies' Garment Workers' Union*. New York: B. W. Huebsch, 1924.

Levinson, Edward. *Labor on the March*. New York: Harper & Brothers, 1938.

Levinson, Harold M. *Determining Forces in Collective Wage Bargaining*. New York: Wiley, 1966.

_____. *Unionism, Wage Trends, and Income Distribution, 1914–1947*. Michigan Business Studies, vol. 10, no. 4. Ann Arbor: University of Michigan Press, 1951.

Lewis, John L. "Labor and the National Recovery Administration." *Annals of the American Academy of Political and Social Science* 172 (Mar. 1934): 58–63.

Lichtenstein, Nelson. *Labor's War at Home: The CIO in World War II*. New York: Cambridge University Press, 1982.

Lichtman, Allan J. "Critical Election Theory and the Reality of American Presidential Politics, 1916–1940." *American Historical Review* 81 (Apr. 1976): 317–50.

Livernash, E. Robert. "Wages and Benefits." In *A Review of Industrial Relations Research*, pp. 79–144. Madison: Industrial Relations Research Association, 1970.

Lorwin, Lewis L., and Wubnig, Arthur. *Labor Relations Boards: The Regulation of Collective Bargaining under the National Industrial Recovery Act*. Washington, D.C.: Brookings Institution, 1935.

Loth, David. *Swope of G.E.* New York: Simon & Schuster, 1958.

Lowitt, Richard. *George W. Norris: The Persistence of a Progressive*. Urbana: University of Illinois Press, 1971.

Lubin, Isador. *Miners' Wages and the Cost of Coal*. New York: McGraw-Hill, 1924.

Lukes, Steven. *Power: A Radical View*. London: Macmillan, 1974.

Lynd, Robert S., and Lynd, Helen Merrell. *Middletown in Transition: A Study in Cultural Conflicts*. New York: Harcourt Brace & Co., 1937.

Lyon, Leverett S. *The National Recovery Administration: An Analysis and Appraisal*. Washington, D.C.: Brookings Institution, 1935.

McFarland, C. K. "Coalition of Convenience: Lewis and Roosevelt, 1933–1940." *Labor History* 13 (Summer 1972): 400–414.

_____. *Roosevelt, Lewis, and the New Deal, 1933–1940*. Fort Worth: Texas Christian University Press, 1970.

McQuaid, Kim. "The Frustration of Corporate Revival during the Early New Deal." *Historian* 41 (Aug. 1979): 682–704.

Martin, George. *Madam Secretary, Frances Perkins*. Boston: Houghton Mifflin, 1976.

Marx, Karl. *Capital*, vol. 1. New York: Modern Library, 1936.

Matles, James J., and Higgins, James. *Them and Us: Struggles of a Rank and File Union*. Englewood Cliffs: Prentice-Hall, 1974.

Michels, Robert. *Political Parties: A Sociological Study of the Oligarchical Tendencies of Modern Democracy*. 1915. Reprint. New York: Free Press, 1966.

Miller, Ann Ratner. "Components of Labor Force Growth." *Journal of Economic History* 22 (Mar. 1962): 47–58.

Mills, C. Wright. *White Collar: The American Middle Classes*. New York: Oxford University Press, 1951.

Mills, Frederick C. *Economic Tendencies in the United States: Aspects of Pre-War and Post-War Changes*. New York: J. J. Little & Ives, 1932.

Mitchell, Broadus. *The Rise of Cotton Mills in the South*. Baltimore: Johns Hopkins University Press, 1921.

Moley, Raymond. *After Seven Years*. New York: Harper & Brothers, 1939.

———. *The First New Deal*. New York: Harcourt Brace & World, 1966.

Montgomery, David. *Workers' Control in America: Studies in the History of Work, Technology, and Labor Struggles*. New York: Cambridge University Press, 1979.

Moulton, Harold G. *The Formation of Capital*. Washington, D.C.: Brookings Institution, 1935.

Munn, Robert F., ed. *The Coal Industry: A Bibliography and Guide to Studies*. Morgantown: West Virginia University Library, 1965.

Murchison, Claudius T. *King Cotton Is Sick*. Chapel Hill: University of North Carolina Press, 1930.

———. "Requisites of Stabilization in the Cotton Textile Industry." *American Economic Review*, supp., 23 (Mar. 1933): 71–80.

———. "Southern Textile Manufacturing." *Annals of the American Academy of Political and Social Science* 153 (Jan. 1931): 30–42.

Murphy, Bruce Allen. *The Brandeis/Frankfurter Connection: The Secret Political Activities of Two Supreme Court Justices*. New York: Anchor Press, 1982.

Myers, Robert J., and Bloch, Joseph W. "Men's Clothing." In *How Collective Bargaining Works*, edited by the Twentieth Century Fund, pp. 381–449. New York: Twentieth Century Fund, 1942.

Myers, William Starr, and Newton, Walter H. *The Hoover Administration: A Documented Narrative*. New York: Scribner, 1936.

Nash, Gerald D. "Franklin D. Roosevelt and Labor: The World War I Origins of Early New Deal Labor Policy." *Labor History* 1 (1960): 40–52.

———. "Herbert Hoover and the Origins of the Reconstruction Finance Corporation." *Mississippi Valley Historical Review* 46 (Dec. 1959): 455–68.

Nash, Michael. *Conflict and Accommodation: Coal Miners, Steel Workers, and Socialism, 1890–1920*. Westport, Conn.: Greenwood Press, 1982.

National Bureau of Economic Research, Conference on Price Research. *Report of the Committee on Prices in the Bituminous Coal Industry*. New York, 1938.

National Industrial Conference Board. *The Competitive Position of Coal in the United States*. New York, 1931.

National Recovery Administration. *Report of the President's Committee of Industrial Analysis*. Washington, D.C.: U.S. Government Printing Office, 1937.

Neumann, Franz. "The Change in the Function of Law in Modern Society." In *The Democratic and the Authoritarian State: Essays in Political and Legal Theory*. Edited by Herbert Marcuse, pp. 22–68. New York: Free Press, 1957.

Norris, George W. *Fighting Liberal*. New York: Collier Books, 1961.

Northrup, Herbert R. *Boulwarism*. Ann Arbor: University of Michigan Press, 1964.

Nourse, Edwin G. *America's Capacity to Produce*. Washington, D.C.: Brookings Institution, 1934.

Ogburn, William F. *Progress and Uniformity in Child-Labor Legislation: A Study in Statistical Measurement*. 1912. Reprint. New York: AMS Press, 1968.

Olson, James Stuart. *Herbert Hoover and the Reconstruction Finance Corporation, 1931–1933*. Ames: Iowa State University Press, 1977.

Otey, Elizabeth L. "Women and Children in Southern Industry." *Annals of the American Academy of Political and Social Science* 153 (Jan. 1931): 163–69.

Ozanne, Robert. "Impact of Unions on Wage Trends and Income Distribution." In *Wage Determination: Market or Power Forces?* edited by Richard Perlman, pp. 104–25. Boston: D. C. Heath, 1964.

Parker, Glen Lawhon. *The Coal Industry: A Study in Social Control*. Washington, D.C.: American Council on Public Affairs, 1940.

Patterson, James T. *Congressional Conservatism and the New Deal: The Growth of the Conservative Coalition in Congress, 1933–1939*. Lexington: University of Kentucky Press, 1967.

Peel, Roy V., and Donnelly, Thomas C. *The 1932 Campaign: An Analysis*. New York: Farrar & Rinehart, 1935.

Perkins, Frances. *The Roosevelt I Knew*. New York: Viking Press, 1946.

Perlman, Selig. *A Theory of the Labor Movement*. New York: Macmillan, 1928.

Perlman, Selig, and Taft, Philip. *History of Labor in the United States, 1896–1932*. New York: Macmillan, 1935.

Pope, Jesse E. *The Clothing Industry in New York*. New York: Columbia University Press, 1905.

Potter, David M. "The Historical Development of Eastern-Southern Freight Rate Relationships." *Law and Contemporary Problems* 12 (Summer 1947): 416–48.

Radosh, Ronald. "The Corporate Ideology of American Labor Leaders from Gompers to Hillman." In *For a New America*, edited by James Weinstein and David W. Eakins, pp. 125–52. New York: Random House, 1970.

————. "The Myth of the New Deal." In *A New History of Leviathan*, edited by Ronald Radosh and Murray N. Rothbard, pp. 146–87. New York: Dutton, 1972.

Rae, John B. *American Automobile Manufacturers: The First Forty Years*. Philadelphia: Chilton Co., 1959.

Ramirez, Bruno. *When Workers Fight: The Politics of Industrial Relations in the Progressive Era, 1898–1916*. Westport, Conn.: Greenwood Press, 1978.

Rayack, Elton. "The Impact of Unionism on Wages in the Men's Clothing Industry, 1911–1956." *Labor Law Journal* 9 (Sept. 1958): 674–88.

Rees, Albert. *New Measures of Wage Earner Compensation in Manufacturing, 1914–1957*. National Bureau of Economic Research, Occasional Paper no. 75. New York, 1960.

Robinson, Dwight D. *Collective Bargaining and Market Control in the New York Coat and Suit Industry*. New York: Columbia University Press, 1949.

Rogin, Michael P. "Voluntarism: The Political Functions of an Anti-Political Doctrine." *Industrial and Labor Relations Review* 15 (July 1962): 521–35.

Rollins, Alfred B., Jr. "Franklin Roosevelt's Introduction to Labor." *Labor History* 3 (Winter 1962): 3–18.

Romasco, Albert U. *The Poverty of Abundance: Hoover, the Nation, the Depression*. New York: Oxford University Press, 1965.

Roos, Charles F. *NRA Economic Planning*. Bloomington: Principia Press, 1937.

Rosen, Elliot A. *Hoover, Roosevelt, and the Brains Trust: From Depression to New Deal*. New York: Columbia University Press, 1977.

Rosenman, Samuel I., ed. *The Public Papers and Addresses of Franklin D. Roosevelt*. 13 vols. New York: Random House, 1938–50.

Rosenof, Theodore. *Dogma, Depression, and the New Deal: The Debate of Political Leaders over Economic Recovery*. Port Washington, N.Y.: Kennikat Press, 1975.

Ross, Malcolm. *Machine Age in the Hills*. New York: Macmillan, 1933.

Rudolph, Frederick. "The American Liberty League, 1934–1940." *American Historical Review* 56 (Oct. 1950): 19–33.

Saposs, David J. "The American Labor Movement since the War." *Quarterly Journal of Economics* 49 (Feb. 1935): 236–54.

Sargent, James E. *Roosevelt and the Hundred Days: Struggle for the Early New Deal*. New York: Garland, 1981.

Schatz, Ronald. "The End of Corporate Liberalism: Class Struggle in the Electrical Manufacturing Industry, 1933–1950." *Radical America* 9 (July–Aug. 1975): 187–205.

Schlesinger, Arthur M., Jr. *The Age of Roosevelt*. 3 vols. Vol. 1, *The Crisis of the Old Order*. Vol. 2, *The Coming of the New Deal*. Vol. 3, *The Politics of Upheaval, 1935–1936*. Boston: Houghton Mifflin, 1957–60.

Schumpeter, Joseph. *Capitalism, Socialism, and Democracy*. New York: Harper, 1950.

Schwarz, Jordan A. *The Interregnum of Despair: Hoover, Congress, and the Depression*. Urbana: University of Illinois Press, 1970.

Seidman, Joel I. *The Needle Trades*. New York: Farrar & Rinehart, 1942.

———. "The Yellow Dog Contract." *Quarterly Journal of Economics* 46 (Feb. 1932): 348–61.

Selznick, Philip. *Law, Society, and Industrial Justice*. New York: Russell Sage Foundation, 1969.

Skeels, Jack. "The Background of UAW Factionalism." *Labor History* 2 (Spring 1961): 158–81.

Skocpol, Theda. "Political Response to Capitalist Crisis: Neo-Marxist Theories of the State and the Case of the New Deal." *Politics and Society* 10 (1980): 155–201.

Slichter, Sumner H. "The Current Labor Policies of American Industries." *Quarterly Journal of Economics* 43 (May 1929): 393–435.

———. *Union Policies and Industrial Management*. Washington, D.C.: Brookings Institution, 1941.

Smith, Robert Sidney. *Mill on the Dan: A History of Dan River Mills, 1882–1950*. Durham: Duke University Press, 1960.

Soule, George. *Prosperity Decade: From War to Depression, 1917–1929*. New York: Rinehart, 1947.

———. *Sidney Hillman: Labor Statesman*. New York: Macmillan, 1939.

Spengler, Joseph J. "Some Economic Aspects of Immigration into the United States." *Law and Contemporary Problems* 21 (Spring 1956): 236–55.

Stein, Leon, ed. *Out of the Sweatshop: The Struggle for Industrial Democracy*. New York: Quadrangle, 1977.

Steinberg, Ronnie. *Wages and Hours: Labor and Reform in Twentieth Century America*. New Brunswick: Rutgers University Press, 1982.

Steindl, Josef. *Maturity and Stagnation in American Capitalism*. Oxford University Institute of Statistics, Monograph no. 4. Oxford: Blackwell, 1952.

Stelzer, Irwin M. "The Cotton Textile Industry." In *The Structure of American Industry: Some Case Studies*, edited by Walter Adams, pp. 42–73. New York: Macmillan, 1961.

Sternsher, Bernard. "The Emergence of the New Deal Party System: A Problem in Historical Analysis of Voter Behavior." *Journal of Interdisciplinary History* 6 (Summer 1975): 127–50.

————. *Rexford Tugwell and the New Deal*. New Brunswick: Rutgers University Press, 1964.

Stolberg, Benjamin. "Big Steel, Little Steel, and CIO." *Nation*, 31 July 1937, pp. 119–23.

————. "A Government in Search of a Labor Movement: The NRA and American Labor." *Scribner's*, Dec. 1933, pp. 345–50.

————. *The Story of the CIO*. New York: Viking Press, 1938.

————. *Tailor's Progress*. New York: Doubleday Doran, 1944.

Stone, Katherine. "The Post-War Paradigm in American Labor Law." *Yale Law Journal* 90 (June 1981): 1509–80.

Stoneman, William E. *A History of the Economic Analysis of the Great Depression in America*. New York: Garland, 1979.

Taeuber, Conrad, and Taeuber, Irene B. *The Changing Population of the United States*. New York: Wiley, 1958.

Tax, Meredith. *The Rising of the Women: Feminist Solidarity and Class Conflict, 1880–1917*. New York: Monthly Review Press, 1980.

Taylor, Myron C. *Ten Years of Steel*. Extension of Remarks at the Annual Stockholders Meeting, Hoboken, N.J., 4 Apr. 1938. United States Steel Corporation, 1938.

Tcherikower, Elias. *The Early Jewish Labor Movement in the United States*. Translated and revised by Aaron Antonovsky. New York: YIVO Institute for Jewish Research, 1961.

Thomas, Brinley. *Migration and Urban Development*. London: Methuen, 1972.

Thompson, E. P. *Whigs and Hunters: The Origins of the Black Act*. New York: Pantheon, 1976.

Tolles, N. A. "Regional Differences in Cotton-Textile Wages, 1928–1937." *Monthly Labor Review* 46 (Jan. 1938): 36–47.

Trattner, Walter I. *Crusade for the Children: A History of the National Child Labor Committee and Child Labor Reform in America*. Chicago: Quadrangle, 1970.

Troy, Leo. *Trade Union Membership, 1897–1962*. National Bureau of Economic Research, Occasional Paper no. 92. New York, 1965.

Tryon, F. G. "The Effect of Competitive Conditions on Labor Relations in Coal Mining." *Annals of the American Academy of Political and Social Science* 111 (Jan. 1924): 82–95.

Tryon, F. G., and Mann, L. *Coal in 1923: Minerals Resources of the United States, 1923*. Part 2. Washington, D.C.: U.S. Government Printing Office, 1926.

Tugwell, Rexford G. *The Brains Trust*. New York: Viking Press, 1968.
———. *The Democratic Roosevelt*. Garden City: Doubleday, 1957.
———. *The Industrial Discipline and the Governmental Arts*. New York: Columbia University Press, 1933.
———. *In Search of Roosevelt*. Cambridge, Mass.: Harvard University Press, 1972.
———. "The Protagonists: Roosevelt and Hoover." *Antioch Review* 13 (Dec. 1953): 419–39.
Ulman, Lloyd. *The Rise of the National Trade Union*. Cambridge, Mass.: Harvard University Press, 1955.
U.S. Bureau of the Census. *Census of Manufactures: 1931*. Washington, D.C.: U.S. Government Printing Office, 1935.
———. *Census of Manufactures: 1933*. Washington, D.C.: U.S. Government Printing Office, 1936.
———. *Census of Manufactures: 1935*. Washington, D.C.: U.S. Government Printing Office, 1938.
———. *Historical Statistics of the United States: Colonial Times to 1957*. Washington, D.C.: U.S. Government Printing Office, 1960.
U.S. Bureau of Labor. *Report on the Condition of Woman and Child Wage-Earners in the United States*. 19 vols. Washington, D.C.: U.S. Government Printing Office, 1910–13.
U.S. Bureau of Labor Statistics. "Strikes in the United States, 1880–1936." *Bulletin No. 651*. Washington, D.C.: U.S. Government Printing Office, 1938.
———. "Technological Change and Productivity in the Bituminous Coal Industry, 1920–1960." *Bulletin No. 1305*. Washington, D.C.: U.S. Government Printing Office, 1961.
———. "Wages and Hours of Labor in Cotton-Goods Manufacturing, 1910–1930." *Bulletin No. 539*. Washington, D.C.: U.S. Government Printing Office, 1931.
———. "Wages and Hours of Labor in the Men's Clothing Industry: 1932." *Bulletin No. 594*. Washington, D.C.: U.S. Government Printing Office, 1933.
———. "Wages in Cotton-Goods Manufacturing." *Bulletin No. 663*. Washington, D.C.: U.S. Government Printing Office, 1938.
U.S. Bureau of Mines. *Minerals Yearbook, 1957*. 2 vols. Washington, D.C.: U.S. Government Printing Office, 1959.
U.S. Chamber of Commerce. *Report: Working Periods in Industry*. Washington, D.C.: U.S. Chamber of Commerce, 1933.
U.S. Coal Commission. *Report*, Part 3, Senate Doc. 195, 68th Cong., 2d sess. Washington, D.C.: U.S. Government Printing Office, 1925.
U.S. Commission on Industrial Relations. *Final Report and Testimony*. 11 vols. Washington, D.C.: U.S. Government Printing Office, 1916.
U.S. Congress, Joint Economic Committee. *Productivity, Prices and Incomes*. Washington, D.C.: U.S. Government Printing Office, 1957.
U.S. Congress, Temporary National Economic Committee. *Economic Power and Political Pressures*. Monograph no. 26. Washington, D.C.: U.S. Government Printing Office, 1941.
———. *Economic Standards of Government Price Control*. Monograph no. 32. Washington, D.C.: U.S. Government Printing Office, 1941.

_____. *Hearings: Investigation of Concentration of Economic Power.* Part 26, Iron and Steel Industry, United States Steel Corporation Studies. Washington, D.C.: U.S. Government Printing Office, 1940.

_____. *Industrial Wage Rates, Labor Costs, and Price Policies.* Monograph no. 5. Washington, D.C.: U.S. Government Printing Office, 1940.

_____. *The Structure of Industry.* Monograph no. 27. Washington, D.C.: U.S. Government Printing Office, 1941.

U.S. Department of Labor. *Proceedings of the National Conference for Labor Legislation*, 14–15 Feb. 1934. Washington, D.C.: U.S. Government Printing Office, 1934.

U.S. Federal Trade Commission. *Preliminary Report: Investment and Profit in Soft-Coal Mining.* Washington, D.C.: U.S. Government Printing Office, 1922.

U.S. House of Representatives, Committee on Interstate and Foreign Commerce. *Hearings: Coal Legislation.* Parts 2 and 3. 69th Cong., 1st sess. Washington, D.C.: U.S. Government Printing Office, 1926.

U.S. House of Representatives, Committee on the Judiciary. *Hearings: Defining and Limiting the Jurisdiction of Courts Sitting in Equity.* 72d Cong., 1st sess. Washington, D.C.: U.S. Government Printing Office, 1932.

U.S. House of Representatives, Committee on Labor. *Hearings: Investigation of Wages and Working Conditions in the Coal Mining Industry.* 67th Cong., 2d sess. Washington, D.C.: U.S. Government Printing Office, 1922.

_____. *Hearings: Thirty-Hour Week Bill.* 73d Cong., 1st sess. Washington, D.C.: U.S. Government Printing Office, 1933.

U.S. House of Representatives, Committee on Ways and Means. *Hearings: Extension of NIRA.* 74th Cong., 1st sess. Washington, D.C.: U.S. Government Printing Office, 1935.

_____. *Hearings: National Industrial Recovery.* 73d Cong., 1st sess. Washington, D.C.: U.S. Government Printing Office, 1933.

U.S. House of Representatives, Subcommittee of the Committee on Labor. *Hearings: To Regulate the Textile Industry.* 75th Cong., 1st sess. Washington, D.C.: U.S. Government Printing Office, 1937.

_____. *Hearings: To Rehabilitate and Stabilize Labor Conditions in the Textile Industry of the United States.* 74th Cong., 2d sess. Washington, D.C.: U.S. Government Printing Office, 1936.

U.S. House of Representatives, Subcommittee of the Committee on Ways and Means. *Hearings: Stabilization of the Bituminous Coal Mining Industry.* 74th Cong., 1st sess. Washington, D.C.: U.S. Government Printing Office, 1935.

U.S. Industrial Commission. *Reports.* Vol. 12, *Capital and Labor Employed in the Mining Industry.* Washington, D.C.: U.S. Government Printing Office, 1901.

U.S. National Labor Relations Board. "The Effect of Labor Relations in the Bituminous Coal Industry upon Interstate Commerce." *Bulletin No. 2.* Washington, D.C.: U.S. Government Printing Office, 1938.

_____. *Legislative History of the National Labor Relations Act, 1935.* 2 vols. Washington, D.C.: U.S. Government Printing Office, 1949.

U.S. National Resources Committee. *The Structure of the American Economy.* Part 1, *Basic Characteristics.* Washington, D.C.: U.S. Government Printing Office, 1939.

U.S. Senate, Committee on Banking and Currency. *Hearings: Economic Power of Labor Organizations*. 81st Cong., 1st sess. Washington, D.C.: U.S. Government Printing Office, 1949.

U.S. Senate, Committee on Education and Labor. *Hearings: To Create a National Labor Board*. Parts 1–3. 73d Cong., 2d sess. Washington, D.C.: U.S. Government Printing Office, 1934.

U.S. Senate, Committee on Education and Labor, and U.S. House of Representatives, Committee on Labor. *Joint Hearings: Fair Labor Standards Act of 1937*. Part 2. 75th Cong., 1st sess. Washington, D.C.: U.S. Government Printing Office, 1937.

U.S. Senate, Committee on Finance. *Hearings: Investigation of Economic Problems*. 72d Cong., 2d sess. Washington, D.C.: U.S. Government Printing Office, 1933.

————. *Hearings: Investigation of the National Recovery Administration*. 74th Cong., 1st sess. Washington, D.C.: U.S. Government Printing Office, 1935.

————. *Hearings: National Industrial Recovery*. 73d Cong., 1st sess. Washington, D.C.: U.S. Government Printing Office, 1933.

U.S. Senate, Committee on Interstate Commerce. *Hearings: Bituminous Coal Commission*. Part 2. 70th Cong., 2d sess. Washington, D.C.: U.S. Government Printing Office, 1929.

————. *Hearings: Conditions in the Coal Fields of Pennsylvania, West Virginia, and Ohio*. 70th Cong., 1st sess. Washington, D.C.: U.S. Government Printing Office, 1928.

————. *Hearings: To Regulate Interstate Commerce in Bituminous Coal*. 74th Cong., 2d sess. Washington, D.C.: U.S. Government Printing Office, 1936.

U.S. Senate, Committee on the Judiciary. *Hearings: Thirty-Hour Work Week*. 72d Cong., 2d sess. Washington, D.C.: U.S. Government Printing Office, 1933.

U.S. Senate, Committee on Labor and Public Welfare. *History of Employment and Manpower Policy in the United States*. Vol. 5, *Selected Readings in Employment and Manpower*. Washington, D.C.: U.S. Government Printing Office, 1965.

U.S. Senate, Committee on Mines and Mining. *Hearings: To Create a Bituminous Coal Commission*. Part 1. 72d Cong., 1st sess. Washington, D.C.: U.S. Government Printing Office, 1932.

U.S. Senate, Subcommittee of the Committee on Education and Labor. *Violations of Free Speech and Rights of Labor*. Parts 1–75. 74th–76th Congs. Washington, D.C.: U.S. Government Printing Office, 1936–40.

U.S. Senate, Subcommittee of the Committee on Interstate Commerce. *Hearings: Stabilization of the Bituminous Coal Mining Industry*. 74th Cong., 1st sess. Washington, D.C.: U.S. Government Printing Office, 1935.

United States Steel Corporation. *TNEC Papers*. 3 vols. 1940.

Vadney, Thomas E. *The Wayward Liberal: A Political Biography of Donald Richberg*. Lexington: University of Kentucky Press, 1970.

Vittoz, Stanley. "The Economic Foundations of Industrial Politics in the United States and the Emerging Structural Theory of the State in Capitalist Society: The Case of New Deal Labor Policy." *Amerikastudien* 27 (Winter 1982): 365–412.

————. "World War I and the Political Accommodation of Transitional Market

Forces: The Case of Immigration Restriction." *Politics and Society* 8 (1978): 49–78.

Wagner, Robert F. "Will Congress Choose a Way Out of Unemployment?" *American Labor Legislation Review* 20 (Sept. 1930): 293–96.

Wall, Joseph F. *Andrew Carnegie*. New York: Oxford University Press, 1970.

Warne, Frank J. *The Coal-Mine Workers: A Study in Labor Organization*. New York: Longmans, 1905.

Wechsler, James A. *Labor Baron: A Portrait of John L. Lewis*. 1944. Reprint. Westport, Conn.: Greenwood Press, 1972.

Weinstein, James. *The Corporate Ideal in the Liberal State, 1900–1918*. Boston: Beacon Press, 1968.

Weintraub, David. "The Displacement of Workers through Increases in Efficiency and Their Absorption by Industry, 1920–1931." *Journal of the American Statistical Association* 27 (Dec. 1932): 383–400.

Wiebe, Robert H. "The Anthracite Coal Strike of 1902: A Record of Confusion." *Mississippi Valley Historical Review* 48 (Sept. 1961): 229–51.

Williams, William Appleman. *The Contours of American History*. Cleveland: World, 1961.

Wilson, William H. "How the Chamber of Commerce Viewed the NRA: A Re-examination." *Mid-America* 44 (Apr. 1962): 95–108.

Wolfbein, Seymour Louis. *The Decline of a Cotton Textile City: A Study of New Bedford*. New York: Columbia University Press, 1944.

Wolfskill, George. *The Revolt of the Conservatives: A History of the American Liberty League, 1934–1940*. Boston: Houghton Mifflin, 1962.

Wolfson, Theresa. "Role of the ILGWU in Stabilizing the Women's Garment Industry." *Industrial and Labor Relations Review* 4 (Oct. 1950): 33–43.

Wolman, Leo. *Ebb and Flow in Trade Unionism*. New York: National Bureau of Economic Research, 1936.

———. *The Growth of American Trade Unions, 1880–1923*. New York: National Bureau of Economic Research, 1924.

Wright, Gavin. "Cheap Labor and Southern Textiles before 1880." *Journal of Economic History* 39 (Sept. 1979): 655–80.

Zeigler, Harmon. *The Politics of Small Business*. Washington, D.C.: Washington Public Affairs Press, 1961.

Zieger, Robert H. *Republicans and Labor, 1919–1929*. Lexington: University of Kentucky Press, 1969.

Zinn, Howard. *The Politics of History*. Boston: Beacon Press, 1970.

# Index

NIRA, 205 (n. 2)

Kelly, Clyde, 67, 88–89
Kendall, Henry P., 121, 149
Kent, Fred I., 81, 88, 149
Keynesian economics, 10, 81, 172
Kirstein, Louis E., 139, 149
Knudsen, William S., 150–51, 157

Labor Advisory Board, 138–39
La Follette, Robert, Jr., 79, 88
La Follette Civil Liberties Committee, 157, 161
Lamont, Robert P.: involvement of in bituminous coal industry, 65
Lamont, Thomas W., 163
Lauck, W. Jett: and industrial stabilization, 88–90, 195 (n. 62)
Lewis, David J.: and 1932 coal stabilization bill, 67–68
Lewis, John L., 54, 58–59, 62, 65, 78, 88–89, 131, 161; quoted on conditions in bituminous coal industry, 57; and bituminous coal code, 107; and Guffey-Snyder Act, 112; and National Labor Board, 139; and General Motors "sit-down" strike, 157; and Steel Workers Organizing Committee, 159; and U.S. Steel negotiations, 162–64. *See also* United Mine Workers of America
Lubin, Isadore, 150
Lund, Robert L., 91–92

McMahon, Thomas F., 120–21
Marshall, Leon C., 151
Marx, Karl: critique of capitalism by, 3; analysis of English Factory Acts by, 170
Mellon, Andrew, 74, 184 (n. 19)
Meyer, Eugene, 74
Michels, Robert, 168
Millinery Stabilization Commission, 105
Moley, Raymond, 78; and Brains Trust, 79–81; confers with FDR on recovery

legislation, 82–83, 87; and bituminous coal code, 106–7
Morrow, J. D. A., 112
Moulton, Harold G., 81, 88–89
Murchison, Claudius T., 134
Murphy, Frank, 157, 161–62
Murray, Philip, 159, 163, 167

National Association of Manufacturers, 80, 210 (n. 45); and Thirty-Hour Week bill, 83; and industrial self-regulation, 86, 89–91; and labor provisions of NIRA, 92–93; and National Labor Board, 140; and Labor Disputes bill of 1934, 143; and National Industrial Adjustment Act, 144; and National Labor Relations Act, 149
National Bituminous Coal Commission, 114–16
National Coal Association, 65, 112
National Coat and Suit Industry Recovery Board, 105
National Conference of Bituminous Coal Producers, 113, 116
National Emergency Council, 112
National Federation of Miners and Mine Laborers, 50
National Industrial Adjustment Act, 144
National Industrial Recovery Act, 69, 78, 80, 91–96, 137–39, 147, 171; and garment industry, 98–100, 104; and question of renewal in bituminous coal industry, 113; and labor provisions of Guffey-Snyder Act, 115; and cotton textile industry, 119–21, 124, 127, 130; and Labor Disputes bill of 1934, 143
National Industrial Recovery Board, 147, 209 (n. 35)
National Labor Board, 138–45 passim, 206 (n. 11)
National Labor Relations Act, 7–8, 12, 146–53, 171–72
National Labor Relations Board, 77, 144–46, 149, 161, 172